KEEPING IT REAL

IRISH FILM AND TELEVISION

Edited by Ruth Barton and Harvey O'Brien

WALLFLOWER PRESS

LONDON and NEW YORK

First published in Great Britain in 2004 by
Wallflower Press
4th Floor, 26 Shacklewell Lane, London E8 2EZ
www.wallflowerpress.co.uk

A catalogue for this book is available from the British Library.

ISBN 1-903364-94-9 (pbk)
ISBN 1-903364-95-7 (hbk)

Book design by Elsa Mathern

Printed in Turin, Italy by Grafiche Dessi s.r.l.

791.4309415

CONTENTS

Acknowledgements

The editors would like to acknowledge the contributions of all of the speakers, delegates and volunteers from the *Keeping it Real* conference held in University College Dublin in April 2002. We would also like to acknowledge the support of our colleagues at the Centre for Film Studies, University College Dublin and also of the Irish Research Council for the Humanities and Social Sciences, whose financial support enabled us to organise the event. We would like to thank *Film Ireland* and the Film Archive and Film Library of the Irish Film Institute for their help in the development of this book, and all at Wallflower Press who have supported the project throughout. Finally we would like to thank our families for their generosity and patience.

Notes on Contributors

Steve Baker is a Media and Cultural Studies lecturer and an independent researcher and writer. His interests lie in the relations between media, culture and politics. He lives outside Belfast.

Desmond Bell is currently Professor of Film and Photography at Napier University, Edinburgh, and is shortly to take up the Chair in Film Studies at Queens University Belfast. He has written widely on Irish media and has produced an important body of film work dealing with post-Famine Ireland. His current film, *Rebel Frontier*, will be broadcast by RTÉ.

Elizabeth Butler Cullingford is Professor at the Faculty of Women, Gender, and Literature, University of Texas at Austin. She is the author of *Ireland's Others: Gender and Ethnicity in Irish Literature and Popular Culture* (2002), *Gender and History in Yeats's Love Poetry* (1993) and *Yeats, Ireland and Fascism* (1981) and has published numerous articles including 'Seamus and Sinead: From 'Limbo' to *Saturday Night Live* via *Hush-a-Bye Baby*' (1994) and 'The Stage Englishman of Boucicault's Irish Drama: National Identities in Performance' (1997).

Marcus Free is a lecturer in Media and Communication Studies at Mary Immaculate College, University of Limerick. He has published articles on gender, national identity and football supporter culture, and on television drama, and is co-author of *The Uses of Sport: A Critical Study* (2004).

Paula Gilligan is a lecturer in film theory and practice, modern Irish culture, and audience theory at Dundalk Institute of Technology. Her doctoral dissertation at Trinity College Dublin was entitled *Dream Country: The Ireland Text in French Cinema, 1937–1977*.

Ruth Lysaght researches in the area of language and culture. She also writes for theatre and film. She has spoken on contemporary Irish language filmmaking in conferences around Europe, and has introduced screenings for the schools' programme in the Irish Film Institute. She is currently investigating developments in minority language television beyond Europe.

Brian McIlroy is Professor of Film Studies, University of British Columbia. He is the author of *World Cinema 4: Ireland* (1989) and *Shooting to Kill: Filmmaking and the 'Troubles' in Northern Ireland* (1998). Has designed and written an online university credit distance education course on Irish cinema, which went live in September 2002.

Cahal McLaughlin is a documentary maker and Senior Lecturer in Media Arts at Royal Holloway University of London. He has directed and produced for broadcast television and community organisations, as well as written on film about the 'Troubles'.

Martin McLoone is Professor of Media Studies, University of Ulster at Coleraine. He is the author of *Irish Film: The Emergence of a Contemporary Cinema* (2001), editor of *Broadcasting in a Divided Community* (1996) and *Culture, Identity and Broadcasting in Ireland* (1998) and co-editor of *Border Crossings* (1994) and *Big Picture, Small Screen* (1996).

Barry Monahan has recently completed a PhD at Trinity College. He has taught on a number of graduate and postgraduate courses in film at Trinity College, University College Dublin and the Dublin Institute of Technology, and is currently lecturing on an American and Canadian film course at the University of Birmingham.

Diane Negra is a lecturer in Film and Cultural Theory, University of East Anglia. She is the author of *Off-White Hollywood: American Culture and Ethnic Female Stardom* (2001), co-editor of *A Feminist Reader in Early Cinema* (2002) and editor of *The Irish in US: Irishness, Performativity and Popular Culture* (forthcoming) . She is also co-editor of a special issue of *Camera Obscura* and contributing editor for the forthcoming *Routledge Encyclopedia of Irish Culture*.

Paul O'Brien is a lecturer in aesthetics and cyber-culture at the Faculty of History of Art and Design and Complementary Studies at the National College of Art and Design, Dublin. He holds a PhD in Philosophy from Trinity College Dublin and has published articles on art theory and cultural theory.

Diog O'Connell is a lecturer in Media and Film Studies at Dun Laoghaire Institute of Art, Design & Technology and a PhD student at Dublin City University in the area of Irish cinema.

Sunniva O'Flynn has been Curator of the Irish Film Archive since its establishment in the Irish Film Centre in 1992. Her key role is in the facilitation of access to the Archive collection for students, programme makers and exhibitors. She has contributed to the International Federation of Film Archives' Bulletin of Preservation and has published articles on Irish Newsreel production and distribution. Her most recently published article, 'The Tragedy of Drumcollogher', was published in FIAF's *This Film is Dangerous* (2003).

Lance Pettitt is Principal Lecturer in Media and Popular Culture, Leeds Metropolitan University. He is the author of *Screening Ireland: Film and Television Representation* (2000),

December Bride: Ireland Into Film (2001) and a forthcoming book, *Irish Media and Popular Culture.*

Stephen Rea is an actor and director. He was a co-founder of the Field Day Group and appeared in several Field Day stage productions prior to featuring in Neil Jordan's *Angel* (1982). Has appeared in almost all of Jordan's subsequent films including *Michael Collins* (1996) and *The Butcher Boy* (1997). He received an Oscar nomination for Best Actor for *The Crying Game* (1992). His other work includes *Bad Behaviour* (1993), *Citizen X* (1995), *A Further Gesture* (1996) and, most recently, Leopold Bloom in *Bloom* (Seá Walsh, 2003).

Ted Sheehy is the Ireland correspondent for *Screen International* and *screendaily.com.* He writes a regular column for *In Production*, the Irish film and television trade quarterly. He was editor of *Film Ireland* magazine 1996–2001, and recently curated the programme 'Thirty Years On: The Arts Council and the Filmmaker', held at the Irish Film Centre.

Introduction[1]

Ruth Barton

When Harvey and I were planning our April 2002 conference, 'Keeping it Real: The Fictions and Non-Fictions of Film and Television in Modern Ireland', our ambition was to challenge the canon, and particularly the approaches to Irish cinema, that have become associated with the subject. We anticipated that, like us, the gathering of local and international academics who came together for a weekend of panels, individual papers, screenings and informal meetings would welcome the opportunity not just to hear the familiar songs, but to invent new tunes. We were also hoping to hear from colleagues working in the fields of television, cultural studies and new media and to encourage them to share their ideas with us.

It was, perhaps even more than we could have realised at the time, a moment of transition, not just for Irish society which, having rapidly accustomed itself to the new wealth generated by the dot.com generation, suddenly found that the Celtic Tiger was a vanishing species, and that the economy was, once again, in crisis. In the wake of the atrocities of 11 September, a raft of old certainties no longer pertained, whilst a new nostalgia for an old world order was already becoming evident. On the local front, the filmmaking boom associated with the revival of the Film Board in 1993 was showing signs of coming to an end. Politicians were less committed than ever to the tax incentive scheme, latterly known as Section 481, that had provided local filmmakers with a bedrock of funding, whilst fewer international production companies were being tempted to shoot in Ireland, now one of the most expensive European economies to work and live in. Meanwhile, new initiatives from the Irish Film Board have reversed the recent policy of producing quality, mid-budget films and are now aimed at fostering a mini- and micro-budget film culture based on the expectation of recouping costs in the home market.

No better time, therefore, to review what we termed 'the Fictions and non-Fictions of Modern Ireland' – indeed, to ask the question, is modern Ireland itself a fiction? The title of the conference, and this volume that arose from it, are evidently ironic, recalling a tradition of constructing an Ireland of the imagination that was born in the colonial past, fostered by generations of emigrants for whom Ireland represented a dream of return quite divorced from the social and economic reality of its geographical space and reinforced by a tourist industry that promised the real whilst trading in the fantasy. The sense that Ireland is not so much a real place as a projection of the imagination has been reflected in an issue of nomenclature that has reverberated through recent Irish scholarship. Declan Kiberd's seminal *Inventing Ireland* (1996) has been followed by *Reinventing Ireland* (edited by Peader Kirby, Luke Gibbons and Michael Cronin, 2002), whilst the title of the 1996 conference, 'Imagining Ireland', was echoed in the 'Re-Imagining Ireland' event held in Charlottesville, Virginia in 2003.

The other and related question that we felt needed to be addressed with some urgency concerned the place of Irish film studies within the discourse that had evolved in tandem with the 'new' Ireland. Had Irish film studies become obsessed with the relationship between the state, the nation and cultural representations thereof? Was this a wider problem for Irish Studies? Would the inclusion of 'new' disciplines, such as Irish media and cultural studies, shake up the consensus? Could the up-and-coming scholars, many of whom offered papers at the conference, bring new perspectives to what was in danger of becoming a jaded discourse?

It is useful at this point to trace the evolution of Irish film studies, the discipline that perforce structures this book. It remains the most developed of the academic disciplines within this area – those attempting to work in Irish television have been hampered by the absence of a public-access archive (such as the Irish Film Archive) geared towards scholarly research, and Irish media and new media studies are still in their infancy. Readers are thus invited to view this collection less as an attempt at maintaining the supremacy of this older discipline than as admitting its limitations and its search for new directions.

From the polemics of the venerable Fr. Devane, through the late Liam O'Laoghaire to the trio of Kevin Rockett, John Hill and Luke Gibbons and on to Martin McLoone and Lance Pettitt, Irish cinema has not lacked its critics. It now has its own history, its own canon and is attracting the attentions of a range of writers from what might loosely be called Irish Studies. Any number of institutions, both in Ireland and overseas, offer courses in Irish cinema and the recent surge in local filmmaking has left them with a wealth of films to study.

When the now-canonical textbook *Cinema and Ireland* was first published in 1987, there was no Celtic Tiger, no serious threat of any Coca-Colaisation of the Irish film industry, in fact, no Irish film industry. Instead, as its authors described it, the policies of successive post-Independence governments had created a history of antagonism towards both the watching and making of films that left screen representations of the Irish at the mercy of other filmmaking practices, notably the sentimental vision of Irish-America and the hostile gaze of the last of Britain's imperial lackeys. The book is informed by a dual critique of cultural nationalism and an exploration of identity politics that were to dominate Irish film studies for at least another decade, if not to date. Its publication coincided with the espousal of Irish nationalism and anti-imperialism by the largely London-based left-wing that had enabled like-minded filmmakers such as Pat Murphy, Joe Comerford and Thaddeus O'Sullivan to apply to British sources to fund their avant-garde films. These films in turn became the benchmark for writers in search of a politically-engaged indigenous filmmaking practice. By the time of the appearance of *Border Crossing* in 1994, edited by

John Hill, Martin McLoone and Paul Hainsworth, the problems of Irish cinema were being discussed within the context of European and British cinemas. The core question of how a small country could make culturally-specific films in an environment of co-productions and continued Hollywood dominance absorbed the book's authors. Some, such as Colin McArthur, argued that low-budget filmmaking was inevitably less compromised than works requiring international financing and global audiences; whilst others such as Martin McLoone recognised Hollywood's modernising influence, even if this still did not persuade them to love the enemy. McLoone continued to interrogate the legacy of cultural nationalism in his most recent book, *Irish Film: The Emergence of a Contemporary Cinema* (2000) whilst further working through the implications for Irish cinema of its reliance on global capital. McLoone also nudged Irish film criticism towards a less simplistic attitude to Irish-American filmmakers whose history had already been at least partially retrieved by Joseph Curran in his useful *Hibernian Green on the Silver Screen* (1989).

Lately, a raft of academics, mostly from the English departments of American and British universities, have turned their hands to writing about Irish film. One of the keynote speakers at the 'Keeping it Real' conference was Elizabeth Butler Cullingford whose latest book, *Ireland's Others* (2001), traces the interweaving of themes between Irish literature and film with a particular eye on their implications for gender representations. Two more speakers, Lance Pettitt and Gerardine Meaney, are contributors to the 'Ireland Into Film' series whose brief is to discuss filmic adaptations of literary texts. Chapters on film may be found in recent books by David Lloyd (*Ireland After History*, 1999), Conor McCarthy (*Modernisation, Crisis and Culture in Ireland*, 2000) as well as in collections of essays such as *Ireland in Proximity* (1999) and *Writing in the Irish Republic: Literature, Culture, Politics, 1949–1999* (2000).

This dilution of the film studies gene pool can only be welcome. However, it does beg the question as to whether it has fostered a greater diversity of approaches to analysing Irish cinema (whatever that is) or simply meant more people circling around the same directors and films. Neither analysis is quite accurate since simplifications like this never are. Yet, I sense a feeling among people working in the field that we have found ourselves stuck in the one representational rut. If it isn't the films of Neil Jordan (favoured text: *The Butcher Boy*, runner-up: *The Crying Game*), then it is the postcolonial pack (Joe Comerford, Neil Jordan) or gender (Pat Murphy, *Hush-A-Bye-Baby*, Neil Jordan). The Troubles are always good for a chapter, as is the legacy of nationalism. The same binaries also tend to reappear: city/country, Church/individual, feminine/masculine, colonial/native, global/local.

It is easy to be glib and, of course, one of the big problems is the scarcity of challenging Irish films. You can say that we need to take a painterly approach to analysing the existing works but very few of them have much to boast of in the way of a visual language. I have heard it suggested that the influx of refugees from the English department has cemented an underlying tendency to analyse narrative rather than cinematic effects, but they have also been responsible for a more rigorous application to the amenable films of the hip pomo-poco (postmodern-postcolonial) axis that many people find exciting.

Another consequence of film studies' close relationship with literary criticism has been a certain elitism in terms of theoretical approaches. Films that smack of the 'popular' tend to be avoided, this despite the ascendancy in other academic climates of cultural studies. In this instance, I think that Irish literary studies are even more limited. The social significance of Maeve Binchy anyone? No thanks, but take your pick of essays on Yeats, Synge, Joyce, Friel and Heaney (Elizabeth Bowen and Jennifer Johnston for gender and cultural balance). A bracing analysis of the contribution of popular television, radio, music, dance to Irish cultural life remains to be written.

In the end, the 'Keeping it Real' conference reaped rich rewards; so much so that it is with enormous regret that we are unable to include here the full complement of papers offered to us. The authors included in this collection have relished the challenge of responding to film and media culture on the cusp of change. Whilst many of these authors are familiar names in the various disciplines associated with Irish studies, our list of contributors also includes recent graduates and postgraduate students.

In our opening section, 'Real Histories, New Myths', Elizabeth Butler Cullingford delves deep into a history of ritual humiliation to locate cinematic treatments of the 'prisoner's wife' across an array of films; Lance Pettitt draws on the cinematic history of the gangster to locate the recent spate of Irish gangster movies in a discourse of social containment and aberrant masculinity and Sunniva O'Flynn examines the significance of the clerical collection of films by amateur priests held in the Irish Film Archive. Multiple pasts, as all these writers acknowledge, inform the present or so we may believe; but is the past simply a fiction constructed by the present? 'Real Lives' are the theme of the second section, in which Diane Negra discusses the appropriation by American culture of a regressive Irishness in the wake of 11 September, symbolised by fire-fighter Mike Moran's invitation to Osama Bin Laden to 'kiss my royal Irish ass'. Brian McIlroy also focuses on the dialogue between Ireland and America in a new definition of the Irish exilic and diasporic narrative. Steve Baker questions the relationship between Loyalism and the image of the vampire in a new reading of the film, *Resurrection Man*. Storytelling is the focus of the third section, 'Real Stories'; here Desmond Bell discusses his practice of using found footage, much of it culled from the archival material described by O'Flynn, to illustrate, interrogate and reinvigorate the venerable tradition of storytelling in his film *The Last Storyteller?*; Cahal McLaughlin relates how his documentary, *Telling Our Story*, functioned as a therapeutic narrative, facilitating the community who had experienced the Springhill shootings of 1972 to work through and, in some cases, lay to rest their memories of that day. Paul O'Brien traces the connections between James Joyce's *Ulysses* and internet hypertext and Diog O'Connell challenges our assumptions that Irish narratives reflect Irish culture, locating

Martin Duffy's film, *The Boy From Mercury*, within a universal structure of storytelling. In the fourth section, 'Real Places', Martin McLoone reflects on the new cinematic Belfast that is rising out of the ashes of the Troubles, asking whether it has any sense of identity other than a global placelessness. Ruth Lysaght examines the depiction of the West of Ireland in the popular television Irish-language soap opera, *Ros na Rún*. Paula Gilligan suggests that the attraction of Ireland for a particular group of French intellectuals and filmmakers has been that of finding in it the potential for a return to fascist aesthetics. In the final section, 'Real Paradigms', Marcus Free analyses the public response to the 'Roy Keane affair' as it was articulated on radio and television, finding in it a symptomatic division between the old and the new Irelands, whilst Barry Monahan proposes that a Lacanian interpretative model best offers a framework for analysing the relationship between the spectator and Irish cinematic space. The collection ends with an interview with Field Day founder-member and leading Irish actor, Stephen Rea, in which he discusses with Ted Sheehy his work with Neil Jordan and his wider experience of Irish filmmaking.

It is the hope of the editors that this collection will open Irish film, television and media studies to a wider readership, that it will allow new voices to emerge and that it will encourage existing practitioners to push their work in new directions.

Note

1   An early version of this introduction, entitled 'If You Want to Stay Here, You'll Have to Move On', appeared in *Film Ireland*, issue 85, February/March, 2002, pp. 26–7.

part 1 **real histories, new myths?**

The Prisoner's Wife and the Soldier's Whore: Female Punishment in Irish History and Culture

Elizabeth Butler Cullingford

It is a truth universally acknowledged that a minority group hard pressed by an occupying power must be in want of a secure sexual identity. Women, the potentially porous membranes through which the purity of a beleaguered community may be contaminated, are more closely regulated in times of instability than in times of peace. During the recent Troubles in Northern Ireland the IRA took over the role of community policeman, using various forms of corporal punishment (beating, knee-capping, the smashing of wrists and hands) to discourage crimes like drug dealing, joyriding and theft (White 1988).[1] Irish films and popular novels also subscribe to the belief that the Provos will police the sexual behaviour of an imprisoned comrade's woman. According to Tony Catney of Sinn Féin Prisoners' Department, this belief has a basis in fact:

> Prisoners' wives and girlfriends were expected to be paragons of chastity. In clubs there was the practice where people would check if the woman they fancied was a prisoner's wife or girlfriend. There was also a time when a prisoner would send out word if he heard that someone was going out with his wife or girlfriend, and tell the movement to do something about it. (qtd. in Coulter 1991: 93–4)

If incarceration suggests impotence, an unfaithful wife evokes emasculation, and an army marches on its masculinity.[2] Republican morale had to be sustained by keeping the prisoner's sexual property safe.[3] Jack Holland's 1981 political thriller, *The Prisoner's Wife*, which characterises this extra-legal justice system as 'ghetto politics', offers a representative example of the stereotype:

> Long Kesh kept them together; its walls, wire fences and watchtowers held her more securely than any marriage vows. Now her marriage had entered the public arena of ghetto politics and it was impossible for her to take any steps to break with him. She was trapped. She was the prisoner's wife. (Holland 1981: 27)

In such a situation female adultery, the staple fare of novel writing and movie making alike, entails higher risks than usual. I want to explore the changing relationship of this sensational scenario to historical fact, and to suggest that it has now evolved into a convenient cliché, a hook on which to hang various ideological and political agendas.

In Jim Sheridan's 1997 'ceasefire' film, *The Boxer*, the heroine Maggie tells her father, Republican boss Joe Hamill, that her marriage to an IRA man imprisoned in Long Kesh has long been over, although the social code of their community mandates her continued fidelity: 'I'm the prisoner here', she says, 'You and your politics have made sure of that.' Nevertheless, she intends to leave her husband for Danny Flynn, the man she has always loved. As she speaks, she is juxtaposed with a print of a wild goose taking off over the ocean, a significant component of the *mise-en-scène* that symbolises her longing for freedom, but also borrows from Irish history to suggest that the price of liberty may be enforced exile. In *The Boxer* Sheridan promotes individual female desire as a counterweight to collective Republican 'fanaticism', asking whether Maggie's erotic transgression must inevitably entail her exclusion from her Catholic nationalist 'home'. By aligning its love story with the impulse towards peace, the film mobilises the weight of audience empathy against those members of the IRA who wish to continue the armed struggle.[4]

The Boxer implicitly posits the incompatibility of hard line Irish Republicanism with Irish feminism, but the IRA prisoner's wife is a flexible cultural icon in whom politics, sexuality and narrative aesthetics can intersect to produce quite different ideological results. Given the release of most political prisoners after the 1998 Good Friday Agreement, and the decommissioning of Long Kesh in 2000, this trope belongs to recent history rather than to current events. But an analysis of how 'women's issues' can be appropriated for strategic purposes by male interests (whether they are conservative, radical or liberal) is not yet out of date.

Many Irish media critics have lamented the tendency of native filmmakers to neglect social and economic circumstances in order to refract their politics through the lens of personal relationships.[5] Certainly the story of the Troubles has often been told as an exercise in family values or a version of romantic melodrama, and the words 'Romeo and Juliet' should be expunged from the lexicon of Irish film criticism. Nevertheless, driven by the interlinked imperatives of funding and the box-office, filmmakers with political interests persist in creating audience empathy through relatively conventional techniques.[6] The trope of the prisoner's wife (or girlfriend) offers several narrative advantages: in a society with high incarceration rates it offers a guarantee of authenticity; it interrupts desire with the insurmountable obstacle of the prison wall, and it provides the female character with a choice between fidelity and betrayal, always the source of fruitful triangular complications. Of course, these are the fictional virtues of the motif. In real life the burdens borne by prisoners' wives and families are at least as heavy as those borne by the prisoners themselves.

The trope of the unfaithful prisoner's wife is closely related to the figure of the soldier's whore, the woman who sleeps with a member of the British army of occupation. In both cases, female sexual transgression threatens the masculinity of the colonised native, who has no reciprocal access to the coloniser's women. At the climax of David Lean's film *Ryan's*

Daughter (1970), the local community, unflatteringly represented as a lynch mob, hacks off the long hair of the Irish heroine Rosie in order to punish her affair with a British officer. They accuse her of betraying an IRA arms shipment to her soldier lover, and facilitating his arrest of a Republican hero. Although Rosie has not committed the political treachery of which the mob suspects her, her sexual collaboration is provocation enough, and the punishment is grotesquely eroticised when the crowd strips off her underclothing as well as her hair.

Ryan's Daughter was extremely popular in Ireland; in Dublin it ran for nearly a year (Rockett 1988: 113). Its fictional representation of female humiliation was soon echoed on the streets of Northern Ireland. In early 1971, several young women from the Ballymurphy district of Belfast who were 'fraternising' with the enemy at discos run by the British Army had their heads shaved and were tarred and feathered by members of the IRA. Gerry Adams was popularly suspected of organising these ritual punishments (Sharrock 1998: 76–8). In November 1971 three women from Derry who had been dating soldiers were also shaved, tarred and feathered, and left tied to railings or lampposts, apparently on the orders of Martin McGuinness (Clarke 2001: 47–9). Members of Cumann na mBan, the women's section of the IRA, helped to carry out the sentences. According to newspaper reports, the public spectacle was condoned by large sections of the community: jeering crowds watched without intervening as judgement was inscribed directly on the female bodies that had transgressed (Cowan 2001). How often such scenes were repeated is hard to determine, although one commentator claims a figure of twenty-eight in 1972 alone (Shannon 1989: 59); but the practice had mostly died out by the late 1970s.[7] Because they tapped into the power of sexualised dramatic ritual, however, these incidents had a long afterlife in the Northern Irish imagination, and were as often repeated in fiction as in fact; moreover, these fictions were selectively gendered. At least four men were tarred and feathered by the IRA in 1971,[8] and over the years several other males have received the same punishment, but, with the exception of the hero of Joe Comerford's film *High Boot Benny*, the victims of head-shaving and tarring and feathering are always imaginatively constructed as female.

For example, a 1972 BBC television drama, *A War of Children*, showed a young girl having her head shaved as a punishment for an affair with a British soldier; and a Canadian film made in 1974, *A Quiet Day in Belfast*, climaxes its preposterous and blood-soaked plot with a female tar-and-feathering which is meant to emphasise the grotesque and primitive nature of Irish violence. The female scapegoat also found her way into canonical literature: in his 1975 poem 'Punishment' Seamus Heaney creates an analogy between the 'tar-black' peat-bog corpse of a fourteen-year-old girl who was shaved, blindfolded and subsequently drowned (Glob 1969: 112–14) and her contemporary Derry 'sisters', one of whom was also blindfolded before being shaved.[9] Following the interpretation of P. V. Glob's *The Bog People*, in which he found the photographs of the preserved corpse of the

'Windeby Girl' (Glob 1969: 110–15, 153), Heaney characterises the first-century sacrificial victim as a 'little adulteress' who was punished for sexual betrayal:

> her shaved head
> like a stubble of black corn,
> her blindfold a soiled bandage. (Heaney 1975: 37)

Heaney acknowledges the psychological attraction of an act that defends native masculinity by asserting the tribe's ownership of women's bodies against the forces of the occupying power. In so doing, however, he frankly indicts himself as the 'artful voyeur' of a contemporary pornographic scene:

> Little adulteress,
> before they punished you
>
> you were flaxen-haired,
> undernourished, and your
> tar-black face was beautiful.
> My poor scapegoat,
>
> I almost love you
> but would have cast, I know,
> the stones of silence.
> I am the artful voyeur
>
> of your brain's exposed
> and darkened combs,
> your muscles' webbing
> and all your numbered bones:
>
> I who have stood dumb
> when your betraying sisters,
> cauled in tar,
> wept by the railings,
>
> who would connive
> in civilised outrage
> yet understand the exact
> and tribal, intimate revenge. (Heaney 1975: 38)

This poem has attracted considerable hostile commentary, because in claiming to 'understand' the motives behind the punishment, Heaney appears to condone it.[10] Though he knows the spectacle is ethically indefensible, not 'civilised', Heaney admits that he is seduced both by the 'voyeuristic' erotic attraction of the blindfolded female 'scapegoat' and by the precise dramatic logic of the reprisal: since a woman's hair is a displaced representation of her sexuality, the revenge is indeed 'exact' and 'intimate'. He describes the heads of the Derry women as 'cauled in tar', and the apparently extraneous childbirth metaphor implied by the word 'caul' obliquely suggests anxieties about miscegenation evoked by the idea of 'sleeping with the enemy'. His use of the word 'tribal' may concede too much to the stereotype of the IRA as a bunch of testosterone-fuelled cavemen, but the poem probes the motives of those who watched the tar-and-featherings in silence, and confesses his complicity with them.

The tar-and-featherings of the early 1970s persisted in the popular imagination precisely because they were so extreme and so symbolic. In 1189 Richard Coeur de Lion decreed this bizarre method of punishment for delinquent Crusaders: 'A robber, moreover, convicted of theft, shall be shorn like a hired fighter, and boiling tar shall be poured over his head, and feathers from a cushion shall be shaken out over his head, so that he may be publicly known' (Avalon Project). In its inception, therefore, the punishment involved an essential element of display: it was intended as authorised legal spectacle, less final than a public execution, but equally dependent on an audience.[11] Tarring and feathering has been revived in several places since the twelfth century, but its subsequent manifestations have been outside or aimed against the established law, and its victims have usually been men. For example, American colonial rebels frequently tarred and feathered tax collectors loyal to the British government. After the Boston patriots had employed it as a strategy of anti-colonial resistance, however, the practice came to be seen as medieval (which it was) and inhumane, reflecting more badly on the perpetrator than on the victim. The most famous literary tarring and feathering occurs in *Huckleberry Finn*, when the King and the Duke are run out of town on a rail. Although these sleazy types have just sold his friend Jim back into slavery, Huck demonstrates an ethical and 'natural' response to ritualised mob violence, which amounts to a lynching without the deaths: 'Well, it made me sick to see it; and I was sorry for them poor pitiful rascals … It was a dreadful thing to see. Human beings *can* be awful cruel to one another' (Twain 1988: 290). Such behaviour is primitive and barbaric: 'tribal', in Heaney's unguarded diction. American tar-and-featherings were spectacular, exposing their victims to public ridicule, but they were not sexualised. A specifically female version of this punishment, however, was practiced in twentieth-century Europe. During the Liberation of France, in the period known as the 'épuration sauvage', resistance fighters and other members of the community publicly shaved the heads of female collaborators. Sometimes they stripped their victims naked and forced them to parade through the streets,[12] although they eschewed the more painful and grotesque violence of tar and feathers. Twenty thousand women were shorn during the years 1944–46, more than half of them for what became known as 'collaboration horizontale': sleeping with the German enemy (Virgili 2000: 7, 23, 29). The European practice drew upon the archetypal sexual connotations of head shaving, which was a sanctioned medieval punishment for female adultery (Brundage 1996: 42).

The analogy between humiliating a woman who is fraternising with the enemy and punishing an errant prisoner's wife is obvious: in both cases the community intervenes to restore 'tribal' or 'family' values that have been threatened by unsanctioned female desire. Jack Holland opens *The Prisoner's Wife* with the tarring and feathering of a young woman who has doubly transgressed: she is a prisoner's wife who is also a 'Brit lover', a soldier's whore:

> They hacked at her hair until it stood on her head like stubble in a wheat field after harvest ... The man gripped her around the neck with one arm ... He ran the razor over her head in quick backward sweeps. She winced and groaned as it cut her scalp ... When he finished, the razor was a mass of matted hair and blood ... They pushed her against the cold green iron post, pinning her arms back. The man tied her hands roughly with the rope; when he let go she slid down the post ... The girls lifted the can of tar and poured it over her raw bald skull ... She hung like a scorched corpse from the lamppost. (Holland 1981: 3–4)

This blatantly voyeuristic scene prefigures the novel's climax, in which the Republicans cut off the long hair of the heroine Nora, who is also a prisoner's unfaithful wife. Although Nora has been sleeping with a fellow-Irishman, not with a soldier, the tar pot is already on the boil for her; but a competing faction of the IRA interrupts the ritual at the last minute. At the end of the 1970s Holland, who was born in Belfast, reported on the Troubles for the BBC *Insight* team and has written several non-fiction books about the conflict, was still working from observed fact as well as from inherited cliché. In 1979 the young wife of INLA prisoner Mickey Devine, who two years later was the last man to die on the hunger strike, had a child by her new lover. Two INLA men beat up the couple, whose affair had caused a local scandal, and cut off Maggie Devine's long hair (Beresford 1987: 403–4).

Unregulated female sexuality threatened the Republican movement in directly practical as well as symbolic or psychological ways. Not only was pillow talk potentially dangerous, but stepping out of line left women vulnerable to blackmail by the authorities. *Only the Rivers Run Free*, a series of interviews with Northern women recorded between 1980 and 1983, tells the story of Catherine, a Republican prisoner's wife who became pregnant by another man. Catherine felt that her husband would never forgive her, that prison officers would taunt him with her infidelity, and that the whole community would hold her in contempt. She therefore went to England for an abortion, but she was picked up on her return, and interrogated by the RUC. When they discovered the reason for her trip, they tried to force her to become an informer by threatening to tell her imprisoned husband about her aborted pregnancy (Fairweather 1984: 43–8).

During the 1980s, however, the insights of feminism began to percolate into the Republican movement. In 1980 Sinn Féin created a Women's Department and began serious consciousness-raising, at least amongst its urban intellectuals and among the prisoners themselves, who had more time than their counterparts on the outside to reflect on the larger meaning of the struggle for freedom.[13] In her book about prisoners' families, *Web of Punishment*, Carol Coulter recounts the story of Mary, who visited her IRA husband Roy in prison for seventeen years. In 1986, twelve years into his sentence, she became pregnant: 'I didn't know how he'd take it. I told him and the two of us cried and we sorted it out. I brought her (the baby) over to see him then when she was a few weeks old, so the bond's there between the two of them. She idolises him now, and he her' (qtd. in Coulter 1991: 39). Mary's experience with her community was very different from the stereotype produced by the events of the 1970s: no surveillance, no ostracism, above all, no men in balaclavas wielding shears and carrying pots of tar: 'The neighbours could not be better that time when I was pregnant. Anyway, why should you worry about what people are saying? If you did you'd never get on with your own life. They can say what they like about those flats, but it's a good community' (qtd. in Coulter 1991: 40). The passage of seven years conditioned the different reactions to Maggie Devine's and Mary's extra-marital pregnancies. By the end of the 1980s, Tony Catney insisted, things had changed. 'Men are starting to think: "If I was outside and she was inside, would I remain faithful?" Most men wouldn't. Ironically it has got to the stage where the prisoner can accept something like that better than the community' (Coulter 1991: 94).

This gradual alteration in male attitudes was created by the increasing opportunities for education in the prisons of Northern Ireland, which were eagerly seized by Republicans (McKeown 2002: 129–48). Towards the end of the decade Joanna McMinn's Women's Studies course attracted over two hundred students, who engaged in discussions of 'masculinity, male power and feminist politics' (McKeown 2002: 145–6). As Caffney suggests, the prisoners were ahead of the curve. Margo Harkin's *Hush-a-Bye Baby* (1989) shows Ciaran, a teenage Republican, reacting extremely badly to the news that his fifteen-year-old girlfriend Goretti is pregnant, despite the fact that the baby is his own rather than another man's. Although his masculinity is not threatened, he behaves as though the pregnancy is all Goretti's fault. 'Fuck me! D'ye not think I have enough shit as it is?' he explodes when she tells him the news during a visit to Long Kesh. (Not surprisingly, the 'prison visit' has become a required formula in films about the Troubles.) Goretti responds by rushing out of the visiting cell with the words 'You fucking bastard.' A few months later, however, Ciaran writes Goretti a shamefaced letter of apology containing an offer of marriage. He tells her, 'We talk a lot in here about how things should be to make it better for everybody, and that gets us through, because all this can't be for nothing.' This line is shorthand for the whole system of education and association made possible when the British gradually granted the prisoners' five demands after the 1981 hunger strikes had ended. An older prisoner, fresh from his Women's Studies course, has doubtless alerted Ciaran to the fact that it takes two to make a baby, and that women as well as men need freedom from oppression. But Ciaran's epiphany comes too late: Goretti has got used to the idea that she has choices, and nothing is certain by the time she goes into labour at the end of the film. None of her options – adoption, teen marriage or single parenthood on the dole – look promising, and the end of the film is hardly upbeat, but at least she is aware of alternative possibilities. Deflecting the matrimonial happy ending promised by Ciaran's change of heart, Harkin resists the gendered narrative closure demanded by conventional cinematic techniques.

Orla Walsh has paid tribute to Harkin's influence, but her 1992 film *The Visit* is more optimistic about extra-marital pregnancy in the context of male incarceration. Walsh tackles the stereotypical issue of the unfaithful prisoner's wife in order to subject the potential cliché to critique and revision. As the film opens with the caption 'Belfast, 1987', we hear the heroine Sheila's voice admitting, 'I am scared. I never meant this to happen. Seán might never want to see me again.' A series of flashbacks establishes that 'this' is her pregnancy by her lover, which, as a Republican sympathiser, she understands to be politically as well as morally transgressive. Her anxiety triggers a memory of an evening in a Republican club that precisely replicates the scenario evoked by Sinn Féin's Tony Caffney: as she sits smoking and drinking with two other prisoners' wives, a couple of men at the bar encourage their mate to ask Sheila to dance. He heads off in her direction, only to be brought up short by the sudden warning, 'They're prisoners' wives.' Disgusted by the practical joke, he swiftly returns to the bar: like everyone else, he understands that prisoners' wives do not dance with other men.[14]

Sheila then remembers a previous visit to her husband Seán, who is in Long Kesh serving a twenty-year sentence, and is obviously insecure about his wife's increasing financial and emotional independence and her choice of unsuitable, unmarried girl-friends. Sheila is a part-time teacher who wants to improve her Irish in order to get a full-time job, and she tells Seán that she may go to the Donegal Gaeltacht in the summer (an intertextual nod to *Hush-a-Bye Baby*). Seán is horrified to learn of Sheila's intended companion, 'Not that Debbie one? I've heard she's a real slag, that one.' Sheila replies that Debbie is simply young and likes to have a good time: 'that's still allowed, isn't it?' She wants to talk about their relationship, but Seán is not open to discussion: he is taking an Open University course in Irish and he intends to maintain the gendered balance of power by teaching her the language himself. Obviously his Open University curriculum has not got to Women's Studies yet.

As Sheila starts her journey to the Kesh on the day she is intending to tell Seán about her pregnancy, security cameras follow her every move; but the official surveillance of the state is less disturbing than the eyes of her observant neighbours. What appears to be friendly concern on the part of the acquaintances with whom she shares a black taxi is accompanied by a knowing look; while a simple and kindly-meant conversation can be supportive and menacing at the same time. As she sits in the prison waiting room, an older woman asks her how long Seán is in for, and whether she has any 'wains'. No, says Sheila, obviously conscious of her still-concealed pregnancy, 'we didn't have time'. As if to remind her of the potential consequences of her actions, the woman turns to another friend and asks, 'Did you hear about Teresa Lynch? A dreadful thing to happen to such a nice young girl. She'd beautiful hair too. They said it was for shoplifting but I heard it was for playing around.' The cryptic mention of Theresa's lovely hair and the suggestion that it was cut off for 'playing around' is the only reference to physical punishment in the film. In an interview Megan Sullivan asked Orla Walsh, 'What about the scene which alludes to a woman being watched by her community and to her being tarred and feathered?' Walsh replied, 'Sheila has a reference of this event in her cultural memory, and she knows it could happen to her' (Sullivan 1997: 39). Even in 1992, it seems, the traumatic events of the 1970s can still be evoked as shorthand for the nexus of sexual and political codes that govern the 'wire widow'.

The reference to punishment provokes a flashback to the first intimate interaction between Sheila and the father of her child. Ignorant of the proprieties, since he is just an innocent from Dublin, he asks her out for a drink, and when she hesitates he tells her 'you're not the one in jail'. But she is, and she uses him to break out, coming on with surprising directness: 'With the war, you can get to feel sexy around death. Not because it turns you on, but because you fear death, and the only way to feel alive is to be with someone, to make love.' Sheila's atypical frankness and the phrasing of her sexual invitation may seem unrealistic, but in fact they are borrowed directly from real life. Ten years before the film was made, another woman from Belfast called Sheelagh told the interviewers of *Only the Rivers Run Free*:

> You can feel very sexy around death. It's not because in any way you get turned on by death – not at all. It's because of your own fear, because every death reminds you of your own mortality. And to feel very much alive – making love, and becoming absolutely aroused – is probably one of the very best ways. (Fairweather 1984: 171)

Similarly, while the fictional Sheila 'never intended' the pregnancy, she clearly initiates the sex, which satisfies her need to feel alive again rather than any longing for a replacement male. Her desire is an end in itself. Nevertheless, because Seán is in for twenty years, and her biological clock is ticking, the unintended conception may be a blessing in disguise. Sheila told the woman in the waiting room that she had no children because 'we didn't have time'. By the end of Seán's sentence it may be too late for her to conceive at all. Unlike the schoolgirl Goretti, Sheila has the means to maintain the child: a job as a teacher and a room of her own in Ballymurphy. She is going to tell Seán not only about the pregnancy, but also about her decision to keep the baby.

The prisoner may accept or reject his wife's determination, but whatever happens she will not go to live with the father of her child, who is dismissed in a curiously heartless little scene. This hapless middle-class Dublin character falls victim to Walsh's need to have Sheila make a programmatic feminist declaration of independence: 'This whole thing was never about you or him. It was about me. Everything has always been decided for me. Now I'm going to have my own life. My own life with this baby.' When her lover objects, with some reason, that 'people won't like it', she tells him that she intends to challenge the code that governs the prisoner's wife: 'If this is a problem for people they're going to have to deal with it. Same as Seán.'[15] She asserts that she 'stood by' her man through 'the blanket, the dirt, and the deaths': now, in an amusing reversal of the familiar phrase, she is going to see if he will 'stand by' his woman. If he does, they will 'work something out', and she will stay with her marriage and her political convictions. The film sets a feminist test for the Republican movement, but the final close-up shot, where the radiance of Sheila's smile surrounds her like a halo as she looks at her husband, suggests that, like Goretti's Ciaran, Seán will prove to be educable.

The Visit derives from a story written by one of the 1981 hunger strikers, Lawrence McKeown, and the piece was published in a 1990 issue of the Republican POW magazine *The Captive Voice* that focused on the oppression of women. Yet Walsh suggests that, 'It's less feminist that she's pregnant and would like to stay with her husband'. Her comment is informed by a simplistic view of feminism, which has never demanded *a priori* that a woman should prefer her lover to her spouse. Walsh implies that Sheila's choice places her nationalism over her commitment to women's liberation, because 'women in the North have more in common with their brothers or husbands than they do with their sisters in the South' (Sullivan 1997: 37). But the effect of the film itself is more subtle: it suggests that feminist women need to produce change in their nationalist husbands by articulating their own desires, and that such change is not only necessary but possible.

The trope of the prisoner's wife and the quasi-obligatory scenario of the prison visit have become so familiar that they can be used as the basis for comedy. Neil Jordan's *The Crying Game*, released in 1992, the same year as *The Visit*, restages and re-genders the prison visit as a surreal happy ending. Dil, cross-dressed as a sexy young woman, struts past the ordinary prisoners conversing across open tables towards Fergus, the light of her life, who is enclosed in a bulletproof glass cage. She plays the role of the hyper-faithful prisoner's wife with a determined gusto that sends up the whole idea: she brings Fergus his vitamins because she needs to keep him in shape for the next seven years. The fact that she is really a man is one that Fergus, for all his embarrassment, does not have to deal with yet. Dil's high-camp fidelity is equated with the anti-feminist Country and Western family values of Tammy Wynette's legendary song, 'Stand by Your Man', which rings out as the final credits roll, but in a last twist the cover on the film's soundtrack was recorded by the male country singer Lyle Lovett. Jordan has said that his film ends 'with a kind of happiness' (Jordan 1993: xii): that happiness is constructed through multiple political and sexual reversals.

Neither *The Visit* nor *The Crying Game* is satisfied with the clichés embedded in the injunction, 'Stand by Your Man'. In their very different ways both films measure the distance traveled between 1971 and 1992. Jim Sheridan's 1997 movie *The Boxer*, however, while it derives its action from the years between 1993 and 1997, lifts its treatment of the prisoner's wife from a much earlier period of the Troubles, and plays its Tammy Wynette straight. Unlike *In the Name of the Father* (Jim Sheridan, 1993) and *Some Mother's Son* (Terry George, 1996), *The Boxer* is avowedly fictional, but the central struggle between the modernising and pragmatic IRA leader Joe Hamill and his diehard subordinate Harry McCormick, who feels that peace negotiations are a betrayal of all the martyred dead, transparently allegorises the differences between Adams and McGuinness on the one hand, and Real or Continuity IRA on the other. Yet Sheridan and George, burned by press attacks on their alleged distortion of the facts in *In the Name of the Father*, refuse to be precise about dates.[16] At the re-opening of the boxing club, Ike Weir announces that the Troubles began twenty-eight years ago, thus locating the 'present' of the film in 1997. The political voice-overs at the start of the movie include a statement by Tony Blair, who became Prime Minister in May 1997. Nevertheless, the announcement of a historic truce early in the movie must reflect the first ceasefire of August 1994. The bombing of a Protestant butcher's shop alludes to the IRA's destruction of the Shankill Road fish shop in October 1993, which nearly derailed the peace negotiations. When Harry disrupts the truce by planting a bomb under an RUC officer's car, the historical reference is to the IRA's attack on London's Canary Wharf in February 1996, which brought the first ceasefire to an end. Sheridan has commented:

> Then the IRA set off a car bomb in England and that focused my thoughts. I think violence, taken out of the moral sphere, is a stupid way to solve things. It's fucking neanderthal, so I thought 'I don't want to endorse this' and maybe I should make the film about someone who fights within the rules. (Dwyer 1997)

Sheridan's refusal to relate his fictional events precisely to the historical peace process is emblematised by his shot of the plaque on Ike's coffin, which allows us to see the first three figures of the date, '199', but obscures the last with handful of soil. This chronological coyness, while not in itself problematic, is consistent with the film's resolute and more disturbing ahistoricity on the question of the prisoner's wives.

The inspiration for *The Boxer*, Sheridan has said, came from Barry McGuigan, the former featherweight world champion:

> I saw Barry in 1984 and he was on the television saying 'Leave the fightin' to McGuigan', which was kind of innocent and naïve, but it appealed to me ... And then I thought about the idea of fighting within the rules and fighting outside them. And then I thought of the love story, y'know. First I thought Catholic-Protestant, but that seemed too schematic and then we went for the prisoner's wife. (Anderson 1997)

Sheridan finds the idea of fighting within the rules a compelling metaphor for what he wants to say about the North.[17] But the love story was clearly an afterthought, tacked on to the boxing narrative and its exploration of competing modes of masculinity. Had Sheridan cared more about it he would have seen that by 1997 'the prisoner's wife' was no less schematic a trope than the Catholic-Protestant thing. Even Sheridan's 'reality based' (Crowdus 1997) scriptwriter Terry George, who left Belfast for America in 1981, was happy to operate in a time warp with respect to this aspect of the movie.

While he insists that he is offering self-criticism from within the Republican movement (Crowdus 1998), Sheridan has also called *The Boxer* 'a propaganda film made with Hollywood money' (Barton 2002: 147), and some of the crudeness of the anachronistic gender scenario must have been dictated by that money. The opening sequence, which features a couple getting married in jail, and an IRA-sponsored wedding reception held without the prisoner, is carefully set up to explain the politico/sexual rules of the game to an American audience, and Sheridan demonstrates what happens to anyone who breaches the boundary that marks the body of the prisoner's wife as forbidden territory. A young teenager is seen slipping his hand down the bare back of a slightly older woman as they dance closely together. Two IRA heavies separate them, pull the boy into lavatory, and tell him, 'Her husband's doing five years in prison. If you go near her again I'll shoot both your kneecaps off.' The Republican chief Joe Hamill nails in the point by giving a wedding speech in praise of the altruism of prisoners' wives that is both sentimental and, given the notoriously high rate of marital breakdown occasioned by incarceration, unrealistic. He tells the new bride that he is proud of 'how you stood by your man', and repeats the cliché several times: his own dead wife 'stood by me and remained faithful to the cause', while 'you women who stood by your men will be remembered as the bravest of the district'. Tammy Wynette would have been delighted.

But the reviewer of Sinn Féin's newspaper, *An Phoblacht*, was furious, arguing that the film might have been made in the 1970s:

A central theme of the film is the plight of prisoners' wives (never partners or girlfriends since in this world all are married) and the crass handling of it is cringe-making. At the start a youth at a party is threatened with knee-capping by an IRA man for dancing too close with a prisoner's wife. 'This is a film about the emergence of women in this society', claims Sheridan in the press handout but I believe Republican women and prisoners' families will find it deeply insulting. There are no Republican women in their own right, no women prisoners, only 'the wives'. (Mac Donncha 1998)

One does not have to be a member of Sinn Féin to see that the film says little about the emergence of women in the North of Ireland. The prisoner's wife scenario functions as a convenient propaganda tool with which to discredit the hard line IRA, not as a serious examination of a woman's right to arbitrate her own destiny. The careless handling of this motif is evidenced in the movie's major plot absurdity: the total erasure of Maggie's husband and Liam's father, the IRA prisoner Thomas. Joe salutes Maggie's loyalty to a man whom she never seems to visit in jail, and never talks about. She later tells her father, 'my marriage was over before Liam was born', that is, about twelve years ago; but Joe apparently has not noticed anything amiss.

The backstory of Maggie's marriage is contrived to sanitise her in the eyes of the audience. When her childhood sweetheart Danny was imprisoned for IRA activities there was no community pressure for her to remain loyal to him, because he renounced his Republican politics in jail. But when her husband, about whom we know nothing except that he was Danny's best friend and used to be a boxer, was also imprisoned for IRA activities, she became a real 'prisoner's wife'. Nevertheless she is ethically off the hook with the audience because her affections have been with Danny all along. On his return, she experiences no emotional conflict about abandoning her spouse: she makes all the running in the re-establishment of her previous relationship. The male who stands between Danny and Maggie is not the prisoner but his son, Liam, whose experiment with arson operates as a junior version of the IRA's sexual surveillance of his mother. Liam, however, is eventually and rather too smoothly appropriated by Danny, who will replace Thomas in the paternal as well as the erotic role.

Sheridan has contrived a situation in which Maggie's conflict is solely with an outdated version of the sexual code of the IRA, who will put a bullet in Danny's head if he dares to sleep with a prisoner's wife. By a process of metonymy, this code comes to stand for the desire to continue the struggle, so the sexual liberation of women is seamlessly equated with the pursuit of peace. When Joe tells Maggie that she has got to be sexually 'above reproach' he sounds positively Victorian, but his love for his daughter and his commitment to ending the war eventually lead him to break with Harry, the hardliner who still believes in doing things the old-fashioned way. At the end of the film Harry's opposition to the peace process is dramatically represented not as a political choice, but as an atavistic insistence on Maggie's fidelity to her imprisoned husband. The verbal component of his climactic attack on Maggie and Danny focuses entirely on her sexual transgression: 'I'm not going to let you drive around with a prisoner's wife Danny Boy … You forgetting your wedding ring, you fucking whore you? You're a prisoner's wife. You know what that means, don't you? You fucking whore.' But Joe's decision to get rid of Harry instead of Danny revises the sexual codes. At the end of the film Harry's wife, who also bitterly opposes the ceasefire, cradles his dead body in a pièta pose (Barton 2000: 108). She has given both her son and her husband to the cause of violence, and now she weeps alone. Mother Ireland is barren. Mother Maggie, determinedly reconstituting her unconventional nuclear family, is headed for 'home'.

The bodies of the prisoner's wife and the soldier's whore, shorn or tarred and feathered, tied to the railings or to a lamppost, sometimes hung with placards proclaiming 'Tout', revived the grotesque spectacle of public punishment that had been replaced during the nineteenth century by the less visible operations of modern penal law. Making allowances for differences of historical context and scale, these pathetic figures can be placed beside the witches, midwives, female vagrants and horizontal collaborators who also served as public scapegoats for their communities in times of crisis. They provided an 'example': a warning issued by those who could not invoke State power and therefore revived a brutal form of popular justice. The British, meanwhile, conducted their own medieval tortures in secret, interrogating Irish prisoners by means of the infamous 'five techniques'. The trauma suffered by the male prisoners was brought to light at the European Court of Justice, but the trauma suffered by the women who were tarred and feathered, though it continues to surface in imaginative texts, has seldom been politically acknowledged. Their status is too ambiguous, the uncomfortable witness they bear too closely related to the early careers of current Sinn Féin leaders. Nevertheless, the IRA have apologised to their victims, among whom these women must be included. They cannot be used as a permanent symbol for the relationship between women and Republican nationalism.

Notes

1   Loyalists have done this as well, in gradually increasing numbers (see White 1988).

2   The connection between war and the violent assertion of masculinity is a truism that recent accounts of the use of rape as a military weapon in Bosnia only serve to confirm.

3   Although the wives of Protestant paramilitaries have been subjected to similar pressures, they rarely figure in popular culture (Fairweather 1984: 307).

4   For a detailed and convincing reading of the film see Barton 2002: 99–122. For a negative view of its sentimentality and political absurdity, see McLoone 2000: 76–9.

5   See, for example, the influential Hill (1991: 38), quoted approvingly (in the context of a discussion of conventional narrative forms) by the equally influential McLoone (2000: 73–4). Also see Hill 1998: 150.

6 For a highly sensible defence of Jim's Sheridan's populist approach to filmmaking, see Barton 2002: 4 and passim.

7 Information from the Political Research department, Linen Hall Library, Belfast.

8 See the CAIN Website Chronology of the Troubles. White 1988 carries a photograph of a young man who was tarred and feathered as recently as 1987.

9 For a feminist discussion of this poem, see Coughlan 1991: 103.

10 For the most famous of these responses see Longley 1994: 77–8. In the course of an excellent reading of the poem's ethical ambiguities, Corcoran quotes Conor Cruise O'Brien's negative reaction (1986: 114–17). Both Longley and O'Brien dislike what they perceive as Heaney's political sympathy with the IRA, but David Lloyd, coming from the opposite political position, attacks the 'unpleasantness' of a poetry that seems to confirm the stereotype of Irish 'tribal' barbarity. Lloyd challenges the validity of Heaney's apparent self-criticism: 'As so often in Heaney's work, the sexual drive of knowing is challenged, acknowledged, and let pass without further interrogation, the stance condemned but the material it purveys nevertheless exploited' (Lloyd 1993: 31–3).

11 The classic discussion of the importance of public spectacle to the administration of justice is the section on 'Torture' in Foucault's *Discipline and Punish* (Foucault 1979: 3–69).

12 For a discussion of the spectacle of nudity, see Virgili 2000: 241–4.

13 For a description of this process by Mairead Keane, head of the Sinn Féin Women's Department, see Lyons (1992).

14 For the fullest available discussion of the politics of *The Visit* see Sullivan (1998).

15 My transcription of lines from *The Visit* differs throughout from that of Sullivan (1998). Possibly she had access to a screenplay, although she does not say so.

16 See Crowdus 1997 and Crowdus 1998.

17 Using the work of Allen Feldman on the transition from the 'hardman' to the 'gunman' in working-class Belfast, Barton illuminates Sheridan's Irish version of the 'boxing' film by relating it to local historical circumstances (2002: 108–15).

References

Anderson, J. (1997) 'Love and Politics in Ireland', *Newsday*, 29 December. On-line. Lexis-Nexis.

Avalon Project at Yale Law School. 'Laws of Richard I (Coeur de Lion) Concerning Crusaders Who Were to Go by Sea. 1189 A.D'. On-line. Available at: http://www.yale.edu/lawweb/avalon/medieval/richard.htm

Barton, R. (2002) *Jim Sheridan: Framing the Nation*. Dublin: Liffey Press.

Beresford, D. (1987) *Ten Men Dead: The Story of the 1981 Irish Hunger Strike*. London: Grafton Books.

Brossat, A. (1992) *Les Tondues: Un Carnaval Moche*. Levallois-Perret: Manya.

Brundage, J. A. (1996) 'Sex and Canon Law', in Vern L. Bullough and James A. Brundage (eds) *Handbook of Medieval Sexuality*. New York: Garland, 33–50.

Clarke, L. and K. Johnston (2001) *Martin McGuinness: From Guns to Government*. Edinburgh and London: Mainstream Publishing.

Conflict Archive on the Internet (CAIN): The Northern Ireland Conflict 1968 to the Present. On-line. Available at: http://cain.ulst.ac.uk/index.html

Corcoran, N. (1986) *Seamus Heaney*. London: Faber.

Coughlan, P. (1991) 'Bog Queens: The Representation of Women in the Poetry of John Montague and Seamus Heaney', in Toni O'Brien Johnson and David Cairns (eds) *Gender in Irish Writing*. Milton Keynes: Open University Press.

Coulter, C. (1991) *Web of Punishment: An Investigation*. Dublin: Attic Press.

Cowan, R. (2001) 'McGuinness Exposed', *The Guardian*, 9 May. On-line. Lexis-Nexis.

Crowdus, G. and O. Leary (1997) 'The "Troubles" He's Seen in Northern Ireland: An Interview with Terry George', in *Cineaste*, 23, 1, 24(6). On-line.

_____ (1998) 'Getting Past the Violence: An Interview with Jim Sheridan', in *Cineaste*, 23, 3, 13(3). On-line.

Demonpion, D. (1996) *Arletty*. Paris: Flammarion.

Douglas, M. (1984) *Purity and Danger: An Analysis of the Concepts of Pollution and Taboo*. London: Ark.

Dwyer, M. (1997) 'My Left Hook', in *Irish Times*, 20 September. On-line. Lexis-Nexis.

Fairweather, E., R. McDonough and M. McFadyean (1984) *Only the Rivers Run Free: Northern Ireland: The Women's War*. London and Sydney: Pluto Press.

Foucault, M. (1979) *Discipline and Punish: The Birth of the Prison*. Translated by Alan Sheridan. New York: Vintage.

Glob, P. V. (1969) *The Bog People: Iron-Age Man Preserved*, trans. Rupert Bruce-Mitford. Ithaca: Cornell University Press.

Heaney, S. (1975) *North*. London: Faber.

Hill, J. (1991) 'Hidden Agenda: Politics and the Thriller', in *Circa* 57, 36–41.

Holland, J. (1981) *The Prisoner's Wife*. New York : Dodd, Mead.

Jordan, N. (1993) *A Neil Jordan Reader*. London: Vintage.

Lloyd, D. (1993) *Anomalous States: Irish Writing and the Post-Colonial Moment*. Durham: Duke University Press.

Longley, E. (1994) '*North*: "Inner Émigré" or "Artful Voyeur"?' in Tony Curtis (ed.) *The Art of Seamus Heaney*. Dublin: Wolfhound Press.

Lyons, L. (1992) '"At the End of the Day": An Interview with Mairead Keane, National Head of Sinn Féin Women's Department', in *boundary 2*, 19, 2, 260–86.

Mac Donncha, M. (1998) 'Punch Drunk Plot', in *An Phoblacht*, 5 February. On-line. Available at: http://www.irlnet.com/aprn/index.html

McKeown, L. (2002) *Out of Time: Irish Republican Prisoners Long Kesh 1972–2000*. Dublin: Beyond the Pale Publications.

McLoone, M. (2000) *Irish Film: The Emergence of a Contemporary Cinema*. London: British Film Institute.

Rockett, K., L. Gibbons and J. Hill (1998) *Cinema and Ireland*. London: Routledge.

Shannon, E. (1989) *I Am of Ireland: Women of the North Speak Out*. Boston: Little, Brown.

Sharrock, D. and M. Davenport (1998) *Man of War, Man of Peace: The Unauthorised Biography of Gerry Adams*. London: Pan Books.

Sullivan, M. (1997) '*The Visit*, Incarceration, and Film by Women in Northern Ireland: An Interview with Orla

Walsh', in *The Irish Review*, 21, 29–40.

___ (1998) 'Orla Walsh's *The Visit* (1992): Incarceration and Feminist Cinema in Northern Ireland', in *New Hibernia Review*, 2, 2, 85–99.

Twain, M. (1988) *Adventures of Huckleberry Finn*. Berkeley: University of California Press.

Virgili, F. (2000) *La France 'Virile': Des Femmes Tondues à la Libération*. Paris: Payot.

___ (2002) 'Les Tontes de la Libération en France'. On-line. Available at http://www.ihtp-cnrs.ens-cachan.fr/publications/cahier31/tontes_fr_virgili_31.html

White, P. (1988) 'The Bloody Toll of the Punishment Squads', *Irish Times*, June 2.

'We're not fucking Eye-talians':
The Gangster Genre and Irish Cinema

Lance Pettitt

> Can't you micks make anything but movies about this General guy? It's not like he's
> Al Capone.
>   – Jerry Bruckheimer's 'Head' interviewed by Stephen Walsh, 2003

This chapter examines how the appropriation of the gangster film has figured in the re-articulation of the recent history and cultural memory of crime in the cinema of post-1993 Ireland. My argument is that post-1993, a deep-seated and intimate 'genre memory' of gangster films (Grainge 2003: 9–10) provided a specific context for understanding films about Irish crime. In the light of this position, I want to explore the connections between Irish cinema, gangster films and what Jim Collins calls 'genericity' (Collins 1993: 242–63).

If it is axiomatic that the Irish are central to the emergence and sustained popularity of the classic Hollywood gangster genre, in what follows I do not intend to catalogue a list of characters, actors and directors with Irish lineage. Instead, I want to focus on *The General* (John Boorman, 1998), *Ordinary Decent Criminal* (Thaddeus O'Sullivan, 1999) and *Vicious Circle* (David Blair, 1999) – films that deal with the Dublin 'robber baron' turned 'godfather of crime', Martin Cahill. I want to off-set this analysis with that of two films about the crime journalist Veronica Guerin, *When the Sky Falls* (John MacKenzie, 2000) and the US-funded *Veronica Guerin* (Joel Schumacher, 2003), whose contract murder was allegedly organised by another gang boss, John Gilligan, in 1996.

These films were all released at a time when Irish cinema, television and video audiences were highly culturally competent to enjoy the axial pleasures of gangster films and British television crime thrillers. The gangster genre's established grammar, locale and look were inflected with a 'local' accent to examine concerns particular to Ireland in the 1990s. The most notable example of the former is *Michael Collins* (Neil Jordan, 1996), with its homage sequences to *The Godfather* (Francis Ford Coppola, 1972), whereas contemporary society and crime is rendered cinematically in different registers in films like *I Went Down* (Paddy Breathnach, 1997), *The General*, and *Flick* (Fintan Connolly, 1999), but also television productions like *Making the Cut* (Martyn Friend, 1997).[1]

Just as the first major sound cycle of 'classical' Hollywood gangster films was derived from newspaper coverage, pulp fiction and theatrical sources in the 1920s, the Cahill films amplified and re-mediated an already existing 'mythic' figure generated by the Irish print and broadcast news media.[2] Veronica Guerin's death also produced phenomenal media coverage, and her role within the media itself gave further inspiration for themes regarding the responsibilities of the press. Although Cahill was a self-styled 'ordinary decent criminal' uninvolved in drugs, the potency of these Irish-based films derived from their capacity to remind those living through the 'success' of the Celtic Tiger (Kirby et al., 2002: 1–18) of the drug-ridden, crime-saturated major cities, and of the social despondency and political corruption that characterised the era. Subsequently, the Guerin films equivocate about appropriate methods for responding to the crime wave, simultaneously offering, in the central figure of their eponymous crusading journalist, an endorsement of tactics that sidestep legality, whilst applauding the state clamp-down that expressed itself most visibly in the enactment of the Criminal Assets Bureau (CAB) following her murder in 1996. The politics of popular representation demonstrate the capacity for gangster films to appropriate and rehearse neo-conservative ideologies as well as their potential to offer more searching critiques of crime and its causes.

According to Collins (1993: 242–3), cinematic 'genericity' is prone to produce films that exhibit the broadly divergent features of either 'eclectic irony' or 'new sincerity' that co-exist in postmodern popular culture. Such 'new sincerity' is an effort to represent a mythical nostalgia, a cinematic 'pure' past in the face of anxieties about social miscegenation and cultural multiculturalism. In the USA these anxieties produced the Irish as a reactive, counter-discursive 'white ethnicity' amidst a Latino presence in US popular culture in the 1980s and 1990s (Negra 2001: 229–30 and this volume). 'Eclectic irony' is characterised by increasing reflexivity about origins and 'even more sophisticated hyperconsciousness concerning not just narrative formulae, but the conditions of their own circulation and reception' (Collins 1993: 247–80). To some critics such a condition forms the basis of a debilitating logic of a postmodern, Westernised society characterised by cultural production that betrays a fundamental 'disappearance of a sense of history [and] its capacity to retain its own past' (Jameson 1998: 20 [1988]) and it is 'a pathological symptom of a society that has become incapable of dealing with time and history' (1998: 10). Even if Jameson's conclusion appears here overly pessimistic, earlier in the same essay he discusses what he terms 'pastiche' – a form of 'blank parody' (1998: 5) – and 'the nostalgia mode' (1998: 7–8) in cinema in ways that are pertinent to our discussion of the development of the gangster genre and its dispersive appropriation from one culture to another. Jameson observes of American culture that it is

> exceedingly symptomatic to find the very style of nostalgia films invading and colonising even those movies today which have contemporary settings, as though for some reason, we were unable today to focus on our own present, as though we had become incapable of achieving aesthetic representations of our own current experience. (Jameson 1998: 9)

In Irish culture, renowned in the twentieth century for its rural, traditional and un-modern bias and a very strong sense of its own history, popular cinematic representations relied on but also relished imported images of the urban profanity, individualist and consumerist US culture of which the screen gangsters (and their later Anglo-American television versions) were emblematic (Rockett 2001: 221). The 1990s indigenous prod-uctions strove to capture the look, sounds and emotional landscape of people's experience of the organised crime world as it had been mediated through television and the press, whilst also recalling earlier cinematic images of the Irish and other ethnic gangsters. They did so through 'borrowed' generic conventions that had already been thoroughly indigenised, *pace* Jameson, at the margins of postmodernity.

The narratives of the gangster and Guerin films represent values and ethics under examination in the present generation of Irish society which are expressed thematically as the relations between three broad ideological fields, namely: authoritarian/statist, liberal/humanist and populist/individualist. These fields are distinct but as we shall see, there are interesting points of contact and significant mingling that are played out in the narratives of the films. Briefly, the ideology of authority/state is that which supports interests of Irish Law, the Gardaí, Government and the Church, 'community', tradition; the ideology of the liberal/humanist is identified with middle-class values, professional career ethics, catholicism with a small 'c', the nuclear family, toleration and understanding of a shared humanity and a belief in education/reform for gradual social change and modernity; the ideology of the populist/individualist is concerned to oppose all forms of state/institutional authority (but sees itself as apolitical), replacing it with an alternative ethic of clan/extended family loyalty, is homosocial in nature and based on charismatic individual leadership that is paternalistic. Existing at the margins of the working class and an underclass, it is ruthlessly acquisitive of material wealth and displays status symbols that are otherwise earned 'legitimately' or achieved through 'time served'. It is an ideology that sanctions violence and retributive 'rough justice' against repressive authority and competing business 'enemies', but also against those from among 'its own' who transgress. It promotes the notion of a 'natural' Law and values individual actions as against the Law of the State and consensual decision/action. The populist/individual is embodied on screen in the 'gangster hero' who 'speaks, if contradictorily, for the status quo, for its buried underside as well as its affirmative goals' (Gledhill in Cook 1999: 177).

The five films under discussion here represent variations of conflicts between state authority figures (Garda detectives, judges, politicians, civil servants), populist individualists (gangsters, paramilitaries) and liberal/humanist reformers (sympathetic police, Veronica Guerin). In *The General* and *Ordinary Decent Criminal* the emphasis and screen time falls on the gangster, with the police and authorities providing the necessary dramatic foil in pursuit, caper or (attempted) capture mode with the media playing a minor role. With *Vicious Circle*, the production tried (not very convincingly) to give more emphasis to the personal life of the investigating detective, Finney (Andrew Connolly) and his side-kick, Molloy (Luke Griffin) in the television 'police procedural' crime series mode while the paramilitaries (John Kavanagh) are brought more into play in order to create a triangle of conflicts. Ironically set in Dublin's 'Peace Garden' in Parnell Square, the end of *Vicious Circle* was the film to most blatantly endorse the theory that the Gardaí collaborated with the IRA to remove their blanket surveillance of 'The General', allowing the 'unofficial' army to eliminate a problem that the State could not solve.

With the two Guerin films, rather in the manner of the classic 'G-Men' series but also in examples like *Donnie Brasco* (Mike Newell, 1997), the emphasis of the narrative falls mostly on a police investigation, but with the twist that the decisive Joan Allen and Cate Blanchett roles put the female crime-reporter-as nemesis at the centre of the film's narrative. Although Guerin (Blanchett) or her fictionalised self, Sinead Hamilton, (Allen) are shown to represents a middle-class world of Dublin decency, family life and motherhood, both films also associate her with a degree of lawless individuality and maverick behaviour that suggests affinities between pursuer and pursued, complicating the clear lines of ideological demarcation. Indeed, *The General* and *Veronica Guerin* also share structural similarities, both beginning with the murder of their central character, an event that is then reeled backwards (literally in Boorman's case).

For the remainder of this chapter I want to explore how these broad ideological fields are played out across recurring themes in the Irish gangster narratives, including: the urban space and how it is shaped (and distorted) in the films; capitalism and alternative economies; anti-authoritarianism; sexuality and its aberrant forms; and finally, what I am calling, gangster reflexivity. Where appropriate, I will show how this selective list of topics draws on historical precedents from US gangster films.

By the mid-1990s Dublin was able to 'boast' a cityscape that was sufficiently photogenic for the cinematic requirements of the gangster genre: modern buildings, jostled with dockland warehouses and run-down areas of inner city; refurbished civic, historical architecture and public space (for tourism) contrasted with corporation flats at the edges of the city. *The General* is most overt in portraying these changes in the built environment as they impact on the central character, with Cahill shown to be completely at home in streets and alleyways, and the banks and buildings that he raids. From its opening sequence from a sea-cliff, swooping up the Liffey, over the city, dissolves are mixed with the iconography and harsh music track of the television crime thriller in *When the Sky Falls* to establish urban space but also the specificities of Dublin (Guinness's Brewery features). *Vicious Circle* kicks off with a factory raid but then swiftly goes to aerial shots of Dublin before grounding us at residential street level and establishing the mundane, domestic 'other' life of Cahill. Following its fictionalising, somewhat surreal production rationale, O'Sullivan's film plays freely with its location in a smash and grab technique that has least veracity to an actual Dublin, though the closing heist was shot in the old Irish parliament building, now a Bank of Ireland building.

The Warner Bros. films of the early 1930s were foremost in a tradition that sought to explore the contradictions of urban capitalism and its social effects, notably in films like *The Public Enemy* (1931).[3] Whilst the film may seem to lend itself to a liberal reading, it is worth remembering that Tom Power (James Cagney) meets his grisly end at the hands of a rival gang not the police. Under pressure to be seen not to exploit crime on screen for commercial gain, Warner Bros. framed the film with declarative titles insisting that 'The Public Enemy's not a man, nor is it a character – it is a problem that sooner or later, WE, the public, must solve'. In light of ineffective policing, judicial corruption and asinine legislation, this call could be interpreted as a populist legitimisation of vigilantism by a wider society concerned about a generation of unchecked immigration and in the midst of a Depression. Thus, 'the gangster pictures contributed to the scape-goating … of an ethnic stereotype of criminality' (Maltby 2001: 141).

Boorman's *The General*, operates most clearly out of the 'bio-pic-with-a-conscience' tradition, not only in the way that it deals with Cahill's (Brendan Gleeson) rise to notoriety from his deprived origins in the Hollyfield Buildings, but also because the Gardaí – G-men like – had to adopt some of the intimidation methods of the gangster (Boorman 1998: 113). Crucially, although Boorman had the film shot on colour stock, he did so with the objective of producing a print to be screened in monochrome, a kind of 'retro mode'. Boorman claimed he wanted to avoid colour because it would 'prettify' and 'romanticise poverty', and that 'a black-and-white film approaches the condition of dream, of memory, reaches out into the audience's unconscious' and creates 'a familiar but alien world, a contiguous reality' (Boorman 1998: xvii). It is difficult to square this with the sequences of Cahill junior's (Eamon Owens) early thieving exploits and the older Cahill robbing houses to the soundtrack of Van Morrison ('This is what paradise must be like'), though it does have a compelling 'dream-like' and envisioning quality also picked up in the portrayal of the fictional Michael Lynch in *Ordinary Decent Criminal*, but with a different tone. Boorman's Cahill is cast as a victim figure that resists and rises out of his circumstances, particularly as he defies Dublin Corporation's re-housing (as he sees it, uprooting) of his local community. Early on Gleeson delivers the following from a caravan on the demolition site that once was his home: 'yous are all fucking oppressors of the poor. Civil fucking servants, Garda fucking Síochána, parish fucking priests – get the fuck ouda me house.' Though Cahill finally accepts being moved to Corporation housing in a more middle-class area of Dublin ('to be nearer to me work') and he eventually buys a detached house as well, the shift to a suburban environment bodes ill-fortune. Whilst Boorman and his chief character share a nostalgia about the childhood past (idyllic community poverty), O'Sullivan's Lynch is wilfully inventive and ironic in telling his children about 'the slum flats of Hollyfield, seen through fairytale eyes' (Stembridge 2000: 29) and the *mise-en-scène* 'periodisation' is deliberately artificial and comic for the audience.

This should alert us to the fact that US gangster films of different waves have long been argued to express symbolically an alternative shadow economy of capitalism, corruption and its supportive ideologies. Al Capone famously defended bootlegging as 'business' not crime in the 1920s, and the Mafia's extended 'family' of connections, like the Irish crime gangs in the US, could be seen as a logical and effective response by immigrants in adapting their social structures to American ethics in a new, hostile environment. The representation of Cahill in contemporary Ireland does not lend itself to such an immigrant/adaptation thesis, but Boorman and O'Sullivan offer instead the Irish gangster as a symptom of 'a country shaking off its Catholic past and fumbling toward an uncertain future in Europe' (Boorman 1998: viii), 'a country on the make, where only a few years ago the government declared not one but two moratoria on unpaid taxes' (O'Sullivan 2000: 2) pressing the point that the criminality of the fictional Lynch is consistent with a popular disdain for authority and an extreme version of corruption within corporate capitalism.

The anti-authoritarian strain is evident in all the Cahill films, where he rails against police, priests, civil servants and banks (in another unscripted line, Gleeson's Cahill quips to a queue behind him in a bank: 'isn't it terrible the way they make you wait for your own money?'). This tone gives a mordantly humorous if sympathetic view in particular scenes in *The General*, despite the despicable acts of violence and intimidation that we also witness. A different comic tone pervades *Ordinary Decent Criminal* and is caught well in the playful attitude of Kevin Spacey's entertaining if entirely unconvincing performance. As such these films are close to exemplifying what we earlier termed 'new sincerity' and 'eclectic irony' respectively. The 'General' films are post-Catholic (in the same way as Jordan's *The Butcher Boy* is critical of the institution) but in Boorman's film Cahill is shown attempting to combine a facile Catholicism with nostalgia for an idealised Hollyfield community because it serves his interests. In a short scene between Cahill and Mrs Hogan, a woman whose daughter he is trying to dissuade from testifying in court, Gleeson – in an unscripted gesture – pulls out a crucifix chain to make a calculated attempt to appeal to the mother's sense of community 'solidarity' (Boorman 1998: 109) which is unceremoniously thrown back in his face.

In this moment Cahill's old style 'principles' are brought into sharp relief, as are his dealings with the paramilitaries, where his self-styled image as an 'ordinary decent criminal' who is defiantly 'his own boss' and his avoidance of drugs-related activities carried out by rival gangsters like Tony Felloni (Italian-Irish Dubliner) and John Gilligan set him apart. The 'family firm' ethos of Cahill is, if anything, diluted in Boorman's 'tragic hero' angle, and although low-key, Stott's performance in *Vicious Circle* achieves a credible TV naturalist domesticity about it which scores highly on 'cultural verisimilitude'. In stark contrast,

Stembridge's screenplay makes no pretensions to explain the socialisation of Michael Lynch. At the London screening O'Sullivan claimed that 'the film isn't about Martin Cahill, is it?' (quoted in Pettitt 2000: 24). This production's justification for its apparently glib approach is rooted in its enjoyment of the myth of 'The General' and its playing with the conventions of the genre. O'Sullivan is not attempting to represent the 'truth' of Cahill in a journalistic sense: he is more interested in how the criminal sees himself: 'the only truth for Michael Lynch is the truth that suits his book' (O'Sullivan, 'The World according to Michael Lynch' in Stembridge 2000: 2). O'Sullivan wanted his film to show 'that was Cahill's world and, in a sense, the film had that subjectivity, or is supposed to have that subjectivity – his space that he is in control of, to get this idea across that it was him in authority' (O'Sullivan 2000: 23). Hence the film's departure from straight-faced realism, the heightened sense of screen imagery and the fact that Lynch/Cahill defies history, does not die but rides off into the credits on his motorbike having just stolen a chocolate bar. Audiences in Ireland (Maume 2000) were critical of the film's disregard for facts, cultural verisimilitude, accent authenticity and the abuse of the 'geographic continuity' of Dublin (McCloy 2000: 41).

For all their anti-authoritarianism, Irish gangster films locate an alternative source of authority in the gang or 'firm' as 'family' with Cahill and Gilligan as the 'lord', 'boss', 'General' or 'godfather' controlling a strict hierarchy of power that is as rigorously oppressive as

Figure 1: **Comedic rough justice for gangsters who cross their boss. Brendan Gleeson and Seán McGinley in _The General_ (permission – John Boorman).**

state law or church morality. Boorman's Cahill may seem to champion class oppression, yet he is no socialist – in fact, the tight-knit gang/family is feudal and militaristic (he is the 'General' after all). As with the portrayal of Gilligan in *When the Sky Falls* and *Veronica Guerin*, the gangster's 'family' endorses honour, loyalty and respect for 'rank' and people who step out of line or question things rarely survive. 'Respect', however, is based on the threat of violence, meted out with a perverse sense of 'fairness' and justice (as in the case of a gang member who is suspected of stealing more than a share from a job). In their invocation of 'moral certainties' and apoliticism, the Cahills and the Gilligan figures call for the reinstatement of conservative values at odds to the rest of society, which has become liberal and tries to promote 'new' standards. We may ask whether this in turn expresses an underlying dissatisfaction with the new liberal consensus in a manner comparable with the equivalent British crime cycle (Claire Monk, writing on the revived popularity of British gangster films in the 1990s, attributes the screening of 'traditional' masculinist values to a 'new lad' demographic (1999: 173)).

Indeed, key to these films, as to commentary about their US antecedents, has been the representation of gender and the performance of (especially) male sexuality. Although films have portrayed female gangsters (*Blondie Johnson*, 1933), the genre is primarily associated with screening a particular kind of patriarchal masculinity. That the gangster's world is a homosocial one is self-evident: the subservient roles of 'molls' or wives of classical gangsters are carried through into these Irish variants: 'mots' and spouses are firmly domesticated in the Cahill films, and Gilligan's wife, although she runs their over-blown, *nouveaux riche* equestrian centre in *Veronica Guerin*, is kept strictly on a short rein. Male gangsters are generally more expansive, happier and 'themselves' when they are not domesticated but enjoy freedom and space 'on the street'. The confounding exception to this is Cahill himself who is presented to be a home-loving father, a pigeon-fancier who is content in a domestic environment (one might add, particularly when it is somebody else's house!). However, his domestic space becomes a fortress and a trap to restrict his freedom to do business and eventually the place of his death (*The General*, *When the Sky Falls*). The lesser 'faces' of the all-male gang may have spouses or girlfriends but they indulge freely along with the single lads in gambling, drinking, doing drugs and enjoying prostitute sex – as does Gilligan in *Veronica Guerin*, signifying and accentuating his moral depravity. The level of consumption and pleasure in clothes, motorbikes, inflicting sadistic violence, sex and gambling is an index of the gangster's contempt for the 'workaday' capitalism under which the rest of society obediently works, but its excess merely embodies *in extremis* the underlying principles of consumerism and 'cut throat' competition that drives the wider economy. The notion of the gangster as a deviant individual version of normative society is crucially expressed through the incest motif and homosexuality.

Critics like Fran Mason have noted that the homosocial structure of the gang allows for homosexual desire to be sublimated between older and younger gangster charges like Putty Nose and Tom Power in *The Public Enemy* (Mason 2002: 18) and between gang members (Tom and Mike), as part of strong bonds of friendship, loyalty and trust. In the British film *The Krays* (Peter Medak 1990) the open secret of Reggie Kray's bisexuality was represented as acceptable within the 'swinging' 1960s milieux and screened in a relatively normative manner. In *When the Sky Falls*, in a jacuzzi scene male bodily display on screen is overtly sexualised by framing but homosexuality *per se* is not featured in these Irish gangster films; indeed it is vigorously denied in the quotation from which this chapter draws its title. The line, 'We're not fucking Eye-talians', delivered in a strong Dublin accent by the General when one of his henchmen attempts to embrace him, playfully emphasises the film's roots in a local culture that is, we may infer, homophobic and xenophobic whilst simultaneously referencing and disavowing the classic ethnic screen gangster.

Although the family has been the point of tension within gangster movies since its early years – site of wholesome values, tradition and often operating as a futile moral break on a gangster's excessive behaviour – *Scarface* (originally Howard Hawks, 1932; Brian De Palma, 1983) notoriously explored the incestuous desires of Tony for his sister, Cesca (Mason 2002: 27–8) and was subject to censorship. A correlative of this 'perverse' sexuality in the contemporary Irish gangster films is the *ménage à trois* between Cahill, his wife Frances and her younger sister, Tina, which produced several children (Williams 1998a: 234–9). This unorthodox relationship is represented in the films with conventional tropes of parenting, affection and 'normality'; although it is a target for abusive comment within the narrative by the Gardaí and in the news media it was the object of fascinated curiosity. To the film audience this relationship signifies the heterosexual nuclear family taken beyond its normal bounds, but it is morally demarcated from the incestuous child rape carried out by one of Cahill's own close gang members, 'Gary' (played by Seán McGinley in *The General*), and threatened by gang leader Gilligan (Gerard McSorley) in *Veronica Guerin* on the eponymous heroine's young son.

The final theme that I want to discuss, that of the reflexive gangster, derives from the observation that these films all advert through explanatory inter-titles to their own problematic ontology and to the mythologisation of their central characters. The development and pre-production phases of two of the Cahill films witnessed legal difficulties about the status of script/sources and rights between Merlin Films (Boorman) and Little Bird (O'Sullivan), further illustrating the problematic nature of films based on recent history. Cahill's screen representation as a Dublin gangster and his media mythologisation are not without precedent in Irish culture,[4] and indeed *The General* opens with a declaration that draws attention to its fictionalisation and alias: 'all the events depicted in this movie occurred and contributed to the *legend* of Martin Cahill aka … The General' (my emphasis), yet it is closest to Paul Williams' journalistic account. *Vicious Circle* also moves from 'reality' to 'invention' - its opening caption states: 'Martin Cahill, known as 'The General', and his immediate family are real characters [sic]. Everyone else is this film is invented'. But perhaps Stembridge's script was the most overt in its play both with the 'the real' person and also with the genre. O'Sullivan has said in interview that the film was a deliberate attempt 'to get out of the world of the nitty gritty, the backstreet night-time world of the classic gangster genre' (O'Sullivan, 2000: 23). The Guerin films, even the fictionalised *When the Sky Falls*, use closing credits titles and visuals to carefully contextualise the events screened. Schumacher's 'respectful and emotive film' (Kitson 2003: 32) works too hard with its extended ending, a voice-of-god narrator (that of the police detective, Mullan (Don Wycherly)), giving the impression that her death has not been in vain ('Veronica Guerin's writing turned the tide of the drugs war') and the problems have all gone away (McDonagh 2003: 13).

All three 'General' films contain a recurrent motif of reflexivity concerning the media that is not simply concerned with signifying a hero's 'tragic flaw' but also comments on the process of the mediation of gangsters. It is notable that all these films have sequences that refer to or reconstruct Cahill's aforementioned 1988 interview with RTÉ reporter Brendan O'Brien. Reporters and television journalists in these films are generally seen to be reactive and easily duped by the antics of the fictionalised Lynch or the wily Cahill.[5] These sequences are 'framed' by Cahill/Lynch viewing them at home with Frances/Tina or the gang, showing 'The General's' vanity and sense of self-importance: 'the whole country is in awe of us. We're bigger than Riverdance. We're fuckin' superstars' (Stembridge 2000: 104). Such an attitude of hubris is seen to be Michael's 'tragic flaw'; publicity will be his undoing. The real Cahill did selectively court the attention of some print and television journalists, but was – like Al Capone – extremely wary of media exposure being used by the authorities: 'They want to give the impression that there's a big gangster somewhere. D'y'understand? A dangerous man' (Cahill quoted from RTÉ 1988). In *Vicious Circle*, the O'Brien interview is seen being viewed on television first by the Garda detectives, then intercut with a pensive Cahill (Stott) but with a cheering gang enjoying the spectacle at home on a TV. Stott's reflexive Cahill knows the dangers: 'turn that fucking shite off'.

The screen gangster's self-awareness has long been a trait of the genre ever since a shot and dying Rico asks rhetorically in *Little Caesar* (1930): 'Mother of mercy, is this the end of Rico?' This sense of self-dramatisation, an awareness of their mediated image, is part of the gangster's charisma and power. In two of the contemporary Irish gangster films the narrative features sequences in which the Cahill/Lynch character envisions future events or 'day dreams' them. Lynch repeatedly says 'I see it like this' or 'this is how I see it', 'I tell you how it's going to happen' as he plans his next heist (Stembridge 2000: 48). Whilst there might be a naturalistic explanation here that criminals have to meticulously plan what will happen in order to be successful and not get caught (Boorman 1998: 43–4), this trait indicates that both filmmakers use this envisioning to achieve what Boorman calls 'the truth of the imagination' (1998: x) and the subjective, imaginative truth of a character's own perception through a cinematic technique (O'Sullivan 2000: 23), rather than trying to render a historical, objective truth. Both films then show differing degrees of awareness of the myth-making process within the gangster genre; the funeral sequence in *Ordinary Decent Criminal* begins with 'Classic Mafia movie shot … The entrance to the funeral parlour' but in a moment 'the shot now has a posed look to it' (Stembridge 2000: 142–3) and we subsequently realise that the whole thing is a ruse, concocted by Lynch.[6]

In the struggle to control the gangster's public image, the power of media representation becomes a crucial tool in investigating and combating crime (Innes 1999). Whereas in the 'General' films the gangster was confronted by lone or pairs of dedicated but hampered Gardaí, ineffectual comic cops or paramilitaries, the narrative emphasis in the more recent films falls squarely on the crime journalist Veronica Guerin as nemesis of the villain, a contemporary rival of Cahill's in Dublin, John Gilligan (played respectively as the fictional 'Hackett' by Gerard Flynn and as Gilligan by Gerard McSorley). Guerin, especially in Schumacher's film, is conscious of her role as a journalist opposing crime. When she is brutally assaulted by Gilligan, she goes on television to do an interview and show her injuries. In a telling moment, however, her son Cathal sees his mum's face on the side of a Dublin bus: she is not only myth but commodity, an image advertising the *Sunday Independent* newspaper for whom she works.

MacKenzie's film, fictionalising its subject matter, has a dark, bleaker vision with a convincing feel to its representation of the criminal underworld's sleaziness, but the calculated impact of screen violence is well-directed in key scenes within both films, namely the death of an addict being used by the Gardaí and Gilligan's doorstep assault of Guerin. In Schumacher's production, Brendan Galvin's photography of drug-deprived squalor appears over-produced and Schumacher strives too hard in suggesting an upbeat redemptive present from which to look back at the recent past. In the same way that *Veronica Guerin* borrows the bio-pic tragic structure of *The General*, it also shares a mirrored 'new sincerity' nostalgia. MacKenzie, however, draws on the British crime film tradition – to which his own *The Long Good Friday* (1980) is a notable contribution – but equally the popular British TV cop/crime thriller genre, particularly with its development of female investigators like *Prime Suspect* (Granada, 1991–96, starring Helen Mirren).

Whereas in the classical gangster films, rival gangs, the police or 'private eyes' were dramatic foils, in the most recent pair of Guerin films the villains are pursued, confronted and exposed by a female *journalist* articulating heroic expressions of professional drive and familial decency in the absence of any effective agency by the police and the Irish legislative system. Former journalist colleague and script writer who collaborated on *When the Sky Falls*, Michael Sheridan, has noted that 'in the end, the only story worth telling was her story which also made it less of a gangster film' (Sheridan 2000: 16), but we have already indicated that elements of the characterisation of the screen Guerin character are similar to those of her gangster quarries and there are structural analogies between *The General* and *Veronica Guerin*.

Guerin's character is a post-feminist professional, juggling motherhood, a high-profile career and marriage, and also manages to be an ardent Manchester United fan and drive a fast red sports car (thus capturing male viewer appeal). Being a female journalist (rather than a male cop) makes for a compelling hybrid, and she occupies an intermediary, even outlaw, status between police and politicians even though she reassures them that 'we're on the same side'. Disliked for her methods by Dublin's complacent journalist clique, she forces meetings with Traynor (Ciarán Hinds), using her feminine attractiveness while she arranges with Garda detective Mullan to photograph him for evidence and her scoop. Her reformist campaign, zeal and strong female drive to achieve her aims (to expose the drugs baron Gilligan) are firmly within the Hollywood individualist hero(ine) mode, and little is explained about the poverty or economic conditions in which drugs thrive. As such, the chief strengths of *Veronica Guerin* – a controlled clarity and force of emotive storytelling about a remarkable woman – are also its greatest limitations. Amid the publicity for *Terminator 3*, *Veronica Guerin*'s poster tag-line ('single-minded, single-handed … she tormented the tormentors') strikes a similar note: the lone individual fight is inspiring and universalising. The difficulty with the assertion is that not only are the reassurances of the closing voice-over and inter-titles thin, but the underlying economic and social ideologies that buttress Celtic Tiger Ireland are left unquestioned.

The notion of generic appropriation, historically and in the present, is a useful tool in understanding how the gangster film figures in Irish cinema. It is provocative to consider this cluster of films about crime in contemporary Ireland with Zygmunt Bauman's description of this generation's 'liquid modernity' in mind:

> Our time is auspicious for scapegoats – be they politicians making a mess of their personal lives, criminals creeping out of the mean streets and rough districts, or 'foreigners in our midst'. Ours is a time of patented locks, burglar alarms, barbed-wire fences, neighbourhood watch and vigilantes. (Bauman 2000: 38)

'Popular' film representation is just as capable of generating neo-conservative, populist ideologies and cultural nostalgia as it is of bringing forth challenging, critical questions about Irish society and culture. The re-mediation of Guerin's 'victory' over the gangsters in recent cinema may in fact alert us not only to the persistence of a problem but also an unforeseen, maybe unwelcome, cultural shift in our perceptions of the nature of 'solutions' available to us.

Notes

1   *Making the Cut*, a two-hour pilot feature screened on RTÉ in 1997, was scripted by Scotsman John Brown, with subsequent episodes of the series by Eric Deacon. The series was loosely based on the kind of news stories on crime in Ireland that RTÉ audiences would have been very familiar with. It

was, as Ruth Barton commented, the 'disguised Cahill' narrative. The experience of creative and senior technical talent in British television programmes like *Prime Suspect*, *Cracker* and *Inspector Morse*, plus the budget that allowed for shooting on film ensured high production values that showcased accomplished screen acting performances from a strong mainly-Irish cast. See also 'Ratboy', TV Review in *Film West*, 30 (October) 1997, 58–9. Thanks to Eugene Finn at the Irish Film Archive for alerting me to *Making the Cut*, lending me his copy and helping with other notes/production details in the preparation of this chapter.

2   A key television programme here was the Irish current affairs investigation *Today Tonight* shown on RTÉ, 10 February 1988. In this programme, an astonished television audience witnessed reporter Brendan O'Brien interview the scarily amicable Cahill *in public* outside an unemployment office under the watchful glances of 'under cover' surveillance gardaí on foot and in an obvious 'unmarked' car, who were themselves being filmed by an RTÉ camera crew secreted in a near-by parked car. In this surreal situation, Cahill wittily claimed at one point in the interview that he himself was a freelance 'private detective'. O'Brien played 'himself' in Boorman's *The General* and Blair's *Vicious Circle* in what appear to be re-constructions of this interview with Gleeson/Stott as Cahill in sequences that are viewed on the television by Cahill's gang. For a fuller discussion of *Today Tonight* sequences in relation to the Cahill films and popular culture, see my own *Irish Media and Popular Culture* (Routledge, forthcoming 2005).

3   In the same way that Al Capone, dubbed 'Public Enemy No. 1' by the Chicago Crime Commission in 1930, was then written about in the press to popularise him, so Martin Cahill's media persona as 'The General' was an invention of Irish journalists, as a way of publicising his activities but staying within Irish law.

4   Donegal-born Vincent Coll emigrated to America early last century and became a New York gangster but was killed aged 23. 'Mad Dog', as he became known, was, in the words of his biographer, 'the quintessential Prohibition gangster – a European immigrant who realised that the quickest way to the American dream was via the barrel of a gun' (Delap 1999: 12). Coll was the subject of a recent TnaG documentary *Mad Dog Coll* (Pat Comer, 2000) but also several fiction films, notably *Mad Dog Coll* (Burt Balaban, 1961) and *Mad Dog Coll* aka *Killer Instinct* (Greydon Clark, Ken Stein, 1992). His figure also appears in *The Untouchables* (Brian De Palma, 1987), *The Lawless Years* (TV, 1959–61), *Mobsters* (Michael Karbelnikoff, 1991), *The Cotton Club* (Francis Ford Coppola, 1984) and *Sleepers* (Barry Levinson, 1996) (see Delap 1999: 13). Students of British crime culture history were able to undertake a similar analysis of screen, fiction and journalism of the Kray Twins, Ronnie and Reggie, notorious London-based criminal brothers from the 1960s.

5   See Stembridge (2000: 100–4) and Boorman (1998: 78–80) for the relevant sequences but note that the final edit often differs from the published screenplay. In particular, Cahill's quip to a Garda standing next to him as Gary assaults the camera operator: 'Desperate, isn't it?' is an unscripted ad lib by Gleeson that is in character and perfect Dublin vernacular.

6   O'Sullivan gave a workshop to students at St Mary's College, London in 1999, at which time he was editing the end of the film and discussed the various permutations of shots in this final sequence to achieve this reading of the film.

References

Bauman, Z. (2000) *Liquid Modernity*. Oxford: Blackwell.

Boorman, J. (1998) *The General: Screenplay with Introduction*. London: Faber.

Chibnall, S. and R. Murphy (1999) (eds) *British Crime Cinema*. London: Routledge.

Collins, J. (1993) 'Genericity in the Nineties: Eclectic irony and the new sincerity', in J. Collins, H. Radner and
    A. Preacher Collins (eds) *Film Theory Goes to the Movies*. London: Routledge, 242–63.

Cook, P. with M. Bernick (eds) (1999) 'Contemporary Crime', in *The Cinema Book*. London: British Film Institute,
    172–83.

Delap, B. (1999) *Mad Dog Coll: An Irish Gangster*. Cork: Mercier Press.

Grainge, P. (ed.) (2003) *Memory and Popular Film*. Manchester: Manchester University Press.

Innes, M. (1999) 'The Media as an Investigative Resource in Murder Enquiries', *British Journal of Criminology*,
    39, 2, 269–80.

Jameson, F. (1998) *The Cultural Turn: Selected Writings on the Postmodern, 1983–1998*. London: Verso.

Kitson, N. (2003) [rev] 'Veronica Guerin', *Film Ireland*, 93 (July–August), 32.

Kirby, P., L. Gibbons and M. Cronin (eds) (2003) *Reinventing Ireland: Culture, Society and the Global Economy*.
    London: Pluto Press.

Maltby, R. (2001) 'The Spectacle of Criminality' in J. D. Slocum (ed.) *Violence and American Cinema*. London:
    Routledge, 117–52.

Mason, F. (2000) *American Gangster Cinema*. Basingstoke: Palgrave.

McCloy, S. (2000) [rev] 'Ordinary Decent Criminal', *Film Ireland*, 74 (February/March), 441–2.

McDonagh, M. (2003) [rev] 'A job nicely done, Cate', *Evening Standard*, 4 August, 13.

Monk, C. (1999) 'From Underworld to Underclass: Crime and British Cinema in the 1990s', in S. Chibnall and
    R. Murphy (eds) *British Crime Cinema*. London: Routledge, 172–88.

Negra, D. (2001) 'The New Primitives: Irishness in Recent US Television', *Irish Studies Review* , 9, 2, 229–39.

O'Sullivan, T. (2000) *Ordinary Decent Criminal*, Ikon Entertainment/Little Bird DVD supplementary material.

Pettitt, L. (2000) [rev] 'Ordinary Decent Criminal', *The Irish Post*, 18 March, 24.

Rockett, K. (2001) '(Mis-)representing the Irish Urban Landscape' in M. Shiel and T. Fitzmauurice (eds) *Cinema
    and the City: Film and Urban societies in a Global Context*, Oxford: Blackwell, 217–28.

RTÉ (1988) *Today Tonight* [Reporter Brendan O'Brien] Off-air VHS, Tx. 10 February, 50 mins.

Sheridan, M. (2000) 'True to Death', *Film Ireland*, 76 (June/July), 15–17.

Stembridge, G. (2000) *Ordinary Decent Criminal* (screenplay). London: Headline.

Walsh, S. (2003) 'Bruck & Me', *Film Ireland*, 93 (July–August), 12–15.

Williams, P. (1998, second edn.) *The General: Godfather of Crime*. Dublin: The O'Brien Press.

Black and White and Collar Films:
Exploring the Irish Film Archive Collections of Clerical Films
Sunniva O'Flynn

For many years in my work as Curator of the Irish Film Archive I have been aware of and intrigued by the volume of film material acquired from and produced by members of religious orders. Levels of indigenous professional film production in Ireland were, until relatively recently, very modest. Traditionally, amateur production filled the gaps. Such films were made of places and communities that would probably never have been deemed worthy of a professional camera's gaze, and provide a unique ground-level view of Irish life. Many of the makers of amateur films were clergy, both male and female. Collections of these films have been acquired from religious orders, from parishes and from families of filmmakers who understand the need to accord archival film particular storage provisions to ensure its preservation.

The preparation of this chapter has allowed me the opportunity to explore the subject of filmmaking clergy in Ireland and to examine the significance of their contribution to Irish film history. The phenomenon of a distinct pattern of clerical filmmaking is one which I believe may be uniquely Irish – particularly in terms of the *prevalence* of clerical filmmakers in the amateur filmmaking landscape.

This chapter discusses these clergy people and their films in the context of the Irish Film Archive collection.[1] It will look at the often-ambivalent attitude of the Catholic Church towards the cinema, distinguishing between their cautious, sometimes hostile, reaction to film exhibition and the more positive (often-encouraging) stance taken on film production and the use of film for educational purposes. Primarily though, what follows is an overview of the many religious collections in the Archive, collections which I believe typify particular strands of clerical production.[2]

The Irish Film Archive has been actively identifying, acquiring, preserving and providing access to Irish film collections since the late 1980s. The collection, which now numbers over 17,000 cans of film, all of which can be described as 'Irish' by one definition or another, includes feature films, newsreels, sports films, travelogues, informational and educational films. Amateur or semi-professional filmmakers have made a significant contribution to the collection.

Generally, religious orders are very mindful of their collections and increasingly cautious about provision of access. This caution has arisen from the huge amount of public and media interest in any material relating to the abuse of children in religious-run institutions in past decades and the perceived need to acquire otherwise innocuous footage to illustrate investigative documentaries. The Archive, in its annual presentation to the Society of Church Archivists Summer School, appeals for the transfer of film material to the Irish Film Archive, but it can offer advice on storage, preservation and handling of film to church archivists determined to retain material. Such films are enormously important records of the everyday lives of both adults and children in Ireland of the past, and the role of ordinary clergy in documenting this cannot be underestimated, nor should the value of the films themselves.

Church and cinema – the early years

The influence of the Catholic Church upon the development of Irish cinema was felt from the earliest years of the state. The 1923 Censorship of Films Act, which severely curtailed the content of material which could be seen by the Irish public, had been drawn up in response to a series of debates and appeals from members of the Irish Vigilance Association, the Priests' Social Guild, the Catholic Church and Protestant and Presbyterian groups who were dissatisfied with provisions of an earlier Act. The Act was designed to protect the morals of society from the corrupting influence of the new and powerful medium. The first Irish Film Censor, James Montgomery, was notoriously strict and banned any films that were, in accordance with the provisions of the Act, 'indecent, obscene or blasphemous'.

The Church was also eager to have its say with regard to matters of exhibition. Though the first custom-built cinema had been opened and managed by James Joyce in Dublin in 1909, by the mid-1920s there were still many rural towns and villages without any cinema at all. Audiences were served by travelling shows, whose operators moved from village to village with their portable projectors showing films in town and school halls, often paying scant regard to local by-laws regarding public entertainment. In 1926 an incident occurred which brought the question of regulation into sharp focus.

Drumcollogher was a village in Co. Limerick with a population of about 500 in 1926. In September of that year, William Forde, the local taxi proprietor opened a makeshift cinema above Brennan's Hardware Shop. The first film to be shown there was Cecil B. De Mille's *The Ten Commandments* (1923), a title guaranteed to bring in people of all ages from all corners of the village itself and also those nearby. Tragically, a fire ripped through the premises during the screening and claimed 48 lives. Incredibly, despite the religious nature of the programme, one local cleric saw the tragedy as an opportunity to comment on the evils of cinema. In a letter to the Canon Begley P. P. of Drumcollogher, Most Reverend Dr Fogarty, Bishop of Killaloe said 'This wretched Cinema craze was bound to end in a disaster sooner or later; but this one is appalling, and how sad that it should fall on your village.'[3]

However, apart from issues of control and protection, some members of the Church were genuinely interested in the potential of the medium as an educational and proselytising tool. In June 1936 Pope Pius XI articulated his growing concern with the fast-spreading influence of cinema in an encyclical entitled *Vigilanti Cura – On Motion Pictures*. It advised on the potential for good as well as for evil that lay within this new and powerful medium. The Encyclical outlined the means of action and vigilance that should be adopted by concerned Catholics, including the inspection of films for content, the promotion of desirable films, and even the further censorship of films already passed by the Film Censor. As a result of *Vigilanti Cura*, Catholic commissions were set up throughout the world both to oversee the distribution and exhibition of existing films and to encourage the production of films deemed in accordance with the teachings of Christianity.

Such films had in fact been in production for some time. As early as 1932 The Catholic Film Society of London had produced a film in Ireland entitled *Aran of the Saints*. The film was made in the year of the Eucharistic Congress, at that time the most significant international religious event ever held in the country. The film cited Aran, the most westerly point in Europe, as a holy place populated by people who are also holy, due primarily to the remoteness of the island and its distance from the corrupting influence of modern society. In the film, life for the islanders centres on religious activities – attending mass, communion services, the Angelus and the Rosary. A notable sequence in the film records the funeral of a nine-year-old boy, an event that would probably not have been filmed by a lay person. Such filming highlights the particular relationship that filmmaking clergy have with their subjects. Certainly in relation to religious services, members of the clergy were allowed access that lay filmmakers could not have enjoyed. The presence of priests at religious services was of course required, and by extension the filming of such services by members of the clergy appears to have been acceptable. *Aran of the Saints* is particularly interesting for its depiction of lives which, although Spartan, are peaceful and at times playful. It is in stark contrast to the wild and heroic existence of the islanders struggling against constant hardship and the brutal forces of nature depicted by Robert Flaherty in *Man of Aran* a mere two years later.[4]

In the same year as *Aran of the Saints*, Father Francis Browne, better known for his photographic collections,[5] also made a film. His was a record of the Eucharistic Congress itself, and it provides an interesting counterpoint to the religious anthropology of *Aran of the Saints*. In some respects, Browne's work is typical of that strand of clerical filmmaking which simply records religious procedures. The film, entitled *Eucharistic Congress 1932*, documents the preparation for the event, which took place between 21–26 June 1932. A triumphal demonstration to the world of the strength of the Catholic Church in Ireland, the Congress transformed Dublin city into a brightly-coloured capital filled with an air of carnival, decorated with flowers and banners and bunting. The film faithfully records the atmosphere and the environment, showing the arrival of the Papal Legate and his journey into the city, the many services that took place, and the climax of the devotions – a mass in Phoenix Park which was attended by over 1,000,000 people. Thanks to his experience as a photographer and the excellent vantagepoints which he managed to secure throughout the city – the sheer magnitude of the proceedings is perfectly conveyed.

John Charles McQuaid and the National Film Institute

The Church's direct and organised involvement in film production in Ireland began in earnest in the 1940s. John Charles McQuaid, a Holy Ghost father who had been consecrated as Archbishop of Dublin in 1940, set about implementing the recommendations of *Vigilanti Cura* with the establishment of the National Film Institute (NFI) in 1943. He attempted not only to regulate the manner in which cinema was received by Irish audiences, but also through the establishment of a national educational body, to explore the use of film as a tool for education and enlightenment.

The Institute (now The Film Institute of Ireland) was established under McQuaid's patronage in 1943. Founder members included members of the legal profession, businessmen, educationalists and members of the clergy. Many of its stated aims concerned implementing the terms of *Vigilanti Cura* in terms of protecting and promoting values in accordance with Church teachings though control of distribution and exhibition of 'suitable' films. To this end the Archbishop donated £250 towards the cost of three film projectors for the setting up of three mobile film units. By 1950 the Institute had over 850 films in stock covering such subjects as health and hygiene, agriculture, horticulture, athletics, geography, physics, chemistry and road safety.

The Institute was also instrumental in promoting the production of film for educational purposes, and it is from these activities that a number of films made by Irish clergy were produced. In 1947 Reverend J. J. Toomey, President of St Patrick's Training College offered the college to the NFI as a venue for a Summer Course in Film Techniques (28 July–2 August). There were practical demonstrations on projector maintenance, lectures on documentary techniques and explorations of the Youth and Cinema. A film produced during the course, *NFI Summer School 1947*, clearly shows the participation of a number of priests and nuns eager to learn camera techniques. There is no doubt that the Institute played a significant role in promoting amateur film production among clergy and laypeople from the 1940s to the 1960s. The Institute's information sheets and periodicals, the *Irish Cinema Quarterly*, *National Film Quarterly*, *Irish Film Quarterly*, *Vision* and *Scannán* were distributed to teachers, parents and other interested parties. The magazines often carried articles on film production techniques. An annual amateur film competition was initiated in 1948. As the competition progressed the Gevaert Challenge Silver Cup was awarded, as were substantial prize-monies.

Father Jackie Moran (1913–86) was a frequent recipient of the top award at these events. Between 1938 and 1946 he worked as a missionary in Australia where he recorded his travels on a 16mm camera. On his return to Ireland he was assigned to Daingean in Co. Offaly. It was here that he made his first Irish film in 1951. *Activities of a Country Town* was made for and with the people of Daingean. It is a beautifully-shot record of life in a small Irish town in the 1950s. His camera-work is assured and his familiarity with and respect for the work of his parishioners is evident in every sequence.

The Wayfarer (1965) was an adaptation of Patrick Pearse's poem filmed around Newport, Co. Mayo. This film was an award-winner at the National Film Institute and was later included in the Institute's distributing library. Father Moran's father, James, played the role of the wayfarer himself in the film, and several of the children appearing were his nephews. This appearance of family members is not unusual in the canon of clerical films. More often siblings and in-laws and nieces and nephews appear not as actors but as subjects of home-movies filmed by their clerical relatives while on home visits.

Father Moran was commissioned by various bodies to make films for educational and other purposes. These included films on hurling and football for the GAA and a film on mental health for the South Eastern Health Board. *Adveniat Regnum Tuum* (*Thy Kingdom Come*), another NFI award-winner, was made by Father Moran with Sister Louise Boland of the Little Sisters of the Assumption. The film, made in 1962, portrays the pastoral work of the order in Limerick, Dublin and abroad as they minister to the sick and impoverished in their homes. As in *Aran of the Saints*, where the funeral of a small boy was filmed, *Adveniat Regnum Tuum* demonstrates the unique social position of filmmaking priests and nuns in relation to the subjects of their films. Access to their subjects appears to have been unproblematic even in such sensitive circumstances. The film would have been screened in a controlled environment, not broadcast or screened out of context. It would have been introduced by a member of the Little Sisters of the Assumption and used primarily for vocational or fund-raising purposes.

Parish priests, community and fund-raising films

It would be tempting to argue that the Institute had a central role in encouraging all aspects of clerical filmmaking, but this would difficult to sustain. The fact is that there were many priests producing films *before* the establishment of the Institute or, later, outside the framework of Institute workshops, newsletters and competitions.

Many priests had a more casual approach to filmmaking than Fathers Moran and Browne. Despite the fact that it was a relatively expensive hobby and one that few of their parishioners could afford, it was not much more extravagant than playing golf or betting on horses, and not much more time consuming than involvement in the local Gaelic football club; all hobbies with which their fellow clergy may have been involved. At

Figure 2: Fr Jackie Moran receiving the National film Institute Annual Award for Best Picture from Joseph P. Murphy, Chairman of the Institute (permission – the Irish Film Institute).

a time when church attendances were high and collection boxes were filled at each of the masses, the cost of a camera and film stock would have been quite manageable.

While many clergy people were involved in film production for vocational, fund-raising or educational purposes, others made films simply as records of the communities in which they lived. Many priests focused on church-related affairs: Corpus Christi processions, weddings, communions, confirmations and christenings. Others made films of more secular activities of their parishioners. Their agenda, if it could be called that, is not always as clear as the non-clerical amateur filmmaker. The lay home-movie enthusiast generally records the growth of his or her family for nostalgic purposes. The films of the clerical filmmaker transcend the constraints of the family to document a much larger community. The filmmaking career of priests often outlasted home moviemakers whose interest often only last as long as the childhood of their children. The clerical filmmaker is not limited to the growth of one generation: his interest is with the entire community and with new generations of that community.

Father Tommy Doherty, a Parish priest and later a Canon and an Archdeacon in the Arch-Diocese of Raphoe in Donegal, was by far the most enterprising of film-loving priests in Ireland. In his time he was a filmmaker, a cinema owner and a stand-up comedian – and by all accounts (including two television documentaries[6]) a much loved and very colour-ful character in the parishes where he ministered. Shortly after his ordination in 1927 he was sent to Scotland to serve his apprenticeship. It was there that he bought his first camera – a 9.5mm model on which he filmed in Scotland and the first years of his minis-try in Donegal. He soon graduated to 16mm film on which he filmed activities, religious and otherwise, of the towns of Min a Croise, Convoy, Donegal and Dunfanaghy. As there was no cinema for more than thirty miles his filming caused something of a sensation. He filmed turf cutting, fishing, Corpus Christi processions, weddings, fair days, local beauty spots, the local narrow gauge railway and people going about their business.

Father Doherty also ran commercial cinemas in Convoy and Donegal town. He rented 35mm films from Dublin distributors and supplemented his programme of commercially-available releases with 16mm films of local interest. Those items that guaranteed the full houses were the local events. Those appearing would come along to see themselves on screen. The money raised through the film shows was added to parish funds generated from weekly church collections. Funds were constantly required to maintain the church, the parish house and for new building projects. All new school building and building refurbishments for example were funded through parish collections. Similar fund-raising efforts were made by Canon Cahill in Borrisokane, Co. Tipperary who, in an effort to raise funds for the St Peter and Paul Church in Borrisokane, opened the Stella Cinema in 1957.[7]

We have recently learnt of the activities of another Donegal priest, Father McDyer, who made and exhibited films in Glencolmcille throughout the 1950s. Another cleric who used film to successfully raise funds for community affairs was Father James McGrath, a Dublin-based Augustinian Priest. In the 1950s Father McGrath ran a boys social club – the Our Lady of Good Counsel Boys Club in Thomas Street – a working-class area of Dublin's inner city. He decided that the production of a short film outlining the activities of the club would be a useful promotional and fundraising tool. Funds to produce the film were secured from Guinness Brewery whose premises were also in Thomas Street. McGrath approached professional cameramen Stuart Hetherington and Brendan Redmond to make the film. They produced *Clubs Are Trumps*, which had its premier in the Olympia Theatre one Sunday evening in 1959. Guinness were so impressed with the club and its role in gainfully occupying the youth of Thomas Street that they agreed to fund all future activities of the club.

Foreign priests

An interesting sub-group of the Irish filmmaking priests comprise those who were assigned a foreign ministry but who maintained contact with the old country. The combination of 'inside' and 'outside' point of view provides a fascinating illustration of attitudes towards country and community. Frequently Irish priests who were sent to houses abroad would acquire cameras and bring them home to film the family during holidays. The films were often then brought back to the foreign outposts to share pictures of the old country with new friends. One was Father Holland, a priest based in the UK who came home to Wexford each year and filmed the people and activities there. Fortunately several of these collections have made their way back to Ireland.

Monsignor Jack Hegarty was an Irish priest originally from Ballyduhig in Listowel in Co. Kerry who spent most of his ordained life in San Diego in the US. In 1937 he travelled through Europe on his journey home to visit relations in Ballybunion, Co. Kerry, filming all the way. In Dublin he captured the newly inaugurated President Douglas Hyde leaving Dublin Castle and later in the RDS with Eamon de Valera and German Ambassador to Ireland, Eduard Hempel. Monsignor Hegarty's is probably the only colour film of these events. Amateur enthusiasts were quicker to embrace Kodak's new colour reversal stocks and the Monsignor's 1937 film is a good early example.

Religious orders and school films

Many of the films made by clergy documented the activities of the religious orders. These films, recording ordinations, religious services, reception ceremonies, profession ceremonies and funerals were made purely for the purpose of posterity and were not screened publicly except to members of the order and, occasionally, for their families. The most common location for the clerical camera however is, not surprisingly, the schoolyard. Until recent times more priests and nuns were involved in teaching in Ireland than in medical or missionary work. The films in the archive collection reflect this.

One collection, acquired recently from the Christian Brother's Provincialate in Dublin, is unusual in that it includes both amateur and commissioned, professional films documenting activities of Christian Brothers and their pupils in Ireland and abroad. More often school films are amateur productions. It is possible to identify two distinct types of school films. The first type are those made by priests or nuns who were staff members in the schools in which they filmed. The camera was probably school property and was used either by one skilled member of staff or by whichever staff member requested it for the recording of a particular activity or trip. Inevitably these collections have come from relatively affluent schools. Two recently acquired examples came from boarding schools – St Louis, Monaghan and Castleknock College, Dublin.

The St Louis collection, filmed by Sr Mary Alacoque between 1940 and 1960 comprises over twenty cans of film and includes footage of Carrickmacross and the surrounding Monaghan countryside. Student activities include demonstration of their fashions in the conservatory and participation in St Patrick's Day pageants while their teachers, the St Louis nuns are seen enjoying themselves on holiday in Bundoran. Both pupils and teachers appear unselfconscious in the presence of the camera. Its presence in these schools is not an unusual occurrence.

Father Vincent O'Brien and Father Tom Davitt made the Castleknock films from the 1960s and 1970s. The activities of the pupils – canoeing on the Barrow, trips to Lourdes, swimming in the college pool and indeed participation in St Patrick's Day pageants – demonstrate clearly the privileged lifestyle of these wealthy pupils.

The other type of school film was that made on an occasional basis by parish priests and curates invited in to record the activities of schoolchildren in their parishes. Examples of such films in our collection include those made by Father Courtney in Dublin's East Wall under the title *Snapshots from Church Road (1939–40)* and by Father Jack Delaney in Dublin's Seán McDermott Street in the 1930s. These films are more formal than the others. The children are brought together, marching through the schoolyard in their class groups for a group portrait. It is evident in these films that the children are less at ease in the presence of the camera than in the earlier films, because of the formal nature of the filming process in this case. This in no way undermines the value of the films as pictorial records of entire communities of children who may not otherwise have been photographed, and their value cannot be overestimated.

Father Delaney's collection, for example, provides a vivid moving-image record of Dublin tenement life in the 1930s that, to our knowledge, does not exist elsewhere. Father Delaney was a parish priest in Dublin's inner city and later Dun Laoghaire. His sister Eileen Delaney, in an interview in the *Home Movie Nights* series,[8] spoke of his passion for his camera: 'He seemed to be in advance of the times in that he could see that these were pictures that deserved to be taken and kept.' In the 1930s, Father Delaney was assigned to the parish in Dublin's Gloucester Street, an extremely poor neighbourhood where people lived in densely populated tenements. Here he filmed his parishioners outside their tenement homes, children playing on the streets, marching in the Corpus Christi procession.

The professionals: Radharc films

The most significant and best-known independent production team, religious or other-wise, to emerge in Ireland in the last century was of course Radharc. Between 1961 and 1996 Father Joe Dunn (director), Father Des Forristal (writer) and Father Peter Lemass, (pre-senter) produced over 400 religious programmes subsequently broadcast on Irish televi-sion. As a young priest Joe Dunn had been sent by Archbishop John Charles McQuaid to attend television courses in Manchester and the Academy of Broadcasting Arts in New York. McQuaid, anticipating the imminent launch of RTÉ hoped to situate a production crew concerned with religious matters in a position where they might either run the sta-tion or contribute significantly to it. Funds were allocated for purchase of professional filmmaking equipment.

The Radharc team became noted for their innovative approach and for the integrity and sincerity with which they explored difficult issues in Ireland – issues such as social deprivation, prostitution, homelessness, emigration and juvenile delinquency. Stories ranged from the semi-humorous, the theological and the political to the sociologically groundbreaking. In 1966 Radharc made their first trip to Africa to make the first of many documentaries examining the work of Irish missionaries abroad. They traveled to Africa, North, South and Central America, Eastern Europe, Russia, India and Asia offering a Christian perspective on a wide range of issues: social affairs, justice and peace, the developing world and human rights.

Radharc produced a remarkable body of work which I believe simply continues a firmly-established tradition of filmmaking clergy who, thanks to their particular position in Irish society created a invaluable and unique moving-image record of Irish life in the twentieth century.[9]

Research, reference and reconstruction: the use of clerical collections by contemporary filmmakers

I would like to conclude this chapter with some reference to the use of films from the clerical collections. The Archive is an important resource for research and reference as well as preservation, and it is inevitable, and indeed desirable that filmmakers make use of the collections for the purposes of their own work. It is interesting to examine some of the uses to which this footage has been put in recent years, and to observe the relationship between the original footage, the context in which it has been used, and the level of reference or relationship with the source in films that employ dramatic reconstruction.

During the past decade, extracts from clerical films have been used to punctuate a wide variety of historical and sociological documentaries. However, in recent years there has been a marked increase in the use of these collections by those producing documentary investigations into life within religious-run institutions in Ireland in the twentieth century. Filmmakers have trawled the archive for films which would provide a visual key to life within these institutions. These include *Dear Daughter* (Louis Lentin, 1996), *Sex in a Cold Climate* (Steve Humphries, 1997), *60 Minutes: The Magdalen Laundries* (CBS News NY, 1999), *12 Apostles* (ITV, 2001) and *Stolen Lives* (Louis Lentin, 1999). Together these documentaries have created a public awareness of the abuse of children over decades within these institutions.

The most important documentary dealing with the subject was RTÉ's *States of Fear*, broadcast in 1999. Directed by Mary Raftery and researched by Sheila Ahearn it was a three-part series examining the experience of children in reformatories and industrial schools and in medical institutions from the 1930s to the present day. The programme, which included interviews with survivors of these homes, was underpinned by solid, broad-ranging research unearthing incontrovertible evidence of physical and sexual abuse of children by members of the clergy and of profound negligence by the state. The dramatic public response to the broadcast was instrumental in the establishment of the Laffoy Commission, which addressed the need for full compensation from the state and from the culpable religious orders for victims of institutional abuse.

The series incorporated a considerable amount of archive material. Unlike some earlier documentaries dealing with the subject, only those archive films whose provenance was fully confirmed were used. The programme makers were reluctant to use film extracts that might hurt or expose their subjects. They avoided close-ups or sequences in which children could be easily identified except where the children had been contacted and had authorised their appearance. They were denied access by rights holders to some films relevant to their research but others, such as the families of Father Delaney and Father Moran, were very helpful. One film made by Father Delaney has been used repeatedly in recent years. It was made sometime in the 1930s in the grounds of the convent of the Sisters of Our Lady of Charity in Gloucester Street, Dublin. This convent housed a Magdalene Laundry and Home (which eventually closed its doors in 1996). In itself the film provides valuable insights into life within the Home. The Magdalenes and the nuns are seen engaged in religious ritual and acting playfully before the camera. Their uniforms, hairstyles, their ages and their general appearance are recorded. Extracts from this short film were used in *Les Blanchisseueses des Magdalenes* (Christophe Weber, 1998) and were juxtaposed with contemporary scenes showing elderly former residents of the Gloucester Street Magdalene Home and interviews with the Sisters of Our Lady of Charity.

Likewise fiction filmmakers have also referred to the archive collections. Director Peter Mullan viewed Father Delaney's and other films in the course of research for *The Magdalene Sisters* (2002). Mullan's film depicts the experience of four women within a Magdalene Institution in Ireland in the 1960s. I watched the film, curious as to whether the archive research would be apparent in the reconstruction of various activities. It was most strikingly evident in the character of Father Fitzroy (Daniel Costello), an amateur film enthusiast who in one scene records on his 16mm camera the women (nuns and Magdalenes) in the grounds of the convent in a direct re-enactment of the Father Delaney film. The scenes which follow this reconstruction depict Father Fitzroy sexually abusing a young girl. The priest is an amalgam, conflated from unrelated facts. The characters of the four women in the film are also inspired by but not directly based on real women whose lives within Magdalene Institutions were the subject of the documentary *Sex in a Cold Climate*. There is room for some confusion as to the extent of the fictionalisation in the film, particularly with regard to the presentation of the apparently factual biographical details for each of the women provided at the close of the films.

Other amateur films documenting the everyday lives of such institutions and the orders who ran them have been withheld from programme makers. The owners of rights in these films (that is, the religious orders who made or commissioned the films) have argued that the anonymity of the subjects of the films must be preserved.

Films made by clerics continue to be acquired by the Archive. In recent months films have been donated by the Christian Brothers and by the Jesuit and Salesian Orders in Dublin. While some recently-acquired collections include professional films commissioned by religious orders, more conform to previously identified patterns of amateur clerical production. They are films about ordinary people made from perspectives which are at once intimate and objective. They document the urban and rural, the agricultural and the industrial, the sacred and the secular. Together they constitute a vivid moving-image record of Irish social life in the twentieth century, a record which provides a vital link to the past and which must be preserved for the future. The Irish Film Archive is committed to preserving these films so that they may be permanently accessible – particularly to those individuals or communities who are their subjects.

Notes

1   All clerical collections currently held by the Irish Film Archive and studied here have been produced by members of the Roman Catholic Clergy.

2   The subject of films made by Irish Missionary Orders will not be examined here. The Irish Film Archive is currently working with the Irish Missionary Union to identify, repatriate, digitise, catalogue and preserve films made by Irish missionary orders around the world. These films have not yet been

deposited in the Irish Film Archive.

3   *Irish Independent*, 10 September 1926, 7.

4   For further discussion of this film and these issues, see Harvey O'Brien, *The Real Ireland: The Evolution of Ireland in Documentary Film* (Manchester University Press, 2004).

5   For his work as a photographer *The Irish Times* has called Father Browne (who was born in Cork in 1880) 'the most important documentary historian of this century'. Less is known about his filmmaking activities. We know, from conversations with Father Eddie O'Donnell, Curator of the Father Browne Archive, and from identification of material within the Irish Film Archive collection, of just four films: a film on Irish forestry (c. 1933); *Castle Rising* (1935), a short drama made in the UK; *Waters of Providence* (1949), a record of the work of the Sisters of Charity in the Foxford Woolen Mills, Co. Mayo; there is as yet no trace of a fourth film of which there is documentary evidence – on the Garda Siochana, the Irish police force.

6   'Filling the Fourpenny Seats', produced by Peter Feeney, RTÉ 1985; 'Hollywood Can Wait', UTV (tx. 31 January 1989).

7   For a marvelously detailed account of the establishment and management of The Stella Cinema, Borrisokane, Co. Tipperary (opened 1957) by Canon Cahill (later Dean Cahill P. P.) see Michael Doorley, *Stella Days 1957–1967: The Life and Times of a Rural Irish Cinema*. Dubhairle Publications.

8   *Home Movie Nights* (Alan Gilsenan, 1998).

9   For further discussion of Radharc Films, see Lance Pettitt, *Screening Ireland* (Manchester University Press, 1999).

part 2 **real lives: modern irish identities**

Irishness, Innocence and American Identity Politics Before and After 11 September

Diane Negra

A large and growing body of work has come into existence analysing the rapid transnationalisation of Irishness spurred by Celtic Tigerism. At one extreme in the spectrum of this scholarship we find the suggestion that Irishness is now essentially an impossible category. To borrow a phrase from Colin Graham's *Deconstructing Ireland* the contemporary global environment is one in which 'an idea of "Ireland" [is] produced more often as a citation than an actuality' (Graham 2001: flyleaf). This is perhaps nowhere better illustrated of late than in the recently-released *Charlie's Angels: Full Throttle* (McG, 2003) in which African-American comedian Bernie Mac attempts to infiltrate a Dublin-based tanker controlled by the criminal O'Grady Clan. When his presentation of a driver's license identifying himself as Paddy O'Malley is met with a sceptical reception Mac launches into a comic tirade. 'You never heard of no black Irish?' he asks. 'Who do you think invented the McRib, Lucky Charms, the Shamrock Shake?' This catalogue of associative links delivered by a black comedian is but one example of a popular culture increasingly likely to produce comedy tied to the omnifarious nature of Irishness. The joke here turns on an assumption the film presumes its audience to share, namely that whatever else it may be, Irishness is reliably, invariably a form of whiteness.

In this chapter I want to emphasise the politicised nature of the fantasies of nostalgia and innocence in which Irishness is so often embedded in the US. How does Irishness work for a culture that is at once highly sentimental with respect to its own interests and most often coldly unsympathetic to the interests of others? I will explore certain aspects of an American national expressive culture that strategically mobilises Irishness in its self-narrativisation. Of course, as I have argued elsewhere, the lifestyling of Irishness has been a *bona fide* cultural phenomenon in the US for nearly a decade (Negra 2001: 229–39). Conferring ethnic legitimacy upon white Americans newly beset in the 1990s multiculture, claims of Irishness catalysed a heritage fantasy that has both domestic and touristic functionality. In the late 1990s, the uses of such claims expanded further, with a wave of Irish-American and Irish-themed television sitcoms and dramas giving evidence of the new ways that Irishness figured in a representational lexicon compatible with family values. The commercial exploitation of Irishness in everything from popular music and print fiction to coffee and cholesterol medication advertisements and chain restaurants marked its emergence as the most marketable white ethnicity in late twentieth-century American culture. The strikingly anodyne nature of the Irishness conceptualised in such formats indicated its use value as a consoling ethnic category. The tendency, above all, to use Irishness as a way of speaking a whiteness that would otherwise be taboo, was well underway before the events of 11 September.

As Irishness has acquired the status of an ethnicity at large in American culture, its uses as an imagined state of innocence have become evident in a growing number of commodity categories. For instance, fantasies of innocence are central to the work of Thomas Kinkade, a painter whose specialisation in scenes of cosy homes and picturesque hometowns has struck a resonant chord with the contemporary American middle class. Kinkade, whose phenomenal popularity provides a uniquely literal spin to the phrase 'cottage industry', uses light to thematically convey the warmth of home, the virtues of smalltown life and the fantasy integration of development with unspoiled nature. His success in recent years has been vast, with his landscape paintings, merchandising and most recently serenity-themed self-help books feeding a franchise that in 2000 amounted to more than $2 billion a year in revenue. (Kinkade is the kind of fully mainstreamed artist who has his own shops in malls, a largely unprecedented phenomenon.) *The Irish Times* reported in 2002 that Kinkade's work hangs in one out of every twenty American homes (Campbell 2002: 12).[1]

Art Historian Karal Ann Marling characterises Kinkade's art as 'suffused with nostalgia', arguing that the appeal of the paintings lies in the fact that they 'create a sense of safety and light in a darkened world' ('Despite Elitist Gripes', 2002: B4). Several of Kinkade's works are set in Ireland, notably 'Emerald Isle Cottage' and 'A Peaceful Time'. Reliant on hackneyed images of the warmly-lit, thatch-roofed cottage, Kinkade's Irish-themed work feeds a retreatist American sensibility. For example, in the blurb that accompanies

Figure 3: **Thomas Kinkade's 'Emerald Isle Cottage' links nostalgic Irishness to themes of security and safety.**

'Emerald Isle Cottage' in the 2002 Kinkade catalogue the painter notes that 'To me, Ireland means tradition and stability … charming customs, love of family, a faith as enduring as the austere, ruggedly beautiful countryside itself'. While Irishness, as I shall discuss further, seems increasingly well-suited to re-mythologise the white working class and to stage political innocence, it is used here to fantasise removal from present-day exigencies and the re-embrace of traditionalism. Kinkade's reliance on expressive, often unpopulated landscapes generates a pictorial/geographical innocence in which Ireland, as has frequently been the case in tourist advertising, figures as the site for rejuvenating re-connection with the past.

This impulse is elaborated in certain forms of television drama which feature protagonists who long to be excused from present-day dilemmas of citizenship and family life and to retreat back into history. One example is the CBS made-for-television movie *Yesterday's Children* (tx 16 October 2000) which centralises the production of an 'instant past' through an ingenious yet perhaps inevitable permutation of the heritage narrative – the reincarnation drama. For *Yesterday's Children* the psychic route toward Ireland is linked with American family formation and rejuvenation. Jane Seymour plays Jenny Cole, a 42-year-old Allentown, Pennsylvania mother whose surprise late pregnancy materialises at the same time as a series of dreams of a prior life in 1930s' Ireland. Scenes of family life in the Cole household depict patronising and distant relations between husband and wife (who argue about Jenny's pregnancy) and a classically alienated teenage son. Jenny and her husband Doug had been on the cusp of the 'empty nest' phase, but Jenny's pregnancy occurs just as her only child, Kevin, is making plans to leave home to attend college as far away as possible on the West Coast.

Jenny's dreams become increasingly intense flashes of the life of an abused wife, Mary (Seymour as well), her husband John and their children. Mary loses a stillborn child, and though her doctor warns that she cannot survive another pregnancy, John rapes her and Mary dies giving birth, after entreating her oldest son, Sonny, to keep the children together at all costs. Jenny's mother Maggie is the only one around her who takes her dreams seriously and refers her to a psychiatrist who hypnotises Jenny into further recollections. The psychiatrist soberly informs her that 'These aren't dreams, Jenny. These are your memories', and urges her to discover 'how your life now is connected to her life then'. With this establishment of her proprietary relationship to Irishness, Jenny's heritage journey enables her to recover and legitimise her childhood dreams of Ireland (she begins her quest with sketches of Ireland she had drawn as a child, that reveal the Swords Road in Malahide and a local church). When Maggie gives the family tickets to Ireland, Jenny tracks back to Malahide, where she and Kevin quiz local residents about whether they remember the family of her visions. In her new role and on Irish soil, Jenny acquires a dignity and an agency that she never possessed back home. Notably, her husband and son experience distinct personality changes upon arriving in Ireland. The surly Kevin transforms into

Figure 4: **Dilemmas of citizenship and family life are resolved by a trip to Ireland in** *Yesterday's Children*. Clancy Brown, Jane Seymour and Kyle Howard.

a kind and concerned son, an accessory figure to his mother's identity quest. Doug, who had brusquely dismissed his wife's visions as reveries unrelated to their present life, inexplicably shifts to a position of warm support once he arrives. Jenny's agency is recognised by the local parish priest whose help she enlists – Father Kelly tells her 'The spirit of this woman could be speaking through you to find her children.' When Jenny locates Sonny (a dubiously-accented Hume Cronyn) and is able to gather together Mary's other surviving children (who had been separated since being placed in an orphanage), Father Kelly tells her 'You've done a glorious thing'.

In its emphasis on the positive transformations of the Cole family in Ireland, *Yesterday's Children* well illustrates tendencies discussed above for Ireland to be figured as a therapeutic heritage zone for middle-class, white Americans. Yet it makes a somewhat original intervention as well, drawing from the generic power of the made-for-television movie and its ability to figure quasi-autobiographical stories of women's experience that act to validate female subjectivity.[2] *Yesterday's Children* operates as a narrative of maternal reconsolidation as Jenny reunites and repairs the family of the past as well as the family of the present. Fortified by having intervened upon historical injustices, the Cole family learns to practice better family values through its encounter with a negative historical example. While it means to draw attention to the therapeutic intervention made by Jenny Cole upon an Irish family, *Yesterday's Children* highlights just as decisively the beneficial therapeutic effect that she and her family receive. Her pregnancy no longer a subject of contention and her son transformed, by the conclusion Jenny has symbolically ascended to the role of the revered Irish mother whose innocence and altruism make her unassailable.

Another instance in which pre-11 September popular culture equated Irishness with a re-essentialised, simplified epistemology can be found in a television and radio advertising spot used by Bennigan's Irish-American Bar and Grill, one of the most successful ethnic-themed chain restaurants in the U.S. Heavily broadcast around St Patrick's Day, the ad called 'Pocket Money' features a non-descript guy who celebrates the discovery of $10 in his jeans pocket, and chooses to express his delight by taking himself (and his money) to Bennigan's. In part through its use of stylised intertitles fashioned to resemble those of silent film, the ad tacitly promises to 'turn back the clock' to an era in

Figure 5: **Bennigan's 'Pocket Money' advertisement encodes Irishness as good fortune.**

which $10 was a meaningful amount of money. By linking this to themes of Irishness, Bennigan's perpetuates a long line of popular cultural constructions of Irishness as pleasingly anachronistic. More than this, however, it also cultivates a fantasy of financial innocence. This fantasy has a slightly ugly undertone to it as we witness a ridiculous figure who deems himself 'a wealthy man of means' upon finding $10; yet the prevailing tone of the piece is cheery and upbeat and utterly in keeping with the cultivation of innocence that links the majority of recent presentations of Irishness.

For all these similarities, the experience of national trauma after 11 September clearly necessitated and triggered new ways of speaking regionalism and whiteness through Irishness. At the 25 October 2001 benefit concert held at Madison Square Garden to celebrate the efforts of New York's police and fire departments after 11 September, Mike Moran, a New York City fireman, took the microphone to deliver a feisty challenge to Osama Bin Laden. The rhetorical terms of this mode of address are what interest me and inspire a starting point for this section of my analysis. For at a moment when intense professions of American national identity were the norm, Moran invited the radical Arabic leader to 'kiss my royal Irish ass!'[3]

This episode, which went into heavy rotation as a video clip to promote re-broadcasts of the concert and as an audio clip on New York-area radio stations, speaks forcefully to the emergence of the trope of Irishness as white ethnic legitimacy and empowerment in contemporary American culture. While it is hardly surprising that a reference to Irish identity would emerge at a benefit for police and fire officers (this reference, after all, continues a long-established association between the Irish and policing in America), the circulation of this clip suggests how Irishness has become a crucial discursive platform for articulating white working-class legitimacy and innocence. Amidst the exigencies of politics and the marketplace, invocations of Irishness give shape and substance to nebulous, unstable and/or discredited notions of national and ethnic identity. Moran's remark, in fact, catapulted him to a revered cultural status, with Steve Hochman writing admiringly, for example, in the Los Angeles Times that 'There was simply no bigger, better rock star in 2001 than New York City fire-fighter Michael Moran' (Hochman 2001) Indeed, it seems that Moran was able to inscribe an Irish connection to 11 September that even Bono envied, as he quoted Moran repeatedly during U2's fall concerts and subsequently invoked him again in an appearance on The Tonight Show with Jay Leno.

The resonance of Moran's assertion of white Irishness to others is suggested not only by the fact that it was this moment of the concert that was picked up and re-played incessantly by media in New York, New Jersey and Connecticut. Moran's remark inspired Doug Cogan and Christopher Storc to adapt John Kegan Casey's 'The Rising of the Moon' into 'The Ballad of Mike Moran', a song that celebrates Moran and other fire-fighters.[4] In their promotional website for 'The Ballad of Mike Moran' Cogan and Storc state that the song is meant to 'pay tribute to all of the brave men who lost their lives on 11 September

2001. As songwriters, we hope that it also offers a sense of empowerment to those who hear it' (Cogan and Storc 2001).[5]

This rhetoric of empowerment is striking when we consider that prior to 11 September, the majority of representations of white male firefighters and police officers stressed a sense of anxiety about a perceived loss of status in a society that no longer valued their brand of masculinity. As sociologist Neal King demonstrates, 1980s and 1990s 'cop action films' endlessly rehearsed plots in which guilty white masculinity both recognises itself and strives to re-assert its relevance. In such films,

> cops see their world hurtling into monopoly capitalism and multicultural strife, too busy to defer to working-class joes. The largely white and male ranks of police workers feel that they have lost an esteem they once enjoyed as otherwise unmarked everyman Americans, not simply to declines in discrimination and shifts in industry, but also to the corruption overrunning their world. (King 1999: 12–13)

In this light, the events of 11 September may be seen as something of a boon for a class of white male workers driven by a sense of 'lost ground' and awkwardly positioned in the space between the service and professional classes.[6]

Mike Moran's characterisation of himself as 'royal/white' and 'Irish' and the subsequent elaboration and celebration of these traits indicate something of the use-value of Irishness to the broader American cultural conversation about the heroism of working-class white males that emerged post-11 September.[7] It is important to note here that in the wake of the World Trade Center attack, the New York Fire Department (FDNY) remained 93 per cent white, an astonishingly skewed racial percentage given the multiracial character of urban New York.[8] While Moran or any other member of the New York police or fire departments would have been unlikely to trumpet a proud assertion of whiteness at the concert (the NYPD, after all, drew national attention several times in the 1990s for abuse cases involving racial minorities), Moran crucially identifies himself not just as white, but as Irish. By making these proximate terms, Moran insulates himself from any perception of racism, while Cogan and Storc's song elaborates Moran's bid for identity capital by situating it in a historical continuum of Irish national resistance to British oppression. Ultimately this sort of conservative appropriation of Irishness is highly complementary to American hypernationalism. In fact, it may be seen that aggressive American machismo and sentimentalised Irishness are utterly uncontradictory when framed in these terms. In American culture at present, Irishness may be more and more a pose that enables a hard, masculine Americanness a foray into sentiment and recollection without engendering any deviation from identity as stipulated. On the other hand, and this is where I believe the meanings of Moran's comment exceed anything he may have consciously intended, in naming himself (or at least his representative body part) Irish, Moran was expressing

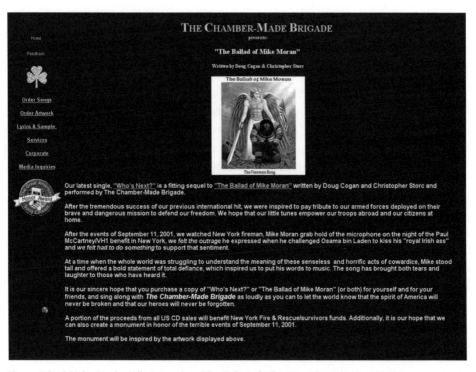

Figure 6: **Post-11 September tributes such as 'The Ballad of Mike Moran' emphasise Irish themes.**

national outrage without the responsibility of citizenship. The attractions of this gambit are evident in the wide circulation and celebration of Moran's remark in both attributed and unattributed forms. One example of the latter can be found in an episode of the Denis Leary sitcom *The Job* in which Leary's New York police officer Mike McNeil, suffering from nicotine withdrawal and a more generalised sense of misanthropy, assaults a Russian taxi driver and is obligated to undergo two weeks of anger management therapy. Leary's abrasive, caustic demeanour proves decidedly at odds with the therapeutic environment and he finally walks out of the session asserting his Irish whiteness as an identity credential.

The celebration of Mike Moran and his Irish-inflected response to the events of 11 September is best understood in my view not as an anomaly but as, in some sense, a highly predictable reaction that draws from a cultural reservoir of associations between Irishness and innocence. It is important to recall that despite the massive sense of shock and sadness experienced by many Americans in the wake of the World Trade Center attacks, there was also a kind of calm and unsurprisedness that suggests that for many, this event represented not so much an aberration as a culmination.[9] Given the broader themes of survivalism and apocalyptic expectancy that have played through American popular culture over the last decade, and the fact that the 1994 attack on the World Trade

Center was a literal rehearsal for the tragically full-fledged destruction of 11 September, it seems credible that many Americans perceived the attacks as a millennial reckoning, slightly delayed perhaps but nevertheless anticipated.[10]

Since the vast majority of millennial-themed destruction scenarios position America (sometimes humanity at large) as guilty of a multitude of sins (hubris, hypercommercialism, grandiosity, environmental neglect and abuse) this cast over the events of 11 September suggests the necessity of exactly the kind of response that was widespread after the attack – the generation of counter-narratives of innocence and virtuous heroism. I want to point out here that Irishness is one ingredient in the broader gendering of the 11 September narrative which cast men as heroes or villains and largely reduced women to the role of mourners, singling out in particular the upper-middle-class suburban white widow in anchoring public grief and designating whose losses we should be concerned with.[11] In these ways, the figure of the affluent suburban widow or the body of the white working-class male rises to exclude others. While I have concentrated on the more sanguine formulations of Irishness post-11 September, there were mournful ones as well, notably the draping of Irish flags at Ground Zero and the massive success of Enya's New Age ballad 'Only Time' in the weeks following the attack with the single becoming essentially the soundtrack for national grief (with the mourning voice kept both Irish and female).[12] It should be noted that a number of accounts have highlighted the heavily Irish-American character of the 11 September victims, both amongst the police and firefighting squads and the financial services employees who made up a high percentage of the casualties. Some have stressed the ubiquity of claddagh jewelry on the victims and the FDNY itself makes available for purchase a Claddagh pin that features the US and Irish flags.[13] A website, IrishTribute.com, was established celebrating the Irish victims of 11 September. Meanwhile newspaper profiles relentlessly figure the events of 11 September in terms of Irishness. A typical example, 'Home of the Brave' – an account of attack-survivor Matt Mellon – notes Mallon's employment with Aon, a corporation named after the Irish word for 'one', his escape from the towers to a place 'as close to home as you're gonna get' (an Irish pub) and finally speculating that his survival can be attributed to 'Irish luck'.

Because Irishness was already in place as a stock element in fantasies of nostalgia and cultural innocence, the Michael Moran phenomenon is actually a predictable response to the traumatic perception of discredited/dysfunctional national identity implicit in coverage of 11 September. In fact, Kirby Farrell's argument would be that in many respects US culture operated in a 'post-traumatic mode' all through the 1990s and this provides a particularly helpful way of understanding the therapeutic functions of commodified Irishness. Deployed across a multitude of representational/cultural sites in the 1990s the experience/endurance of trauma became an ongoing operative metaphor through which many Americans negotiated the vivid prospect of social death under governmental and economic terms that compromised individual and communal health. According to Farrell:

> People may use [the trope of trauma] to account for a world in which power and authority seem staggeringly out of balance, in which personal responsibility and helplessness seem crushing, and in which cultural meanings no longer seem to transcend death. In this sense the trope may be a veiled or explicit criticism of society's defects, a cry of distress and a tool grasped in hopes of some redress, but also a justification for aggression. (Farrell 1998: 14)

In such a climate, the embrace of Irishness as a psychic defence capitalised on popular cultural associations between Irishness and an anachronistic experience of peace, serenity and innocence. The theme of removal to an experience of past serenity coded as Irish illustrates in part the depth of the craving for innocence in contemporary American culture and the further fact that when it cannot generate innocence internally, that culture will appropriate other national/ethnic categories to do so. Indeed, it vividly illustrates Henry Giroux's observation that 'Innocence has a politics' (Giroux 2000: 21).

If before 11 September Irishness was most often invoked to negotiate the traumas of deficient family values or to assuage a sense of capitalism run amok, its flexibility is such that after this seminal event, it could be differently mobilised to stave off an anxious, traumatised perception of American identity. Irish inflections in the post-11 September national discursive environment were hardly confined to Michael Moran and there is currently no better example of the invocation of Irish innocence than the reassembled remains of the Co. Mayo Famine Cottage that sit one block from Ground Zero. Ostensibly a Famine memorial, the cottage is a key feature of the compensatory landscape emerging in place of the post-disaster geography of dislocation and trauma. Out-of-town visitors are likely to tour the area by walking up from Battery Park whose southern end is now home to 'The Sphere', a public art work by Fritz Koenig that stood for thirty years at the World Trade Center and was re-situated on 11 March 2002 in its now half-demolished state. Vendors sell memorial plaques, photo books of the disaster and patriotic paraphernalia in this area of the park, but as one walks north these give way to residual non-commercial displays of photos, tokens and tributes related to the attack victims and the rescuers, and finally to the memorial cottage.[14] Even though functionality and memorialisation coincide here to produce strange juxtapositions (well-dressed corporate workers now neatly zigzag around the still blocked-off areas), the deliberately unstylised, unprettified entrance to the Mayo Cottage is nevertheless startling. One simply steps from the sidewalk into a steep, rocky field (sparsely dotted with plant species imported from Connemara) toward the reassembled remains of the site. With corporate towers looming overhead, this is surely the most anomalous Irish cottage one could ever expect to see. Yet with the former

World Trade Center site literally in view, it is as if one anomaly in the local landscape motivated another.

What is crucial about the Mayo Cottage is that it is essentially a ruin, one which was designed to inspire sombre reflection on a historical experience of loss and displacement, yet it is placed in such a way that its meanings inevitably turn toward the contemporary. Like Ground Zero, it is largely a void space whose elements endow absence with meaning[15] – the cottage 'explains' loss in innocent discursive terms that carry over to the present. Calling upon an understanding of the Famine that has been heightened in America in recent years, the memorial obliquely celebrates the tenacity, endurance and moral unassailability of Irishness. In effect, the placing of one ruin next to another invites us to perceive the sense of injustice many Americans associate with the Famine as equally applicable to Ground Zero. In this respect, the Famine cottage functions as US constructions of Irishness so often do, as a flattering prism for American national identity.

Even if its physical site did not already inspire connections to 11 September, the cottage is also framed within a suggestive rhetoric that makes these connections more manifest. In an exit passageway from the site inscribed with various facts and commentary relating to the Famine, one citation is particularly illustrative of the connections that underwrite this staging of Irish innocence beside Ground Zero:

> The French writer Louis Paul Dubois warned that 'Emigration will soon cause it to be said that *Ireland is no longer where flows the Shannon, but rather besides the banks of the Hudson River and in that greater Ireland whose home is the American Republic'*. (emphasis added)

As vigorous debates continue to play out over the most appropriate way to memorialise the victims of 11 September, the 'borrowed innocence' that accrues to Ground Zero from the Famine cottage has met with a warmly appreciative and politically unproblematic reception. There would appear to be widespread agreement that it is both a poignant and appropriate memorial, though the question of where its memorialising capacities are directed is a complex one, as I hope to have shown.

What these far-flung examples from disparate forms of popular culture illustrate is the functionality of Irishness in American fantasies of political, familial, financial and geographic innocence. They could certainly be further compared to other recent phenomena that work on similar terms, for instance at this writing, historically-based Irish-themed gangster narratives seem to be enjoying a run in the 'prestige picture' category (*Road to Perdition* (2002), *Gangs of New York* (2002)). It is tempting to say that such old-fashioned crime feels almost 'innocent' beside contemporary global terrorism. Indeed the process of activating Irish-inflected discourses of innocence around 11 September might be seen to culminate in *Gangs of New York* which in its conclusion audaciously emulsifies the depiction of brawling turbulent nineteenth-century Five Points New York with an invocation of achievement symbolised by the Twin Towers. The image of the towers is paired with U2's Grammy-winning song 'The Hands That Built America', that also plays over the closing credits and which invokes lyrically the sense of innocence that the Towers are meant to connote visually. The song opens 'Oh my love, it's a long way we've come / From the freckled hills, to the steel and glass canyons', and closes 'It's early fall, there's a cloud on the New York sky line / Innocence, dragged across a yellow line / These are the hands the built America / Ahhh America.' By linking a closed chapter of American urban ethnic history with the sense of loss attached to 11 September, the film's conclusion tries for a sense of political decontamination, that is to say it participates in a broader process of rendering both distant and recent history sentimental and safe.

If I have given the impression thus far that Irishness operates inevitably as a form of political protection in a deeply conservative American popular culture, I would be remiss in not pointing to one recent fiction which strikingly de-sentimentalises Irishness in a post-11 September context. In impressive contrast to reflexive invocations of 'innocent' Irishness (in forms as disparate, as I have illustrated, as reincarnation fantasies and scenarios of dumbed-down consumerism) Spike Lee's *25th Hour* (2002) rigorously interrogates the uses of Irishness as bulwark against the responsibilities of citizenship. From its earliest moments, the film strongly signals that it will reject the contrivances of recent cinema to imaginatively recover pre-11 September New York. Instead, a devastating early sequence insists on both the Towers' absence and the impulse to fill their vacant space in an extended aerial tour of the 'Tribute in Light', the sombre blue beams that temporarily stood in for the towers in early 2002. On his last day in the city before he must report to prison, convicted Irish-American drug dealer Montgomery Brogan (Edward Norton) takes the measure of the place he both loves and hates, his feelings encapsulated in an extended rant delivered to his own mirror reflection in the bathroom of his father's Irish bar. Monty's 'Fuck this city' rant, an astonishing, sweeping condemnation of nearly every ethnic, racial and sexual constituency in multiethnic New York concludes with a now-familiar rhetorical flourish. After bitterly repudiating the interest politics of a wide variety of social groups (including Irish-Americans), Monty invites them all to 'Kiss my royal Irish ass!' Yet in this context the phrase operates very differently from what we have previously seen, its status as a defense mechanism laid bare in a film that elaborates and meditates upon concepts of national and regional identity and that instead of romanticising innocence is unafraid to explore the dynamics of guilt. *25th Hour* thus culminates a flurry of post-11 September references to the Irish body that cumulatively displace an earlier generation's ethnic catchphrase, the blithe (and now very quaint-seeming) 'Kiss me, I'm Irish.'

Further analysis of the kind undertaken here would shed additional light on the ideological components of the Celtic Tiger and the recruitment of Irishness for global capitalism and political insulation. My goal has been to sketch particular conditions of national sentimentality in which Irishness plays quite a large part. These apparently ephemeral phenomena play a strong role in cultivating the attractions of Irishness in contemporary American culture. They interrelate with more pragmatic signs of the embrace of Irish identity in America, signs such as the doubling of applications for Irish citizenship from the US over the last decade, and the quintupling of the Ireland Funds' donor base between 1995–2000 (Dezell 2000: 213, 202–3). More than this, however, they give evidence of a largely undetected but I believe rather widespread historical/cultural dilemma at work in the national psyche – this dilemma finds expression in the longing for an innocent, anachronistic citizenship.

Stephanie Rains, Maeve Connolly and Breandan Mac Suibhne all generously shared with me material related to this discussion, while audiences at the 2002 'Keeping it Real' conference at University College Dublin and the 2003 Notre Dame Irish Seminar offered feedback and encouragement. Przemek Budziszewski helped both in researching and re-formatting several versions of this chapter. A slightly longer version of this essay will appear in my edited anthology, *The Irish in Us: Irishness, Performativity and Popular Culture* (forthcoming, Duke University Press, 2005).

Notes

1   The same article also reported on the development of a themed housing community based on the Kinkade aesthetic.

2   The made-for-television movie has historically been a slot in the network schedule that gives a particular shape and substance to women's experience, as Elayne Rapping so successfully argues in *The Movie of the Week: Private Stories/Public Events*. Minneapolis: University of Minnesota Press, 1992.

3   It is important to point out that as often as not, Moran was cited as having invited Bin Laden to kiss his '*white* Irish ass'. Regardless of the specific construction (whether 'white Irish' or 'royal Irish') both carry similar connotations of a sense of privilege (racial, aristocratic) that is then rationalised/offset by the invocation of Irishness. For a cogent discussion of the symbolic and expressive landscape of post-11 September, see Willis (2002).

4   I am indebted to ethnomusicologist Mick Moloney, who made me aware of some of the historical and thematic connotations of Casey's Fenian anthem.

5   The website address http://www.firemansong.com takes its name from the way that Cogan and Storc's song came to be popularly known by radio listeners.

6   In *American Ground* William Langewiesche discusses the proprietary and preferential status of the 'uniformed personnel' at Ground Zero, briefly linking the tribalism that dominated recovery and removal work to the white ethnic cultures of workers' outerborough neighborhoods and families. (Langewiesche 2002: 154–5).

7   'The Ballad of Mike Moran' constitutes an example of the way that Irishness is used to convey the pride and defiance of white working-class masculinity, while '9/11', a CBS television 'special event' broadcast

in early March 2002 used Irishness in a more elegiac mode. The highly-publicised and well-watched documentary account of the World Trade Center collapse through the perspective of a probationary firefighter and two French filmmakers closes with Ronan Tynan's 'Danny Boy' as the soundtrack accompaniment to a montage of firefighter photos.

8   Niall O'Dowd asserts that it also remains 92 per cent Catholic, 'with those of Irish and Italian roots forming the overwhelming majority of the firefighters' (2002: 52). He does not provide a source for this information.

9   The most common expression of this was the widely-reported observation of those at the scene of the attack and those who watched it by television that they had somehow 'seen this before'.

10   Bill Luhr made exactly this point during a roundtable discussion on 'The World Trade Center Disaster and the Media', held in the University Seminar in Cinema and Interdisciplinary Interpretation at Columbia University on 21 February, 2002.

11   In their book on female firefighters, police officers and emergency medical workers, Susan Hagen and Mary Carouba cite 'the invisibility of women at Ground Zero' and note that 'the media presented story after story about "the return of the manly man" and made daily unapologetic references to "the brothers" and "our brave guys"' (Hagen and Carouba 2002: xi–xii).

12   I am grateful to Kevin Rockett for reminding me of the ubiquity of Enya's music in September and October of 2001, and its relevance to the dynamics of ethnicity and gender I attempt to sketch here.

13   See 'Sonuvagun, If It Isn't Dominion,' for an example of journalism that stresses the Irish dimensions of 11 September. An example of the Claddagh pin can be found at http://www.fdnypins.com/pins.htm.

14   It should be noted that these displays, although officially non-commercial, often welcome donations to firefighter, police and other emergency personnel organisations and have prominently-placed collection baskets.

15   The very muteness and simplicity of the cottage were, it might be argued, all the more necessary in the face of events so staggering they prompted a kind of crisis of public eloquence. When articulate, sensitive assessments on the order of Rudolph Giuliani's pronouncement that the losses at the Trade Center would surely be 'more than any of us can bear' were made, they were repeated again and again as a kind of public consolation. More often, the response to 11 September was a babble of ineloquence (of the kind available twenty hours a day on cable television) and otherwise, a kind of speechlessness. An article detailing the lack of forceful original rhetoric in the upcoming annual commemoration ceremony noted 'speechlessness may also suit the times. Politicians are not trained in oratory, and their audience is skeptical and impatient. In a society fragmented by race, ethnicity and class, it is harder to find language and allusions that resonate widely and to find meanings that can be broadly embraced' (Scott 2002: 31).

References

Blair, J. (2001) 'A Rousing Rock Show for a Wounded City', *The New York Times*, 21 October, B10.

Boym, S. (2001) *The Future of Nostalgia*. New York: Basic Books.

Brooks, D. (2000) *Bobos in Paradise: The New Upper Class and How They Got There*. New York: Touchstone.

Campbell, D. (2002) 'Land of the Twee', *The Guardian*, 8 July, 12–13.

Cogan D. and C. Storc (2002) *Fireman's Song*. On-line. Available at http://firemansong.com

'Despite Elitist Gripes, He's America's Most Popular Artist', *The Chronicle of Higher Education* (22 February 2002), B4.

Dezell, M. (2000) *Irish America Coming into Clover: The Evolution of a People and a Culture*. New York: Doubleday.

Dwyer, J. 'Sonuvagun, If It Isn't Dominion.' *The New York Times Magazine* (11 November, 2001).

Farrell, K. (1998) *Post-traumatic Culture: Injury and Interpretation in the Nineties*. Baltimore: Johns Hopkins University Press.

Giroux, H. A. (2000) *Stealing Innocence: Youth, Corporate Power and the Politics of Culture*. New York: St. Martin's Press.

Graham, C. (2001) *Deconstructing Ireland: Identity, Theory Culture*. Edinburgh: Edinburgh University Press.

Hagen, S. and M. Carouba. (2002) *Women at Ground Zero: Stories of Courage and Compassion*. Indianapolis: Alpha.

Harris, D. (2000) *Cute, Quaint, Hungry and Romantic: The Aesthetics of Consumerism*. New York: De Capo Press.

Hayden, T. (2002) *Irish on the Inside: In Search of the Soul of Irish America*. New York: Verso.

Hochman, S. (2001) 'Pop Music; Pop Eye – Start Spreading the News: A New York Firefighter Upstages the Superstars.' *Los Angeles Times*, 23 December 2001.

Keane, S. (2001) *Disaster Movies: The Cinema of Catastrophe*. London: Wallflower Press.

Langewiesche, W. (2002) *American Ground: Unbuilding the World Trade Center*. New York: North Point Press.

King, N. (1999) *Heroes in Hard Times: Cop Action Movies in the U.S.* Philadelphia: Temple University Press.

Lichte, S. (2001) 'Home of the Brave', *World of Hibernia* 7, 3.

Negra, D. (2001) 'The New Primitives: Irishness in Recent U.S. Television', *Irish Studies Review*, 9, 2, 229–39.

O'Dowd, N. (2002) *Fire in the Morning: The Story of the Irish and the Twin Towers on September 11*. Dingle: Brandon.

Rapping, E. (1992) *The Movie of the Week: Private Stories/Public Events*. Minneapolis: University of Minnesota Press.

Scott, J. (2002) 'The Silence of the Historic Present', *The New York Times*, 11 August, 29.

Smyth, P. (2002) 'A Field in New York that is Forever Ireland', *The Irish Times*, 20 July, 12.

Willis, S. (2002) 'Old Glory' in *South Atlantic Quarterly*, 10, 2, 375–83.

Exodus, Arrival and Return: The Generic Discourse of Irish Diasporic and Exilic Narrative Films

Brian McIlroy

Film is particularly adept at detailing in a visceral way and, equally importantly, in an emotional manner, a diasporic and exilic experience. This experience carries deep resonances in Irish life and only now may it be relegated to historical memory as work opportunities have opened up at home, particularly for those secondary school graduates who have passed the once aptly-titled Leaving Certificate. In the 1990s, in the wake of the so-called Celtic Tiger economy, the trend in emigration has been reversed. Peadar Kirby (2002: 55) reports that Ireland in 1998 experienced a net immigration of 22,800 people. Nonetheless, emigration/immigration narratives have informed and continue to inform popular cultural representations of the Irish in films, such as the ones studied here: Irvin Kershner's *The Luck of Ginger Coffey* (1964), Martin Scorsese's *Gangs of New York* (2002), Atom Egoyan's *Felicia's Journey* (1999) and Nichola Bruce's *I Could Read the Sky* (1999). The corpus of films in this genre is plentiful, and would include New York-based and inspired Irish-immigrant films – Jimmy Smallhorne's *2by4* (1998) and Bill Muir's *Exiled* (1999) – discussed by Martin McLoone (2000: 186) as indicative of an ongoing interest in blue-collar Irish ethnicity and its intersection with themes of masculinity and racism.

Historians Donald Harman Akenson (1993) and Kerby Miller (1985) have taken up the task of detailing Irish emigration and have mapped a remarkable terrain for others to tread. In particular, they have argued that the Irish rapidly assimilated into American culture, notably through inter-ethnic marriage, and quickly moved out of the ghettoes in which they initially found themselves, earning, as they did, the sobriquet of 'lace-curtain Irish' or members of an *arriviste* middle class. Of particular sociological interest is the research of Liam Greenslade (1992) who adapts the theories of Frantz Fanon on the effects of colonialism to draw attention to the remarkably high incidence of Irish people who live in England diagnosed as suffering from mental illness. Cultural critics must, I think, initiate a discussion of the various species that belong to the genus of artistic productions that mediate this diasporic and exilic condition. By so doing, we contribute to the understanding of the effects of this experience on individuals. Emigration and the subsequent immigration are also at the core of the Irish experience. We tap into not just history, folk memory, perceived and real national and ethnic injustices, but also may broaden historical accounts of the disparate experience of the Irish immigrants through analyses of cultural representation.

The impact of immigration is often expressed via memory-pictures of the homeland, themselves filtered through trauma and nostalgia. Irish diasporic and exilic films naturally utilise exodus, arrival and return narrative structures. But any consideration of this genre would expect to struggle to find a suitable framework for describing, firstly, the great exodus from Ireland to North America, Australia, England, New Zealand and other territories due to famine, political and/or religious prejudice or simple economic advancement; secondly, the difficulties of these immigrants' settlement and assimilation in their adopted country; and thirdly, the return for some of these immigrants to their native land. This tripartite structure provides the platform on which a diasporic and exilic generic discourse is played out.

In theoretical terms, perhaps the one major film critic to address specular displacement is Hamid Naficy. In 1993, he published *The Making of Exile Cultures* on the use of local cable television stations and programmes run and produced, respectively, by the Iranian community in Los Angeles. He pinpoints their exile experience as liminal, or on a threshold between two cultures. What Naficy proposes for the cultural critic to consider is a case study of one group's reaction to enforced travel and resettlement. The Iranian Revolution in 1978–79, added to the eight-year-long Iran-Iraq war, drove many hundreds of thousands of people out of Iran seeking a better, or simply safer, life. Many of these individuals became refugees in North America. They faced numerous challenges, among which a foreign culture and a foreign language figured strongly. Naficy traces the development of Iranian television programming in Los Angeles, discovering that it is typified by secular and royalist emphases, within which constant reference to the homeland is evoked.

In his wide-ranging 2001 study, *An Accented Cinema*, Naficy distinguishes between and among ethnic filmmakers, exilic filmmakers and diasporic filmmakers. To Naficy, ethnic filmmakers are typically American-born individuals, such as Woody Allen and Martin Scorsese, who have made their careers by exploring their own ethnic group in America. I would extend the phrase to ethnic films (by contrast, Naficy's aim is to reassert the primacy of auteurist approaches within film studies, and to bring attention to the courage of individual filmmakers) in which category one could put the Irish gangster films *State of Grace* (Phil Joanou, 1990), *Miller's Crossing* (Joel and Ethan Coen, 1991) and *Road to Perdition* (Sam Mendes, 2002), works which utilise Irishness as a confident adjective rather than as an unstable noun. Naficy regards diasporic filmmakers as economic migrants by choice, including second generation immigrants, who are consumed by statelessness, his examples including black British films *Territories* (Issac Julien, 1985) and *Handsworth Songs* (John Akomfrah, 1986). He sees exilic filmmakers as unwillingly absent from their country, and thereby obsessed with the homeland. It is arguably true that both perspectives are at work in Irish and Irish-related films within this genre, and are not mutually exclusive, and that inclusiveness allows us to give recognition to this wider Irish community, pushing critics and commentators to reconsider what the nature of Irish cinema is. Inevitably, this genre places the national under a form of erasure, an instability that is both hybrid and transnational.

Naficy speculates that what distinguishes the exile from the emigrant (both of whom, he argues, deny the grief of loss) is a lapse by the former into childhood narcissism inflected by images of the lost homeland and by dreams of a glorious return. Naficy rightly implies, however, that these feelings of loss, and the various strategies to counter them, are worked through – or simply exhibited – in art, performance and cultural production in general. Exilic discourse has naturally been theorised as mapped onto the experience of race (notably African-American), yet the act of immigration occurs within races and is undoubtedly more frequent. This commonality demands that we consider it carefully as it impacts on social and national relations much more forcefully than we may think. It also confronts a weakened identity formation within a deterritorialised psychological landscape, and it is one of the side-effects of globalisation or, more historically, the rule of Empires.

Naficy provides a checklist of the ways such instabilities are evoked. He does not claim that specific formal strategies distinguish ethnic, exilic and diasporic films, but rather points to a cluster of techniques not usually found in combination in mainstream film. While exilic films are prone to more experimentation, diasporic films, since they are forward-looking, have greater potential for assimilation. In exilic films, then, it is common that the visual style is motivated not by action but by words and emotions, conveyed by an uneven pace, claustrophobic interiors, static shots of a rural homeland imaginary, and a concentration on transit points – boats, trains, buses. The narrative structure is often sparked by voice-over narration, native music, juxtapositions, flashbacks and a structured absence which laments lost people and places. The characters speak the dominant language with an accent and are often alienated and alone. Their general subject is identity and a journey forwards and backwards in search of a stable mental state/home. These features are most prominent in exilic films, less so in diasporic films, and may only be hinted at in ethnic films, such as *Road to Perdition*. In both diasporic and exilic films, however, historicisation is a necessary process, where a character will attempt to account for or recount his or her perceived failure. In turn, the homeland is often represented as a traumatic memory in exilic films, associated with an event in the past that was the catalyst for departure.

In a more abstract manner, the audience is made aware of the tendency to embrace heightened emotions, a melancholy mood, hybridity, liminality and even a fetishised tactility of objects, sounds and gestures (see Laura Marks' thoughts on a haptic cinema, 1999).

Studies in this genre have thus far been mainly historical and in the nature of a survey (see Curran 1989, Lourdeaux 1990, McIlroy 1999, Mulkerns 1999, Pettitt 2000,

Rockett 1994, Slide 1988, Woll and Miller, 1987). Recently, Diane Negra (2001a) has made a theoretical turn to the field of cultural studies, focusing on star actress Colleen Moore in the 1920s. Born an American, Moore was nonetheless promoted by her producers as a safe and wholesome Irish immigrant, perfectly suited to stirring up a nostalgic past in its audience. Negra (2001b) sees similar uses of Irishness in recent Irish-American characters on television series in the late 1990s, programmes freighted, however, with the apparent responsibility to reassert a white, heterosexual, ethnic identity in the face of many Black and Latino shows. Generally, however, there has been no specific theorisation of this popular Irish genre, which naturally reproduces itself – Jim Sheridan's *In America* (2003) being the most high-profile release to date of films concerned with the 'coming to America' narrative. *In America*, with its themes of illegal arrival (via the Canadian border), of loss (the family's youngest child has died) and its sense of claustrophobia (the family moves into a dilapidated tenement building teaming with other illegal immigrants, and visually rendered as ill-lit, cluttered and menacing), drawn from Sheridan's own recollections of life as a newly-arrived immigrant in America, suggests the exilic filmmaker, though Sheridan more correctly belongs to the category of diasporic practitioner. Hence, I would argue, some modification needs to take place in order to apply Naficy's ideas to Irish emigrant/immigrant narratives.

Naficy's work provides us with theoretical tools to revisit this genre, and to put the Irish experience within the forefront of contemporary work on migrations and diasporic studies. In what follows, I touch upon briefly the way in which the trauma of separation from Ireland seems less pronounced in those films that relate to the experience of the Irish in Canada and the United States as distinct from those of the Irish in England. Arguably, this is because my Canadian and American examples – *The Luck of Ginger Coffey* and *Gangs of New York* are diasporic films, whereas my 'English' examples – *Felicia's Journey* and *I Could Read the Sky* are exilic films. Diasporic films, then, are about the process of integration and redefinition starting with arrival while exilic films are about the trauma of departure, do not envisage assimilation and are backward looking.

Canada and the United States – the stuff that dreams are made of?

The Luck of Ginger Coffey is an adaptation of the Irish writer Brian Moore's 1960 novel, and the latter also wrote the screenplay. Moore's early fiction fluctuated between diasporic statelessness (*I Am Mary Dunne*) and exilic nostalgia (*Fergus*) (see McIlroy 1988 and 1989), although this particular film narrative is mainly diasporic. Ginger has lived up to a year in Montreal, along with his wife and teenage daughter. His wife has decided they are to return to Dublin, and has her suitcases already half-packed, and trunks already sent on. But Ginger has been unwilling to commit to buy the boat tickets. He strives to keep his dignity while his family struggles to pay the rent and even eat. Eventually, he takes a job as proofreader at the local newspaper, but its low pay convinces his wife to leave him. His daughter elects to stay with her father, who must now take a second job delivering diapers to make ends meet. But even this sacrifice is not enough, and he watches his wife take up with a senior co-worker at the newspaper. Feeling exhausted and emasculated, he drinks the night away and ends up being arrested for urinating in public, with his heavily-accented joviality mistaken by the francophone officer as an attempt at bribery. His day in court, however, attended by his wife, allows him to face a degree of historicisation, for he must account for his behaviour by explaining his life's problems. He admits that he has not provided for his wife and child. The charge is dismissed, and he and his wife take a slow walk in the snow back to her apartment.

This open ending leaves unclear what their futures will entail. We are struck throughout the film by the claustrophobic interiors, the accented Irish voice of Ginger in the face of dominant English and Scottish tones. In one scene, when he argues with his wife at the newspaper office, the two-shot is 'crowned' by a picture of Queen Elizabeth, raising the question whether the 'Dominion' of Canada is just another form of prison for these characters. What this film develops more than others is the theme that the children of immigrants are more able and desirous of fitting in to the new culture, illustrated by the daughter's enthusiasm to go to an ice-skating party. She does not seem to suffer the indecision afflicting her parents. But perhaps that is to emerge later in her life. As a diasporic film, *The Luck of Ginger Coffey* is imbued with melancholy, suggested in its slow, often uneven pacing. We are privy to a seemingly endless number of shots of Ginger walking in the snow, getting on and off buses, entering cold, forbidding buildings. There is almost a documentary feel to the film created by the removed camera treatment. The film is a study of the trauma of arrival and the difficulty of assimilation. The homeland is never visualised or romanticised; Ginger never believes that a return to Ireland is an answer to their struggles. His wife Vera asserts her independence in Canada not just by leaving him, but by seeking a job, taking up with another man, letting her daughter live with Ginger, and rejecting any pull of religion to curtail her conduct. Ginger and Vera's relationship and their self-perception of themselves have arguably been enhanced by the knowledge of their diasporic statelessness.

Acts of definition and redefinition are also taken up by Martin Scorsese's *Gangs of New York*, a diasporic film rather than an ethnic one, not because the filmmaker is not Irish, but because the film focuses on Irish arrival and assimilation, and because it puts the state under question. The film explores the world of the Five Points, the lower eastside of New York, alighting briefly on 1846, and then mostly 1863. These two dates are not arbitrary. The first alludes to the Irish famine years, while the latter pitches us into the era of the American Civil War, incorporating the anti-black, anti-draft and anti-immigrant riots of the period (see Ignatiev 1995). The arbitrary stoning of newly-arrived Irish is not exactly a warm welcome. We are introduced to Priest Vallon, the leader of the Dead Rabbits, an ethnic Irish gang that loses the challenge for dominance of the Five Points to Bill the Butcher and his 'Nativists'. By the latter term, we deduce that they are the American-born descendants of those who fought the British for independence in the 1770s. The waves of Irish immigration, the abolition of black slavery and the liberalising stance of Abraham Lincoln's tendentious government threaten these nativists' sense of control. In an odd way, it is essentially a Protestant versus Catholic struggle, with both groups overshadowed by larger nation-building events around them. The entrance of the troops *stylistically* recalls Eisenstein's Odessa Steps sequence but the content is inverted in political sympathy, for here Yankee liberalism uses force (with Scorsese's apparent approval) to suppress recidivist tribal conflicts. With the knowledge that Scorsese first thought of adapting Herbert Asbury's 1928 book in the 1970s, it is tempting to draw an Irish parallel which depicts the naïve hope of the time that British troops entering Northern Ireland would overcome the sectarian strife. We know differently, of course, and perhaps Scorsese realized this naïveté by ensuring that the last shot we see in the film is Priest Vallon's son, Amsterdam, escaping the city which magically dissolves into the New York skyline of pre-11 September. The World Trade Center's Twin Towers are a potent reminder that violent conflict has not been erased from the American psyche or from New York's history; on the contrary, Scorsese seems to suggest that ethnic violence defines it (a somewhat simplistic erasure of the global dimension to the issue).

Amsterdam Vallon seeks revenge because of the killing of his father, but he achieves his overall success by mobilising and reinventing the Dead Rabbits while simultaneously using the ballot box (albeit disingenuously), and the iconography of the Catholic Church in relation to martyrdom to press the Irish Catholic ethnic case. A ballot and bullet strategy with a sprinkle of religion has many contemporary Irish resonances. As an Italian-American, Scorsese is clearly on the side of the new immigrants – indeed Amstersdam's friend has an Italian surname – but one can argue that the film's politics are fruitfully confused in places to further establish its credentials as a diasporic film, making allegiances provisional. The audience sympathises with the new-arriving Irish, who are abused and often conscripted for the army straight from the arriving boat (truly one of the great inclusive crane shots in cinematic history), and yet also has some sympathy for the nativists, who are only slightly less poor. For Scorsese, then, the Immigrant/American is a Derridean both/and construction. Scorsese himself is an Italian-American ethnic filmmaker who has made an Irish diasporic film.

England – the Old Enemy?

One of the filmmakers Naficy relies on for much of the structure of his book is the Canadian Atom Egoyan; it is, in retrospect, fitting that this disconnected Armenian, who was born in Egypt, and who immigrated to British Columbia at the age of three, would be the director of the film version of William Trevor's *Felicia's Journey*. The sense of dislocation so clearly apparent in Egoyan's earlier films, such as *Speaking Parts* (1989) and *Exotica* (1994), is brought to bear here on the relationship between Ireland and England. Within the structure of the film, flashbacks tell us the reason for Felicia's sudden departure to the English Midlands: she has become pregnant by an Irish boy who has joined the British army. For Felicia's father, she has disgraced the family's name twice over – by being pregnant outside wedlock and by consorting with a man reinforcing the power of imperial Britain. Hence his outburst that she has the 'enemy' within her.

These scenes of the father's anger are filmed in the small-Irish-town atmosphere, replete with an imposing stone church and in the countryside strewn with the ruins of ancient stone buildings. To this clichéd tale of woe, Egoyan grafts Trevor's narrative of how the young girl is taken in by Hilditch, the serial killer. Felicia is a transient, living at first in a bed and breakfast, then a shelter, and finally in Hilditch's house, narrowly escaping her own murder. Felicia's narrative is punctuated with transit points – the ferry boat to England, the bus station, the bus stop where she says goodbye to her boyfriend, the endless walking under and over bridges, and the car rides with Hilditch. The serial killer arranges the abortion to 'cleanse' Felicia, and as she undergoes the procedure, she dreams of a happy family scene back in Ireland where her son is eagerly awakened by her father. Further, the time has come for her boyfriend to be accepted as the father of her son. It is another imaginary glorious return, as a foetus is literally sucked out of her. Felicia is representative of that other short exile to England that thousands of Irish women must take every year to receive abortion services. The positive ending, if we can call it that, is that Felicia remains in England to build a new life, though we sense her Irish past will continue to haunt her dreams. The desire of the main character to return successfully to Ireland is found in *Felicia's Journey* and *I Could Read the Sky*; at the same time, both films associate Ireland with trauma.

This notion of a haunting past is developed thoroughly in Nichola Bruce's *I Could Read the Sky*, an adaptation of a Booker-nominated work by Timothy O'Grady and Steve Pyke. Like Philip Donnellan's unbroadcast documentary *The Irishmen: An Impression of Exile* (1965) (see Pettitt 2000: 85), Bruce's film is a meditation on the Irish working-class in England. While the film disrupts chronological time and material space, a fairly straightforward narrative of the elderly Irish male immigrant in England is established. In this instance, the nameless man grew up in the country in the west of Ireland, and because he was not the first born male in the family, he could not inherit the farm. This is his first loss. He travels to work in England where he does odd-jobs all his life, punctuated by the sadness in losing touch with his brother Joe, the death of his Uncle, father, mother and, finally, his wife Maggie.

In the man's reverie and contemplation – his historicisation – we see his liminality. He lists all the things he could never do in England, including 'acknowledging the Queen

… follow cricket … speak with men wearing collars … understand their jokes…' He is an alienated individual, locked visually in a small rented apartment with only his memories to transcend his existence. Again, we see in his visions a return to transit points (more obsessively than in diasporic films) of boat, train and car; we see a structured absence of lost people – family, friends, lovers; we see a focus on sadness, emotions and inaction. Synaesthesia is also common, where all his senses are markers of loss – 'I have a sound inside of me but I can't find it', 'I could taste the brine of tears coming into my mouth'; 'Her touch, light as a small breeze'; and after his father's burial, he could smell the burning of a fire. Furthermore, fetishised objects and clothing convey the then and now. Of note here is the accordion he brings from Ireland, but after his work accident in England, he struggles to play; it remains, however, in his room. The second-hand jacket his mother bought him at a market, with the label 'J. Brady', is particularly poignant. He wears another's jacket, and even uses this name for his own at work. His cousin's soliloquy sums it up best: 'We are unknown and unrecorded. We have many names but none our own.' Dissolves, juxtapositions and static shots meld with the shards of Irish culture desperately clung to in England – the radio to listen to Gaelic games, and the pub where storytelling, dance and song can announce the familiar, if only for a short time.

Perhaps Naficy's major challenge in his work, and in any application and nuanced modulation of his theories to Irish-related films is the fluidity and instability of the categories of ethnic, diasporic and exilic films and filmmakers. As we have seen, this is most evident in *In America*, a film that effectively breaches many of the categories nominated by Naficy. What distinguishes *Road to Perdition*, for example, from the bulk of films discussed here is that it, alongside numerous other films with second- or third-generation Irish characters, presents Irishness as a fully assimilated ethnicity. I would propose therefore that, as well as taking careful note of Naficy's visual pointers to the construction of exilic and diasporic narratives, we should consider the common thread that binds together these films to be the theme of Irishness under stress. This is particularly related to a sense of past trauma and thus reverses the convention of Ireland as functioning as therapeutic location. Where Luke Gibbons (2002) has argued that Ireland exists in *The Quiet Man* (1952) as the locus for Sean Thornton's working through of an event in his American past, these films propose the opposite – that in America or Britain their immigrant characters may find refuge from their Irish past. Whether forward-looking diasporic films, such as the mainstream *Gangs of New York* or backward-looking exilic films, such as the highly textured and experimental *I Could Read the Sky*, a rhetoric of loss and grief burns at the core of these works, and reveals their distinctive discourse.

References

Akenson, D. H. (1993) *The Irish Diaspora*. Belfast: The Institute of Irish Studies and The Queen's University of Belfast.

Curran, J. M. (1989) *Hibernian Green on the Silver Screen: The Irish and American Movies*. Westport, Conneticut: Greenwood Press.

Gibbons, L. (2002) *The Quiet Man*, Cork: Cork University Press.

Greenslade, L. (1992) 'White Skin, white masks: psychological distress among the Irish in Britain', in *The Irish in the New Communities*, vol. 2 of Patrick O'Sullivan (ed.) *The Irish World Wide: History, Heritage, Identity*. Leicester and London: Leicester University, 203–25.

Ignatiev, N. (1995) *How The Irish Became White*. London and New York: Routledge.

Kirby, P. (2002) *The Celtic Tiger in Distress: Growth with Inequality in Ireland*. New York: Palgrave.

Lourdeaux, L. (1990) *Italian and Irish Filmmakers in America*. Philadelphia: Temple University Press.

Marks, L. (1999) *The Skin of the Film: Intercultural Cinema, Embodiment and the Senses*. Durham, NC: Duke University Press.

McIlroy, B. (1988) 'Naming the Unnamable in Brian Moore's *I Am Mary Dunne*', *Critique: studies in contemporary fiction*, 30, 2, 85–94.

____ (1989) 'Displacement in the fiction of Brian Moore', *English Studies in Canada*, 15, 2, 214–34.

____ (1999) 'Cinema, Irish' in Michael Glazier (ed.) *Encyclopedia of the Irish in America*. Notre Dame: University of Notre Dame Press, 150–3.

McLoone, M. (2000) *Irish Film: The Emergence of a Contemporary Cinema*. London: British Film Institute.

Miller, K. A. (1985) *Emigrants and Exiles: Ireland and the Irish Exodus to North America*. New York: Oxford University Press.

Mulkerns, H. (1999) 'Film in the Fifth Province', *Cineaste*, 24, 2–3, 50–5.

Naficy, H. (1993) *The Making of Exile Cultures: Iranian Television in Los Angeles*. London and Minneapolis: University of Minnesota Press.

____ (2001) *An Accented Cinema: Exilic and Diasporic Filmmaking*. Princeton: Princeton University Press.

Negra, D. (2001a) *Off-White Hollywood*. London and New York: Routledge.

____ (2001b) 'The New Primitives: Irishness in recent US Television', *Irish Studies Review*, 9, 2, 229–40.

Pettitt, L. (2000) *Screening Ireland: Film and Television Representation*. Manchester: Manchester University Press.

Rockett, K. (1994) 'The Irish Migrant and Film', in *The Creative Migrant*, vol. 3 of Patrick O'Sullivan (ed.) *The Irish World Wide: History, Heritage, Identity*. Leicester and London: Leicester University, 170–91.

Slide, A. (1988) *The Cinema and Ireland*. Jefferson, NC: McFarland.

Woll, A. L. and R. M. Miller (1987) 'Irish' in *Ethnic and Racial Images in American Film and Television Historical Essays and Bibliography*. New York: Garland, 261–74.

Vampire Troubles: Loyalism and *Resurrection Man*

Steve Baker

The question of the representation of Ulster loyalism on film has aroused little serious inquiry, Brian McIlroy's *Shooting to Kill* (1998) being the first sustained study into how the politics of northern Protestants have generally been elided on film. However, two recent films, Thaddeus O'Sullivan's *Nothing Personal* (1995) and Marc Evans' *Resurrection Man* (1998), have brought what are apparently loyalist protagonists to the centre of the big screen, although neither film really engages with the politics of that community in any sustained or serious way. Instead loyalism is appropriated on both occasions to represent and explore violent masculinity.

Nothing Personal at least perhaps aspires to political cinema, acknowledging in its credits a debt to Gillo Pontecorvo's *The Battle of Algiers* (1965), which re-created the struggle for Algerian independence. However, O'Sullivan's film is very different in its content and style. Where Pontecorvo's depiction of political insurrection was served by *cinéma vérité*, *Nothing Personal* is more readily comparable to contemporary films like those of Quentin Tarantino, displaying a similar penchant for 1970s chic and the cinematic iconography of urban gangsterism as *Reservoir Dogs* (1992) and *Pulp Fiction* (1994).

Resurrection Man too establishes itself in a tradition of gangster films, when in an early scene its murderous protagonist, Victor Kelly, is pictured as a young boy in the projection room of a cinema watching James Cagney as Tom Powers in *The Public Enemy* (1931). Powers may be proposed as a role model for Victor but as I will argue here *Resurrection Man*'s harrowing representation of psychopathic violence owes at least as much to the conventions of horror as gangster films. Indeed it is *Resurrection Man*'s affiliation with horror that makes it the most intriguing and troubling cinematic representation of violent loyalism.

In *Resurrection Man* Victor Kelly is the leader of a loyalist gang whose homicidal behaviour is rooted in his sexual dysfunction. His libido is sated only by bloody murder. Certainly his relationship with his girlfriend Heather is without any tangible sexual contact. They never share so much as an on-screen kiss and she goes so far as to suggest that their relationship is never consummated, despite her own sexual yearning. To emphasise Victor's deviance from sexual 'normality' the film makes a clumsy allusion to homosexuality but ultimately Victor's murderous loathing of Catholics is laid at the door of his weak father and overbearing mother, with whom he seems to have an almost incestuous relationship. Mother and son are witnessed dancing, embracing and exchanging romantic dialogue from old films, the sexuality of their relations confirmed by the mother's jealous dismissal of Heather, Victor's prospective girlfriend. In this way *Resurrection Man* employs a loyalist killer to reflect upon warped psycho-sexual desires, with nothing to say about the politics of loyalism, its ideals or its motivations.

Despite this general disregard or disinterest in the political specificity of loyalism, *Resurrection Man* evokes one of the most wretched periods in Northern Ireland's history with thoroughly harrowing and graphic scenes of torture and assassination. In particular the film recalls the notorious loyalist gang, the Shankill Butchers, that terrorised Belfast in the mid-1970s. The gang derived its name on account of a preference for torturing its victims with knives, axes and meat cleavers before murdering them. While *Resurrection Man* would make no claim to historical accuracy, the example of the Shankill Butchers seems to have provided the pretext for the film's exploration of the fascinating depths of human depravity. In effect it is psychology, rather than history or politics, that informs Evans' representation of violent masculinity in the guise of loyalism.

There is nothing new in this apparently apolitical treatment of the conflict. Ireland has long provided British, American and latterly Irish filmmakers with an assumed location for violent primordial passions. John Hill has elaborated on the tendency in cinema to regard violence in Ireland as 'a manifestation of the Irish "national" character' (Hill 1988: 147) and more recently Martin McLoone has noted with regret the propensity of recent films, including *Resurrection Man*, to 'recycle the myth of atavism' regarding the conflict in Ireland (McLoone 2000: 84). Violence, therefore, tends to be shorn of its political and historical context and reduced to the bloody-mindedness and inherent malice of the Irish.

Ignoring politics does not guarantee apoliticism. Films that neglect the political rationale for paramilitary violence in Ireland obstruct genuine efforts to understand the conflict. Such ignorance always serves somebody's interests – usually those committed to the maintenance of the status quo. In this instance, *Resurrection Man* contributes to an already popular perception of loyalist paramilitaries as essentially monstrous. Certainly the use of knives by the most notorious exponents of loyalist violence, the Shankill Butchers, and the ritualistic character of their killings, helped to facilitate the notion of a primitive impulse. That impression of primeval motives is clear in a journalistic appraisal of loyalist paramilitaries written after the massacre of seven people in a Greysteel bar in 1993:

> The massacre in Greysteel has once again illustrated one of the most striking features of loyalist terrorists: that for sheer hot-blooded, vengeful savagery they can often leave the IRA standing. The IRA uses murder as a cold-blooded and clinically calculated means to a political end; loyalist assassins often leave the unmistakable impression that they are men who enjoy their work. (McKittrick 1994: 301)

Once configured as savage and monstrous, loyalism simply seems to defy rational explanation and forego modern political discourse. As such there may appear little point in pursing any serious inquiry into its political motivation. That reluctance to engage meaningfully with loyalism impoverishes our understanding of the Northern Ireland conflict. At the same time, it may suit a section of loyalism that would prefer to avoid having to give a political account of its violent actions. Being designated as inherently monstrous means never having to explain yourself.

Certainly there are conscientious sections of loyalism that are concerned about the low regard in which they are held by the world at large. It is a recurring lament at grassroots and community forums in loyalist areas and some loyalists suspect they know why their reputation abroad is so lamentable. As an anonymous contributor to one community discussion put it: 'We knew full well that the media were short-changing us when it came to representing "our" side of the story, but what *was* our side of the story? We couldn't even explain it properly ourselves' (Hall 1984: 8).

Those loyalists will hardly recognise their 'side of the story' in *Resurrection Man*. At the same time loyalist efforts to articulate that story in commercial cultural forms have been hard to discern. Irish nationalism and republicanism have maintained a cultural dialogue, both within and beyond their immediate political constituencies, and have achieved some commercial successes in the process. Loyalism on the other hand seems to have kept its sullen silence, described variously as 'autistic' (Butler 1991: 102), 'disabled by an imaginative exclusiveness' (Brown 1985: 8) and suffering 'bowler-hatted inarticulacy' (Nairn 1977: 242).

The trope of the tongue-tied loyalist is a popular one but in truth there is nothing tongue-tied about the Reverend Ian Paisley and the raft of loquacious street orators made in his image. Neither are northern Protestants cultural*less* – a tedious assumption that ignores the fact that even loyalists have access to broadly the same commodity culture as their contemporaries. In addition loyalism can refer to a political lexicon that is rich in symbolism, narrative and ritual. Yet unquestionably loyalism has either failed to seriously engage with its political contemporaries, or it has apparently given up seeking the affirmation and good will of those others. There is certainly an element of contrariness underlying an anti-Agreement unionist's response to David Trimble's Nobel Peace prize. The Democratic Unionist Party's deputy leader, Peter Robinson, described Trimble's award as 'a vivid example of rewards offered to those who are prepared to jettison principle and reward terrorists. *Better to be scorned by the world*' (McKittrick 1999: 191; my emphasis). Similar isolationist sentiments are echoed by the predominantly loyalist supporters of the Northern Ireland football team, who chant from the terraces of Windsor Park: 'Nobody loves us and we don't care' (Bruce 1994: 63). It seems that some loyalists understand their isolation from the good opinion of the world, they know themselves as pariahs and have come to wear that pariahdom as a badge of principled defiance. In this respect there are some shocking correspondences between the representation of horrific loyalism in *Resurrection Man* and the self-image of some loyalist groups.

While *Resurrection Man* resembles a gangster film, displaying the currently fashionable iconography of 1970s gangster chic, it is deeply indebted to the horror film, in particular the vampire and slasher sub-genres. Victor's peculiar relations with his mother recall the oedipal issues at the heart of Alfred Hitchcock's *Psycho* (1960), a film that surely set the psycho-sexual standards of all subsequent slasher films. Like Norman Bates, Victor's weapon of preference is a knife, wielded as a phallic symbol of dysfuntional masculinity and like Norman, Victor seems to prefer the *mise-en-scène* of the bathroom while slaughtering his victims. He cuts the throat of a Catholic man in the toilets of a loyalist bar, taking obvious sexual pleasure from the ejaculation of blood that stains the mirror above the sink. Gasping and panting, as if in a post-coital moment, he regards his warped reflection through the sanguinary surface of the mirror. Towards the end of the film he is ensconced in the Tombe Street public bathhouse, which offers a gargantuan recreation of *Psycho*'s notorious shower scene, with its pipes, porcelain and blood-stained shower curtains. These sequences situate Victor within and associate him with a thoroughly abject milieu.

Julia Kristeva in her essay on abjection asserts the abject status of sweat, pus, blood, piss and shit, all the things that our bodies expel and we wash away in order to live (Kristeva 1982: 3). The abject is that which is 'radically excluded' from the civilised environs of the subject where it continues to threaten and fascinate (1982: 2). That Victor eventually takes up residence in a derelict bath house, a place associated with human ablutions, is a measure of his exclusion from civilised society. Interestingly Victor's father, wise to his son's involvement in the spate of vicious murders, describes him as a 'wee shite'. The description further emphasises Victor's affinity with gross materiality. It is also an indication of the father's feelings of guilt at having begot such a monster. Calling Victor a 'wee shite' identifies him with feelings of shame and disgust that might similarly accompany bodily functions.

Estranged from his weak father, Victor is doted upon by his mother, Dorcas, the dreadful matriarch of the Kelly household. Dorcas belittles her weak husband, indulges her murderous son and ultimately acts as an apologist for his homicidal behaviour. As Barbara Creed has explained, the construction of the maternal figure as abject is a feature of many horror films and in *Resurrection Man*, Dorcas Kelly is cast in the tradition of this 'monstrous feminine' (Creed 1993).

Creed offers a Kristevian analysis of horror films, grounding the genre in 'ancient religious and historical notions of abjection – particularly in relation to the following religious 'abominations': sexual immorality and perversion; corporeal alteration, decay and death; human sacrifice; murder; the corpse; bodily wastes; the feminine body and incest' (1993: 9). *Resurrection Man* is fairly comprehensive in its application of the generic conventions that Creed associates with the horror genre.

The film's very title is an immediate indication of its intentions to employ a religious discourse but while in Christian theology the resurrected Christ is the harbinger of eternal life, Victor promises a lingering and tortuous death to his victims. Murder is his stock-in-trade but the manner in which Victor assassinates his victims, studiously lacerating them, establishes that these acts are not generic gangster 'hits'. There is a heavy element of ritual involved in the killings, confirmed by the apparent communion the patrons of the loyalist bar achieve through the brutal beating of a Catholic man, John Maguiness. The sequence recalls the practice known as 'rompering', or the 'romper room', which characterised a number of sectarian murders in the early years of the Troubles. Victims were often abducted at random then taken to back rooms or garages where they were tortured and beaten before being shot.

Maguiness is captured by Victor and presented at the loyalist bar like a sacrificial lamb but it is the apparent unity achieved by the men in the act of identifying and then savagely assaulting the Other that the scene seeks to emphasise. The loyalists urge each other on in the assault; they wink at each other, laugh, pull faces, dance and slap each other on the back. Significantly the scene includes a distinctly misogynistic form of banter. As one assailant declares loudly to one of his accomplices: 'Here, Hacksaw, you can come round my place anytime, give the wife one of them kicks.' The association of the victim with a woman suggests that he is being inferiorised by the aggressive assertion of communal masculinity. The Catholic man is taking a beating 'like a woman' because women 'take' beatings. Masculinity in this instance is defined by, and depends upon, the ability to 'give' such a beating.

One woman literally takes a beating in the film. Elizabeth is assaulted by her drunken husband in the bathroom of their home. Ryan, her abusive spouse, is a Belfast journalist who takes a dubious interest in the murderous activities of Victor Kelly. An association between Ryan's wife-beating and Victor's sectarian violence is made early on in the film. A sequence that shows Victor mutilating his first victim is followed by a shot of Ryan waking on the settee, evidently after having spent the night drinking. The scene switches to the mutilated body of Victor's first victim left in an alleyway. Then we are returned to Ryan, now in the bathroom where he wipes fresh blood from the mirror. As the film progresses it becomes clear in flashbacks that Ryan has beaten his wife in the bathroom of their home while drunk the night before. The image of blood on a bathroom mirror is recalled later when Victor kills John Maguiness in the toilets of the loyalist bar. Juxtaposing Ryan's misogynistic violence with Victor's sectarian violence assumes their similarity; both men, it is suggested, are united in a specifically masculine form of cruelty. In this way the political motivations and rationale of loyalist violence are displaced in favour of a discourse concerned exclusively with sexualised forms of aggression.

In *Resurrection Man* the representatives of vicious masculinity, Victor and Ryan, rendezvous in the Tombe Street bathhouse. The bathhouse represents the lavatory milieu writ-large, which played host to some of the abuses perpetrated by both men earlier. While the 'romper room' is the site of malignant forms of homosociality, the bathhouse is the rank interior of the perverted male mind. Darkie Larche, Victor's ailing and ageing rival in the community, is already in residence. Having lost the loyalty of his paramilitary colleagues and the affections of Heather, usurped on both accounts by Victor, he sinks into drunken impotence. In effect he seems to have been robbed of the two characteristics that defined his masculinity. The first is recourse to violence through paramilitarism and the second is heterosexuality, discernible in his relationship with Heather. Larche is a man with an identity crisis and the bathhouse provides a suitably abject environment in which dysfunctional males sink into self-mortification. By the time Ryan arrives on the scene Victor has subjected Larche to multiple stab wounds. The journalist finds Victor blood-stained and crouched vampire-like over his rival's body in a bath tub, mutilating him with a knife.

Victor's blood lust has distinct vampiric overtones. Similarly the nomenclature 'resurrection man' hints at some association with the undead. In the course of the film it is suggested that Victor, with his gaunt features and pallid complexion, undergoes a sort of corporeal alteration and comes to resemble a living corpse. On his last visit home his mother draws attention to his spectre-like presence and comments on his emaciated condition: 'Victor son, you near put the heart out of me. I thought you were a ghost so I did. Ach son you're like a rake.' By this stage he is resident in the appropriately named Tombe Street bathhouse, his very own crypt.

The vampyric motif is continued in *Resurrection Man* through the nocturnal hours that Victor keeps. He is very rarely pictured in daylight. He seeks out his victims at night, directing his gang from the back seat of the car. His forte for finding his way through the city with his eyes closed draws an admiring comment from one of his accomplices: 'I'm fucked if I know how he does that. Did you swallow a map of this place or something, Victor?' His navigational skills seem bat-like, relying on sonar. Ultimately Victor's demise is presaged by his loss of navigational competence. He guides the gang into dead ends eventually ending up at the docks where he fires off a few rounds of ammunition. Initially he seems to be firing aimlessly out to sea but in a subsequent point-of-view shot it appears that he is shooting at the rising sun as it tries to burn through the haze and gloom over Belfast. The scene of Victor caught in sunlight portends the end of his reign. As with all the best ghoulish and vampire myths, sunlight is terror's nemesis. Significantly then when Victor is gunned down outside his mother's house it is in broad daylight.

Resurrection Man shares a number of similarities with that most enduring of vampire myths, Bram Stoker's *Dracula*, first published in 1897. Both Victor and Stoker's Count assume the aura of the outsider. Dracula is 'a dark stranger' from the east (Stoker 1897/ 1993: 224). Victor, as played by Stewart Townsend is similarly cast as an exotic outsider, replete with swarthy good looks. Heather opines that he 'looks like a foreigner', a property that is attributed by one loyalist to Victor's father being a 'taig'; a derogatory term for a Catholic. This doubt surrounding the Protestant integrity of Victor's parentage is thrown up on a number of occasions by his rival, Darkie Larche, as a way of emphasising Victor's difference from the community and undermining his position within it. In this way Victor's sense of being an outsider and therefore vulnerable, is implicated in his violence. He strives for subjective and social integrity by committing heinous acts of violence against a religiously defined Other. At the same time the impetus behind Victor's violence directed at Catholics may also lie in a sense of self-loathing on account of the suspicion about his father's religious affiliation.

Ultimately *Dracula* and *Resurrection Man* offer thrilling tales of sexuality and violence and both locate their monsters in geo-political universes of uncertainty, threat and disorder: Victor Kelly in late-twentieth-century Ulster and Dracula in nineteenth-century Eastern Europe. That Stoker's demon emerges out of Transylvania may have been a deliberate strategy of the author's designed to play with the anxieties of his contemporary Western readership aware of the political unrest in Eastern Europe and conscious of how that instability offered a threat to the peace of the continent. In *Resurrection Man*, Marc Evans seems to have considered loyalist Ulster a similarly terrifying prospect for modern cinemagoers.

The ease with which loyalism has been appropriated as a figure with which to terrorise the imaginations of cinema audiences is cause for concern but the complicity of some sections of loyalism in their horrific image and reputation is equally alarming. Any masked group that can burst into a crowded Greysteel bar on Halloween night in 1993 and shout 'trick or treat' before indiscriminately spraying the interior with gunfire, is arguably participating in (indeed, revelling in) the construction of its own abject reputation. This complicity is most depressingly demonstrated by a popular wall mural in working-class Protestant areas that depicts loyalism as 'the undead'. A revived corpse, dressed in a traditional red army tunic signifying Britain's imperial past, charges across a battle-scared and apocalyptic wasteland clutching a tattered Union flag in one hand and a sword dripping blood in the other. In the background the iconography of Irish nationalism in the shape of the 'Free Derry' wall is burning. In the foreground a fallen Irish patriot, indicated by a green tunic, lies prostrate at the feet of the resurrected imperial cadaver. This is loyalism as 'resurrection man', an apparent confirmation and celebration of loyalism's abject status.

Kristeva refers to the abject as 'disturbing identity, system, order', it is that which 'does not respect borders' (1982: 4). Indeed Dracula's ability to fascinate and terrify bourgeois Victorians lay precisely in his transgression of spatial and temporal boundaries. He was at once the 'dark stranger' or threatening immigrant in their midst and a feudal anachronism violating their modern sensibilities. His disregard for borders palpably demonstrated his defiance of the boundary between life and death, a condition designated 'undead'.

Similarly the forces of agreement in Northern Ireland today are troubled by their own 'undead' in the shape of loyalist and republican diehards that the Good Friday document proposed to lay to rest. There remain dissident republicans who look to the unquiet graves

Figure 7: **Loyalist wall mural in Bond Street, Derry.**

of their 'fenian dead' for legitimacy, while the symbolic resurrection of a British imperial cadaver depicted in loyalist wall murals suggests that loyalism has been doing a little grave digging of its own.

In a period defined by Tom Nairn (2000) as 'after Britain', loyalism is in the distressing position of bearing witness to its own passing. The old ways may be dying but what will replace them is still undetermined. As Antonio Gramsci warned, this can be a period of 'morbid symptoms' (Gramsci 1971: 276), among them the likeness of a political nosferatu displayed on the gable walls of some loyalist housing estates. What underlies this self image of loyalist abjection is a palpable sense of loss – loss of constitutional position, political integrity, territory, industry and work, and perhaps even the loss of an assumed superiority.

All, however, is not entirely bleak within northern Protestant politics. There are progressives whose contribution to the political process has been fulsome and enlightened. By the same token not all loyalist wall murals are entirely dystopian, although most are determinedly militaristic. With the inception of the peace process one mural on Belfast's Shankill Road offered a more affirmative vision. In the background three crosses (presumably representing the scene of Christ's crucifixion at Calvary) are silhouetted against a setting sun. But this dispiriting landscape is superseded by the slogan 'New Life' in large, bold lettering. In style and content this mural is the antithesis of the previous one. While it also employs the theme of resurrection, it is one more in the spirit of the Christian definition evoked in the popular title of the document signed on 10 April 1998 at Stormont – the Good Friday Agreement.

Still, the grim image of the 'resurrection man' is a reminder of the despair and alienation felt in some working-class Protestant areas. Here they clearly know that in the eyes of their

Figure 8: **'Resurrection'. Wall mural.**

contemporaries they appear unlovely and unloveable. In this respect, *Resurrection Man* sheds no useful light on loyalism's morbid condition at this time: it serves only to confirm it. Certainly filmmakers should not set out to flatter, nor should they be uncritical of loyalist subjects, but a commitment to a more politically-engaged cinema might better illuminate the Troubles in Northern Ireland and the current malaise at the heart of loyalism.

References

Brown, T. (1985) *The Whole Protestant Community: The Making of a Historical Myth*. Derry: Field Day.

Bruce, S. (1994) *The Edge of the Union: The Ulster Loyalist Political Vision*. Oxford: Oxford University Press.

Butler, D. (1991) 'Ulster Unionism and British Broadcast Journalism 1924–89', in Bill Rolston (ed.) *Media and Northern Ireland: Covering the Troubles*. Basingstoke: Macmillan, 99–121.

Creed, B. (1993) *The Monstrous Feminine: Feminism and Psychoanalysis*. London: Routledge.

Gramsci, A. (1971) *Selections from the Prison Notebooks*. London: Lawrence and Wishart.

Hall, M. (1994) *Ulster's Protestant Working Class*. Belfast: Island.

Hill, J. (1988) 'Images of Violence', in Kevin Rockett, Luke Gibbons and John Hill (eds) *Cinema in Ireland*. London: Routledge, 147–93.

Kristeva, J. (1982) *Powers of Horror: An Essay on Abjection*. New York: Columbia University Press.

McIlroy, B. (1998) *Shooting to Kill: Filmmaking and the 'Troubles' in Northern Ireland*. Trowbridge: Flicks.

McKittrick, D. (1994) *Endgame: The Search for Peace in Northern Ireland*. Belfast: Blackstaff

____ (1999) *Through the Minefield*. Belfast: Blackstaff.

McLoone, M. (2000) *Irish Film: The Emergence of a Contemporary Cinema*. London: British Film Institute.

Nairn, T. (1977) *The Break Up of Britain: Crisis and Neo-Nationalism*. London: Verso.

____ (2000) *After Britain: New Labour and the Return of Scotland*. London: Granta.

Stoker, B. (1897/1993) *Dracula*. London: Penguin.

part 3 **real stories: narratives in fiction and non-fiction**

Telling Tales: Narrative, Evidence and Memory in Contemporary Documentary Film Practice

Desmond Bell

Many film makers are acutely aware that an effective synergy between film theory and production practice can only be plotted within a common critical culture. My own film practice has drawn upon a wide range of archive material and narrative strategies in order to explore aspects of Ireland's post-Famine past. In this chapter I seek to make sense of this body of documentary work by drawing upon a range of recent critical writing on documentary practice. This autocritical approach seeks to bring the rigour of critical theory to the core of the creative process, hopefully illuminating our work but also testing the precepts of criticism.

The films

The Hard Road To Klondike (1999) drew on a rich reservoir of early film material in order to retell the story of Mici Mac Gabhann's tramp through frontier America to the Yukon. *The Last Storyteller?* (2002) concerned itself with the work of the Irish Folk Lore Commission and its veteran collector Seán Ó hEochaidh. *Storyteller* used similar archival strategies to those employed in *Klondike* to retell some of the fairytales and folk tales collected in Donegal from the 1930s to the 1950s. The films were made primarily for Irish television but seen worldwide on the festival circuit. Interestingly, some critics have questioned their documentary auspices specifically in relation to the verisimilitude of what is portrayed. These anxieties seem to arise largely out of the particular use of archival sources. I have been accused on occasions of an irreverent and ahistorical use of 'found footage'. Doubts have been raised about whether either piece is actually a documentary at all.

Both projects were based on autobiographical and other documentary sources. *Klondike* was adapted from Mac Gabhann's account of his upbringing in Donegal and subsequent travels as a migrant labourer in Scotland and the US. His story was recorded and transcribed by Seán Ó hEochaidh and subsequently published in book form, first in Irish and subsequently in an English translation. *Storyteller* draws on Ó hEochaidh's field diaries and on his collection of fairytales published by the Irish Folk Lore Commission (1977) under the title *Síscéalta Ó Thír Chonail: Fairy Legends from Donegal*.

Both films involved extensive historical research on Irish migrant workers and on the folk belief and social practice of the northwestern sea board. Both draw on a rich reservoir of archival images, both still and moving, portraying rural life in the west of Ireland from the 1930s to the 1950s. The archival collages, which are a feature of both works, use actuality material and fiction clips. Some of the former is professionally shot and some of home-movie origin. No attempt is made to distinguish between them as storytelling resources. In both films archival sequences are removed from their original filmic context, whether this be within a work of drama or a documentary, and are employed as a narrative resource within new story structures. In other words the archive material is not used as it is in many television documentaries – to illustrate a didactic argument primarily established via an authoritative voice-over. Nor is it used, as in certain historical and ethnographic films, as visual evidence of the way things were in a way of life that is now gone.

And so, as with other found-footage work, the question arises: are these films documentaries? Is the director involved in some sleight of hand in this blurring of the boundaries between fact and fiction? Or is this part of both the historical character and the contemporary condition of documentary film practice?

Let me list the issues that I wish to explore here: the evidential status of the photographic archive within the contemporary documentary film; the use of voice-over and related issues of subjectivity; the role of fictive tropes and strategies within factual filmmaking. How should we as filmmakers evaluate the evidential and expressive status of the still and moving archival image within documentary film practice? What, in other words, are the ethical, epistemological and creative issues involved in handling the shifting boundary of fact and fiction in the creative documentary?

The critical context

Despite the reassuring familiarity of Grierson's definition of the documentary film as the 'creative treatment of actuality', we remain uneasy with documentary films which seek to 'fake it' by employing filmic artifice. Documentary gains its social significance within what Bill Nichols terms a 'discourse of sobriety' (Nichols 1991: 3), where informational and factual criteria remain sovereign in the creation of the work. Certainly in the institutional context of British public service television, any suggestion that a producer has been 'over-creative with the actuality' leads to a moral panic. Reviewers and journalists purportedly concerned with defending the ethical auspices of the form speak out against such films with great indignation.

The indexical character of the photographical image is still seen by many to underwrite the documentary's claim to factuality. The photographic image signals the presence of the camera on the scene at the historical moment of image capture. The photographic emulsion seems to embalm the historical event, preserving it and delivering the image to the present as a 'second-degree original' (Paech 1989). The photograph thus enters the archive as perhaps the most powerful means of documentation and preservation of historical events.

However, in an age of postmodern scepticism (and of digital manipulation) the traditional claims of the documentary to provide objective knowledge of the social world have come under scrutiny. The relationship between, on the one hand, the indexical and evidential basis of the documentary film and, on the other, between the figurative and fictive has often been seen as a conflicting one. Indeed as the Rodney King case has indicated, the widely different evaluations of the video footage of the LAPD assaulting King produced as evidence during the legal proceedings suggests that even the most unconstructed of moving-image sources, in this case the images of a domestic camcorder, can be subject to radically different, 'contradictory but credible', interpretations (Bruzzi 2000: 21).

I try to address these issues as they have manifested themselves in my work. In this task I have found it useful to draw on the work of a number of critical theorists. Bill Nichols (2001), for example, offers us a typology of documentary forms, tracing the evolution of non-fiction film from an expository mode, still favoured by television and characterised by the use of an obtrusive and omniscient voice-over, through the observational and interventionist modes associated with *cinema verité*, to what he calls a 'performative' mode which characterises some contemporary documentary films which inscribe the filmmakers within the text. Whatever my reservations about this rather unilinear conception of the historical development of documentary, I would be the first to admit that his discussion of a range of contemporary film, including found-footage work, has been illuminating for me.

Visual anthropologist Catherine Russell (1999) has also written perceptively about the found-footage film and explored the relationship between archival-based films and ethnographic concerns within the emergent field of visual cultural studies. Similarly Harvard historian Robert Rosenstone (1995) has made the claim that the most grounded contribution to the critique and renewal of historical practice has come from a body of contemporary documentary which tests ideas about truth and power, subjectivity and knowledge. Finally, in my attempt to explore the relation between traditional Gaelic storytelling and film form, I have found it useful to draw upon the work of the theorists of 'Third Cinema', in particular the reflections of Teshome Gabriel (1986) on the role of oral narrative, mythology and popular memory within non-Western cinemas.

The performative documentary and the use of found footage

As Nichols tells us, performative documentary offers its viewer neither the objective summation of events promised by the expository mode nor the lived immediacy and voyeuristic thrills of the observational. Instead filmmakers draw on a disparate set of resources – found footage, re-enactment, personal sources and sentiments – and different creative strategies – experimental collage, use of vernacular voices, visual forms of telling

– in order to communicate a much more partial but often emotionally charged and questioning account of an issue or event.

According to Nichols, the performative mode is characterised by both formal innovation (experiments in using and reframing found footage, the inclusion of the film-maker's presence and performance within the film, recourse to fictional strategies, the development of visually-led forms of telling) and by a certain scepticism with regards to the truth claims of filmmakers, their interviewees and the entire cinematographic apparatus. Within this approach, questions of authority (who knows and who gets to speak) and of evidence (the verisimilitude of presented observation and testimony) are problematised and a much greater emphasis is placed on the subjectivity of the filmmakers than on the objectivity of the photographic medium. Reality is no longer captured unproblematically via the camera lens but patterned via the filmmakers' aesthetic constructions.

In *Film of Her* (1996) and *Decasia* (2002) filmmaker Bill Morrison has drawn on the Library of Congress early paper collection to explore the historical materiality of the cinematic. He employs similar techniques of inflecting archival material to those pioneered by Hungarian filmmaker Peter Forgacs. Forgacs' earlier work *Wittgenstein* (1994) had a profound impact on me when I first saw it in Budapest in the offices of Magyar Television. In it Forgacs reworks amateur home-movie footage taken in 1930s and 1950s Hungary to evoke the Austrian philosopher's reflections on language, vision, suffering and death. There is absolutely no referential relationship between the words of Wittgenstein that we hear intoned by an actor and the archival images we see of a bourgeois family at play often in a rural setting. Yet, by slowing sequences down, reframing shots, and using digital wipes, Forgacs allows word and image to resonate in a manner that profoundly illuminates our understanding of both.

These and other highly expressive found-footage works seem to pose a series of questions about the status of the archival image and more generally about the truth practices and subjectivity of documentary film. My own films, *The Hard Road To Klondike* and *The Last Storyteller?*, pursue the same creative strategy although they are characterised by a much stronger narrative steer. My work seeks to respond to the original source material through its roots in a Gaelic oral tradition of storytelling.

Catherine Russell takes up the argument in her paper on found-footage filmmaking. From the outset she acknowledges that there are many different types of found-footage film. These range from historical documentaries which seek to assemble archival sources as evidential support, to collage films committed to modernist experiment with the archival palate, to the scratch video approaches now found in rock videos and on MTV. My own films would seem to combine features of the historical documentary with some of the formal features of the collage film.

For Russell each of these forms shares a common feature: 'In the process of being appropriated, the original image gives over its meaning to the new text and is manipulated by the new filmmaker on the level of the signifier' (1999: 240). Within the found-footage film the meaning of the archival elements is transformed as these images are compiled in a new text. The original material is used in ways that pose serious questions for both documentary theory and for ethnographic practice.

Russell draws upon Walter Benjamin's theorisation of memory and representation as an aesthetic of ruins and traces. The ruin, for Benjamin, is both the most material and most symbolically powerful form of the allegorisation of history; its fragments are a testimony to what has gone before, but are indicative of a loss that can never be repaired (like the photograph). Benjamin, Russell believes, offers a critical solution to one of the recurrent problems faced by post-structuralist thought, 'how to theorise cultural memory without mystifying it as an original site' (1999: 8).

The found-footage film does not seek to offer the immediate, indexical access to the past promised by the original photographic sources from which it is assembled. In the found-footage film the images are all mixed up. Combined under a montage principle, they establish a different sort of relationship with the past. The relationship of archival element to historical event becomes a *figurative* rather than a referential one.

For Russell, 'its intertextuality is always also an allegory of history, a montage of memory trace which the filmmaker engages with the past through recall, retrieval and recycling'. Accordingly, 'The complex relation to the real that unfolds in found-footage filmmaking lies somewhere between documentary and fictional modes of representation opening up a very different means of representing culture' (1999: 238). The found-footage film then, like the performative documentary more generally, plots a space between fact and fable.

The vernacular voice-over

The Hard Road To Klondike seeks to remain faithful to a traditional practice of storytelling while drawing on the figurative powers of the photographic image. The general theme is Irish emigration. The film recasts the autobiographical recollections of one particular migrant worker using a wide range of archival sources to illuminate his story. Stephen Rea narrates the film from a script based on *Rotha Mór an tSaoil* (1959), Mac Gabhann's transcribed and published account of his travels. This was a book I had been given to read as a child and which is familiar to a generation of Irish schoolchildren through its use on the Leaving Certificate Irish curriculum.

Mac Gabhann's distinctive story speaks to a wider experience of colonised peoples and of diaspora, not only via his account of his passage to the new world but in his relation to the native American peoples he encounters in Montana and later in the Yukon. It is Mac Gabhann's capacity as a storyteller to lift his narrative out of the sentimental reminiscence and to address issues of solidarity and difference between his experience as a Gael and those of the Indians marginalised by miner-settlers like himself that shaped our reading of his text.

Gabriel has coined the term 'hetero-biography' to identify a modality of autobiographical narrative found in third cinema:

> I do not mean autobiography in its usual Western sense of a narrative by and about a single subject. Rather I am speaking of a multi-generational and trans-individual autobiography, i.e. a symbolic autobiography where the collective subject is the focus. A critical scrutiny of this extended sense of autobiography … is more than an expression of shared experience; it is a mark of solidarity with people's lives and struggles. (1986: 58)

Klondike seeks to offer a filmic treatment of memory and the past which, in Gabriel's terms, stands as, 'both a representation of popular memory and as an instance of popular memory itself' (1986: 59). The key to this is its handling of the visual archive, both still and moving, *in conjunction and counterpoint with a particular sort of voice-over*. In marked contrast to the authoritative and disembodied voice of the expository documentary, the film employs what I call a *vernacular voice* (that is a voice-over that in its commitment to storytelling reveals its own partiality).

The voice-over has acquired a terrible reputation as a documentary device within 'smart' film circles. This is to no small degree due to its insensitive use within factual programming, where its tone is often didactic. The 'voice of God' narration can easily overwhelm the visual aspect of the film reducing the complexities of the image to a tautological confirmation of what we are being told. It does not have to be like this. In the work of directors like Buñuel, Franju, Ford and Marker, we find different varieties of voice-over narrations that are ironic and detached, poetic and partial, vernacular and engaged. In a film like Cozarinsky's *One Man's War* or Marker's *Sans Soleil*, the use of such a voice can have a profound impact on the 'reality effect' of the documentary film. Exposure to the films of Chris Marker with their ironic, probing and highly individual voice completed my conversion to a 'revisionist' position on the voice-over, rejecting the orthodoxy of practitioners of *cinéma vérité* that it should never be used.

Clearly the use of the vernacular voice within documentary film raises particular issues. Among these is that of point of view and of the truth status of the enunciated. In fiction the establishment of a point of view is usually signalled by camera perspective (indeed that is one of the original meanings of the term). Within the documentary the qualities of voice-over – its timbre, cadence, resonance and acuity – are often more important than a visually-established point of view. Certainly the choice of Stephen Rea as the narrator of both *Klondike* and *Storyteller* was critical for me, as his skill as an actor and familiarity with the Donegal vernacular were crucial in establishing both tone and point of view. He had tackled a vernacular voice-over in *The Butcher Boy* (Neil Jordan, 1997) several years earlier. In this film he voices the reflections of Francie as an adult looking back on the horrific events of his childhood; a voice, which as Martin McLoone notes, 'retains the idioms and striking language of the original and which again disturbs the audience by being both strange and displaced while at the same time utterly logical in its own terms' (2000: 215).

What distinguishes the *Klondike* voice-over from the ironic postmodern voice employed in the Cozarinsky and Forgacs films is its rootedness in a storytelling tradition and its attention to the role of narrative in relaying popular memory. In both films while interview testimony is included to provide additional sources and perspectives, the films achieve their narratological unity in Rea's performances, an aspect of *Klondike*, I might add, which came in for some criticism at the European Documentary Network conference in Lisbon in May 2001 where delegates found my use of an actor to be inappropriate to the ideals of documentary.

Documentary as a radical form of memory

Gabriel argues that 'Memory does something else beside telling us how we got here from there: it reminds us of the causes of difference between popular memory and official versions of history' (1986: 53). Does it therefore matter that the archival images we see in these films are sometimes quite inappropriate in terms of their historical and chronological status?

Within *Klondike* these filmic elements seek to evoke and retrieve a distant but knowable past. While it is reassuring to believe that the archival image given life within a film offers unmediated access to history, it might be more accurate to see its use as essentially allegorical. For the filmic montage based on found footage is always a figuration of the past rather than a simple index of it.

Take for example the sequence portraying the arrival of Mici Mac Gabhann in New York in the 1890s on board an emigrant ship. Rea voices Mac Gabhann's commentary:

On the eleventh day it was announced we were coming near New York. I gathered myself and tried to move around a bit.

New York was like a dream. I gazed wide-eyed at Manhattan and wandered through its streets in a daze.

This scene is 'covered' visually with a montage made of the following elements: a sequence from the Kalem 1910 fiction feature *The Lad From Old Ireland* showing emigrants on the deck of passenger boat; live action photography scenes of Liberty Island and lower Manhattan and of tenements and homeless people on the streets of the lower east side;

a sequence from Edison's New York Paper Collection, circa 1897, showing a cop moving on a street trader, a scene posed for the camera; a sequence from *The Lad From Old Ireland* showing the hero (played by Kalem director Sydney Olcott) on the New York quayside caught up in the bustle of the port; a trick film sequence (speeded up time-lapse) of the erection of a cinema from the Edison New York Paper Collection, circa 1897; a sequence from the Edison variety *What Happened on 14th Street*, 1896, girl's dress lifted by rush of hot air from a sidewalk vent.

This montage involves fictional elements, actualities of New York, short varieties of staged incidents and contemporary footage capturing the historical resonances of the city. As in other found-footage films, no attempt is made to discriminate between the different sorts of footage, though at one point the soundtrack with its dubbed sound of a cine projector at work does explicitly invite the audience to peep into a cinema of attractions. As Russell notes:

> The work of filmmakers who have experimented with the documentary status of the archival image evokes alternative, invasive and dialectical forms of temporality and history. Recycling found images implies a profound sense of the already-seen, the already happened, creating a spectator position that is necessary historical. (1999: 241)

I guess when we were assembling this sequence we had in mind the historical reality that for many of the newly-arrived emigrants their first port of call in the city may well have been the nickleodeons of Broadway to view Edison varieties like *What Happened on 14th Street*. With their introduction to cinema came also a new way of remembering. Cinema became both a conduit delivering 'the shock of modernity' but also as it developed its power of storytelling, a reservoir of memory.

Beyond the salvage paradigm

The Last Storyteller? directly addresses the ethnographic as a 'discourse of representation'. It also explores the role of folk lore as popular memory. Folk lore has had a bad press within metropolitan critical traditions, associated as it has been with regressive nostalgia towards a rural past and racialisation of culture. Yet as contemporary scholars have shown (for example, Ó Giollain 2000), it can be read as the language and popular memory of the subaltern. For Gabriel popular memory can be understood as the 'oral historiography of the Third World' (1986: 54) and as such provides a rich reservoir of sources for a radical cinema which, in turn, acts as a caretaker for this narrative tradition.

From the outset, *Storyteller* alludes to a number of historical synchronicities and anthropological dilemmas. In 1935 Seán Ó hEochaidh was a twenty-two-year-old fisherman from Donegal about to begin his career with the Irish Folk Lore Commission. Seán and his fellow collectors were dispatched to the Gaeltacht in an attempt to preserve the remaining crop of folk stories told by the last generation of traditional *seanachaí*. That same year critic Walter Benjamin completed his classic essay *The Storyteller and Artisan Cultures*, lamenting the disappearance of the figure of the storyteller within peasant and artisan culture and tracing the implications of the eclipse of oral tradition. Shortly before Seán began his work, *Man of Aran* (Robert Flaherty, 1935) was completed, a film which portrayed an ethnographic present with the sensibility of a primordial past.

Each of these three cultural practices represented in the film was conducted within what has been labelled by postmodern anthropology as a 'salvage paradigm'. As James Clifford tells us, this ethnographic approach reflects, 'a desire to rescue "authenticity" out of destructive historical change' (1987: 121). Even the title of our film alludes to the pervasive influence of such a mentality within folk-lore practice. *The Last Storyteller?* also seeks to critically reframe the notion of salvage though it recognises that both photography and folk lore can be read as attempts to conserve a popular memory, not as a nostalgic vision but as 'a look back into the future' (Gabriel 1988: 65).

The use of found footage together with vernacular voice is the key here. In a middle section of the film, Ó hEochaidh, in a voice-over provided again by Rea, describes his journey into the Blue Stack Mountains, one of the most remote areas in Ireland and still a monoglot Irish community in the 1940s. The region is represented by means of a reconstruction, with an actor seen cycling through a contemporary Donegal mountainscape. Seán recalls recording a particular story from a renowned storyteller Máire Nic a Luin (whom we see in a clip from a 1976 film). The story *The Widow and the Red Haired Girl* is then retold using the following visual elements: archival black-and-white footage of men ploughing from the 1950s documentary *An Irish Village*; archival black-and-white footage of a young girl from 1950s home-movie source; archive [colour] of harvesting from 1940s home-movie footage rendered black-and-white; archive image of young girl again (black-and-white) with digital manipulation to give her red hair; archive of trick film footage (black-and-white) of boys playing, shot by an Irish priest in the 1950s which reverses actions sequences to humorous effect.

In assembling these 'true fictions' we harness an imaginative template to both retell the transcribed folk tale and to place its performance within its original cultural location and moral economy. For me the challenge was to use found footage together with a range of other strategies to engage a contemporary audience and reveal the continuing capacity of these tales to narrate concerns about difference, marginality and power. I also wanted to explore the relation between fairy belief and the magic of the cinema, and to suggest parallels between the spectatorial pleasures of cinema and the enthralment of traditional storytelling. We tried to do this by re-inscribing documentary images within the context of the folk tale.

Figure 9: **The red-haired girl signals to the fairies (permission – Desmond Bell).**

However, *The Last Storyteller?* is not a nostalgic lament for an eclipsed oral tradition and the 'folk society' which engendered it. Its engagement with gaelic alterity, signalled through the vernacular voice-over and its focus on the practice of storytelling even as it tells a story, escapes the clutches of romantic fictionalising and irrendentist nationalist longings. In performing an act of historical salvage with regards a premodern, celtic moral economy, it is intended to provide a critical imagining of a postcolonial and postcapitalist world.

The challenge remains one of, as Benjamin put it, 'how to theorise cultural memory without mystifying it as an original site'. *Storyteller* recognises a transition within popular culture from a modernist world of 'magical' cinema to a digitally slick, postmodern one of visual turbulence. Like traditional anthropology, the archival film performs a salvage operation, rescuing cultural artefacts and traditions 'for posterity'. The found-footage film becomes then a second order act of salvage. In an age of 'visual toxicity' we are salvaging the salvaged.

Clearly the archive image can only do this work when the indexical properties of the photographic image are put in brackets and the image *qua* sign attended to. At the same time the archival image alludes back to a 'profilmic past' and to the relationship of the

Figure 10: **Seán Ó hEochaidh, folklorist, age 76 (permission – Desmond Bell).**

camera to what was once an ethnographic present. This referentiality is as true of fictional found images as it is of ones with factual auspices (which incidentally may be one of the reasons that in the making of *Klondike* we were able to draw with equal fluency on fictional material as actualities).

Our use of found footage seeks to acknowledge the essential ambiguity of the documentary image. Certainly in our use of the archive we seek to remain sensitive to its duality. As we have found again and again when selecting images with which to tell our historical stories, while the indexicality of the image chosen does not make it more real in any absolute sense, it does seem to grant to the image the power to effectively represent the past as an engaging story and a lesson for the future. In reinscribing these images in new narrative contexts (or in this case older, more traditional oral narratives) we hopefully encourage the viewer to question the status of the representations they encounter.

In the found-footage film the indexical images of our cinematic past can be seized upon and their dialectical potential released in order to produce, as Benjamin would have understood it, a 'radical act of memory'. The creative documentary provides for an ethnography of representation and recall rather than of presence and the primitive, facilitating an opening to different histories and marginalised voices and to the 'time of the other'. Hopefully our chosen archival images alluding to a specific ethnographic and historical subject – the marginalised folk culture of the western sea board – can celebrate historic forms of communality, struggle, memory and dignity which can illuminate our future.

References

Bell, D. (1990) 'Media Studies in the Information Age: Towards a Critical Regionalism', *The Media Education Journal*, 10, 12–14.

Benjamin, W. (1968) 'The Storyteller: Reflections on the Works of Nikolai Leskov, in Hannah Arendt (ed.) *Illuminations*. New York: Schocken Books, 85–107.

Bruzzi, S. (2000) *New Documentary: A Critical Introduction*. London and New York, Routledge.

Clifford, J. (1987) 'Of Other Peoples', in Hal Foster (ed.) *Discussions in Contemporary Culture*. Seattle: Bay Press.

Gabriel, T. (1989) 'Third Cinema as Guardian of Popular Memory: Toward a Third Aesthetic', in Paul Willemen and Jim Pines (eds.) *Questions of Third Cinema*. London: British Film Institute, 53–64.

Mac Gabhann, M. (1959) *Rotha Mor an tSaoil*, Dublin: Foilseachain Naisiunhta Teoranta, trans. 1962, Valentine Iremonger. London: Routledge.

McLoone, M. (2000) *Irish Film: The Emergence of a Contemporary Cinema*. London: British Film Institute.

Nichols, B. (1991) *Representing Reality: Issues and Concepts in Documentary*. Bloomington: Indiana Press.

_____ (1994) *Blurred Boundaries: Questions of Meaning in Contemporary Culture*, Bloomington and Indianapolis: Indiana University Press.

_____ (2001) *Introduction to Documentary*. Bloomington: Indiana University Press.

Ó Giollain, D. (2000) *Locating Irish Folk Lore: Tradition, Modernity, Identity*. Cork: Cork University Press.

Ó hEochaidh, S., M. Ní Néill and S. O'Catháin (1977) *Síscéalta Ó Thír Chonaill: Fairy Legends From Donegal*. Dublin: Comghairele Bhéoloideas Éireann/University College Dublin.

Paech, J. (1989) 'The Mummy Lives!', in Willem de Greef and Willem Hesling (eds) *Image, Reality, Spectator: Essays on Documentary Film and Television*. Leuven/Amersfoort: Acco, 57–65.

Russell, C. (1999) *Experimental Ethnography: The Work of Film in the Age of Video*. Durham and London: Duke University Press.

Rosenstone, R. (1995) *Visions of the Past: The Challenge of Film to our Idea of History*. Cambridge: Harvard University Press.

Telling Our Story: Recording Audiovisual Testimonies from Political Conflict

Cahal McLaughlin

One summer's early evening in July 1972, shortly after the breakdown of a ceasefire between the IRA and the British Army, British soldiers opened fire on the Springhill housing estate in Belfast. In the ten minutes that followed, five unarmed civilians – two of them children and one the local priest – were shot dead and several others were injured. It was a mini 'Bloody Sunday', but without any political cost to the perpetrators. No official investigation was carried out and there has been little media representation of the incident other than the news coverage of the time.[1] The Springhill Massacre is just one of the thousands of events remembered as lived experience by the immediate community but incorporated by society into a collective history known as 'the Troubles' – 25 years of political violence over the constitutional status of Northern Ireland.

Following the Downing Street Declaration and the 1994 ceasefires by republican and loyalist paramilitary groups, a number of victims' and survivors' organisations attempted to address the hidden traumas of a quarter of a century of violence.[2] Part of the work of these organisations has been to record first hand testimony. Surprisingly, only a few of them have made use of audiovisual media. Two of the best-known productions from those which have done so are *Night Rider* (1999) directed by Harmen Elisa Brandsma and commissioned by An Crann, and the Northern Visions produced *…and then there was silence…* (2000) directed by Simon Wood for The Cost of the Troubles Study. One of the survivors' organisations that revealed an early interest in audiovisual material was the West Belfast-based Victims and Survivors Trust (VAST). VAST is politically non-aligned, and campaigns on issues of justice while also running workshops and classes for personal and socially therapeutic purposes. This group had established a website and had video-recorded many of their commemorative events.[3]

VAST invited me to work with them in the Spring of 2000. They wanted to produce a short documentary on video that would both offer survivors an opportunity to 'tell their story' and to encourage others to come forward and to add their stories to the archive that VAST was hoping to build (in the manner of the Shoah Foundation). I had directed and produced broadcast and community documentaries over a twenty-year period[4] and the collaboration with VAST came out of my research into recording testimonies from political conflict. As the documentary was intended for 'promotional' purposes and was to have an accessible narrative, we chose the story of the Springhill shootings from the many violent incidents that had occurred in West Belfast during the Troubles.[5]

Some research had been done the previous year with the production of a pamphlet and a locally-organised public inquiry. [6] Other circumstances also aided the telling of this story – there were witnesses still alive, including some who were injured. The incident occurred in daylight, so these individuals had had a clear view of events. It would be possible to film in the actual locations with witnesses as guides to and interpreters of past events. Most importantly though, and what made this story all the more important, was that the case still required closure. No prosecutions had ever been brought, which gave our project of recording the testimony of survivors a personal relationship with the process of remembering and healing underway throughout the country.

Storytelling and public acknowledgement

The performance of storytelling can be regarded as part of a therapeutic process. Although Marie Smith claims in *Personal Accounts from Northern Ireland's Troubles: Public Conflict Private Loss*[7] that some people may be better served by their silence than by telling their story, my conclusions after many interviews with survivors mirrors that of Dori Laub, the psychoanalyst, who has recorded testimonies from Holocaust survivors for his Yale University video project. Laub has written in *Testimony: Crisis of Witnessing in Literature, Psychoanalysis and History*,[8] that some survivors began to find a narrative and uncover connections that were lost as they told their story to him, important elements in the healing of wounds caused by trauma. He writes, 'Survivors need to tell their story in order to survive' (Felman and Laub 1992: 78). Although Renos Papadopolous, an analyst who has worked with Bosnian ex-camp prisoners, acknowledges, 'there were times when our shared silence was honouring the unutterable … ultimately, the healing of these painful experiences due to atrocities may [lie] … in returning to more 'traditional' forms of healing based on assisting people to develop appropriate narratives.'[9]

As Laub states of one of his subjects, 'What ultimately matters is the experience itself of giving testimony, of living through testimony, of reclaiming his position as a witness', (Felman and Laub 1992: 85). The clearest example of this in this documentary was the testimony of Martin, who was severely injured in the shootings. Before recording, we met with Martin and his wife, Bernie, and other survivors in the local community house. Martin appeared to have a stutter and also asked Bernie to accompany him to the recording location. Bernie explained that she was too busy and he should do it by himself. Reluctantly he agreed. But a transformation occurred when we went to the site of the shooting, the camera was turned on and he began to tell his story. He had told his story many times before, but this was the first time in front of a camera. He grew in confidence and articulacy as the story unfolded.

This raises the issue of public acknowledgement. Brian, another of our interviewees, states that the first time he told his story publicly was 27 years after the event at a locally

Figure 11: **Martin points to the permanent injuries that he sustained (permission – Cahal McLoughlin).**

organised public enquiry. He told us that 'I was never asked once about what happened. I was never counselled about what happened.' Shoshanna Felman, the literary critic, also writing in *Testimony*, analyses Claude Lanzmann's *Shoah* (1985):

> To testify is not just to record a fact, but to address another, to appeal to a community. To testify is not only to narrate, but to commit oneself, and the narrative to others … to take responsibility for the truth, which goes beyond the personal, in having general validity' (Felman and Laub 1992: 204).

This is something that VAST is conscious of. They, and the storytellers in *Telling Our Story*, want to tell their stories to the public, to be listened to and to be acknowledged. Stanley Cohen, in his *States of Denial: Knowing About Atrocities and Suffering*,[10] highlights the key difference between knowledge and acknowledge, with the latter implying acting on knowledge. Acknowledgement suggests a development where healing is possible.

Creative collaboration

Most audiovisual productions involve some degree of collaboration and we wished to push this notion as far as possible. *Telling Our Story* was a collaboration between three sets of people – VAST, the survivors who used the Springhill Community House as their focal point, and myself. We all met prior to filming to discuss the project. Each explained their motivations and hopes for the project. I myself was thoroughly interrogated. I was asked who I was and what I wanted to get out of this; fair and proper questions which reflected a mistrust of the media resulting from decades of misrepresentation and stereotyping.[11] Even recently, broadcast television has a tendency to rely on survivors merely to authenticate its 'reports' as otherwise related by journalists and so-called 'experts'.[12]

Since part of my intention had been to leave behind conceptual and technical skills as well as a film, we used VAST's own digital camera rather than broadcast grade equipment to record the material. One of the VAST members acted as sound operator, others as assistants, and the organisation's Management Board were the producers. The group had not yet acquired post-production software, so the piece was edited at my university in London.[13]

Each stage was discussed and agreed with VAST and the participants, from the initial decision to choose what particular story and what questions to ask, to where to record and how a narrative could be constructed in post-production. While the relationship between documentary director and subject has traditionally been one of power over another, some have attempted to redress this balance, most notably Jean Rouch with his approach of 'participatory ethnography'.[14] However, this was limited to the viewing of material and discussions with the participants. The power of representation still lay with the director. My own collaborative protocols[15] arise out of the Workshop movement, a UK network of film and video groups, many of which empowered participants by ultimately allowing them a veto on the material.[16] In the process of producing *Telling Our Story* each rough cut was sent to VAST and the participants for discussion and a final edit was screened to and discussed by an audience of all those involved, a practice also employed by Rouch.

The decision to record the interviews at the site of the original shooting was to encourage a recreation of the atmosphere through direct representation of the environment. We hoped that the location would become a 'character' in itself, and that it would tell its own story. We planned to use as few cutaways as possible to allow the people and the landscape to tell the story. We also planned to make minimum intervention as 'interviewers' because we wanted to encourage the survivors to tell the story in their own way in as far as that was possible. We were aware as documentary makers that we were taking decisions which could control the direction and shape of the final story, but we strove for a collaboration where the participants would have the space to decide what they wanted to include and what to omit, a relationship that we hoped was reflected in the title, *Telling Our Story*. The interviews were edited to create a sense of witnesses describing an event as it happened. One of our subjects, Rosemary, who saw her friend Margaret shot dead, found it difficult to be interviewed. Both girls were aged thirteen in 1972 and Rosemary's responses as an adult recalling the emotions of that moment in time were terse and hesitant. We decided to use her material anyway because this very inarticulateness conveys some of the strains of conjuring up traumatic memory.

The choice of location and the use of a hand-held camera were to play a significant part in the overall aesthetic of the documentary. In one scene one of the survivors, Brian, relates what happened when he arrived at the site of the shooting. He was 16 years old at the time and was returning home from another part of the city. His revisiting of the physical space in the film enables him to more easily revisit it emotionally. He retraces his steps, figuratively and literally, he refers to the street layout, points to the timber yard where the shots came from and to the community centre. He takes us, the audience, on a narrative and a physical journey. The hand-held camera accompanies him. We are usually looking at him, but we sometimes follow his eyeline as he points to a building and the camera wheels around to see it. We, the audience, are encouraged to visit with him another space as well as another time.

Because there was a minimum crew, with the director operating the camera and asking occasional questions and a sound recordist standing out of shot and behind the camera, Brian addresses the camera operator. His eyeline is therefore generally directed towards the camera and so directly to the audience. The sound recordist operated a boom and allowed independent use of the camera to pan away from him, to follow his pointing, and to see what he sees but still allowing us to hear him.

While the recording of reality can only ever minimise mediation, never remove it, the address to camera encourages this minimising and engages the audience more closely with the storyteller. This is part of the philosophy of what American director Errol Morris has dubbed 'first person cinema', a project he has been developing since the 1990s. It inevitably raises the question of performance though, and, in a sense, Brian, like any interview subject, is performing. Stella Bruzzi argues in *New Documentary: A Critical Introduction*,[17] that performance always occurs in front of the camera, but that the representation of the person it contains is no less authentic for this. For his part, in *Representing Reality* Bill Nichols describes how people become what he terms 'social actors':

> I use 'social actor' to stress the degree to which individuals represent themselves to others; this can be construed as a performance. The term is also meant to remind us that social actors, people, retain the capacity to act within the historical arena where they perform. The sense of aesthetic remove between an imaginary world in which actors perform and the historical world in which people live no longer obtains. (Nichols 1991: 42).[18]

Brian's 'performance' in *Telling Our Story* is inherently linked to the authenticity of the location and his personal experiences there, so much so that on occasions he ignores the hierarchy of production and takes charge of the direction. When he describes the

Figure 12: **Brian describes witnessing two deaths next to him (permission – Cahal McLoughlin).**

shooting of the two men on either side of him, he moves around the camera forcing it to follow him (we see the shadow of the boom in this motion). He also presses up against an imaginary wall and leans out to look to his left. As he demonstrates the bullet flying over his head and the body slumping back against him there is almost a tangible connection with the past. Later, when Brian is discussing the affects on him and his community, he looks down averting the camera's gaze, subverting the normal convention of matching eye line with the interviewer/the camera. Although we, the audience, no longer have his look he invites us to a painful place in his thoughts.

Additional material

We allowed for some additional material to be added to the testimonies at post-production. A memorial had been created by local people that included a mural on white tiles. Within this composition were portraits of the dead, a landscape of the temporary single-story houses, which have since been replaced by brick two-storey houses, and images of newspaper coverage at the time, which alleged that the dead were 'gunmen' or had been shot by loyalists. Close-up recordings of these were used to illustrate some points made by the survivors. The strategy was to limit images to those found in the vicinity. The decision not to use television archives was based partly on costs, but also to encourage viewers to hear and see what the storyteller tells and shows us, not what black-and-white footage edited for television news might suggest.

The other non-storytelling images which were employed involved a degree of recreation, but falling short of reconstruction. We planned that when the edited narrative came to the point when a fatal shooting occurred we would zoom in quickly to the physical position where we imagined the shot came from. This could not be achieved easily during the recording of the interview so we recorded it afterwards. In post-production we added the sound of a single shot or series of shots, again reflecting the incident, to the quick zoom image to exaggerate the impact. We wanted this to mirror the suddenness of the original shootings that occurred without warning and to interrupt the narrative. These images and sounds were then followed by an image of a painted portrait of the person shot with a contrasting silent soundtrack.

At an early rough-cut stage, these particular post-production additions caused discussion within the VAST Board. Some members of the Board were concerned that the impact of this quick zoom and sudden noise might re-stimulate pain for the viewing survivors, or other survivors of violence, and be too traumatic. While accepting this possibility, the Board balanced it with the need to reflect in some way the original trauma and agreed to keep the effects as they occurred in a context which justified them, i.e. they had an impact but weren't sensationalist, and were followed by a moment's silence and a portrait.

The other non-testimony material added at the post-production stage included two pages of text at the very beginning to establish context. Since the documentary was not an investigation into the incident, something that would have needed larger resources in order to access British Army and Royal Ulster Constabulary files, but made up of the stories of the survivors, the text restricted itself to giving factual information as to the date, time, location and numbers involved. It also reported that compensation had been paid by the government and that no one had ever been prosecuted for the attack. We chose to use text in order to avoid the disembodied and authoritative narrator's 'voice' which would have increased mediation between the participants and the audience.

The documentary was book-ended with impressionistic sounds. A foreboding rhythm was employed at the beginning over street shots of Springhill, with its imposing 'peace' wall, and children posing for the camera as a brief introduction to the area is offered. The sound does not match the images of orderly houses and children at play, suggesting discordance. A bass heart beat sound ended the documentary over images of the garden and mural, the credits and Martin walking off-screen, visibly severely injured.

One of the most difficult parts of the discussion after the final screening, which was made up of participants and their families, the VAST Board and staff and invited members of the community, concerned the fears of one of the participants, raising issues that reflect wider tensions in the North. He had moved out of the area and was working in a mixed political environment. Sectarian tensions were increasing in the area and he felt concerned for his family. He was worried that if the documentary was seen publicly in the area, he could be identified as someone who was critical of the British Army and conclusions could be drawn that he was a republican sympathiser and so a legitimate target for loyalist paramilitaries. Debate centred upon the paradox that on the one hand the distribution of the documentary would raise important issues but that on the other there was an understandable fear of retaliation. The decision was therefore taken to restrict the screening of the tape to controlled environments such as community centres and festivals. This reflects a tension generally in the North that has persisted since the ceasefires. While there is no declared war, low-level political violence, particularly in Belfast, acts as a break to many promising developments such as the collective need to tell stories of the recent past, most of which were difficult, if not impossible, to tell at the time, because of the sheer level of violence occurring in parallel to the immediate and intimately experienced violence of those affected.[19]

Closure

While accepting the impossibility of complete closure for trauma narratives, we can accept degrees of closure, stages that people can work towards where experiences can be integrated into their lives, rather than dominate and distort them.

The Springhill shootings occurred thirty years ago. There was no police investigation, certainly none that interviewed any civilian witnesses or survivors. There has never been a closure in the sense of either all of the facts being interrogated or legal justice being applied. The survivors reflect a sense of frustration and anger at this public lack of closure, but in different ways. The differences between Brian and Martin are reflected in the difference of their social status as well as the difference of their wounds. Martin is physically injured, with a metal plate in his head. He has a limp and is visually disabled. His past is embodied in the present. He cannot forget or be allowed to forget the past and must live it daily. This is illustrated by his anecdote about his sister-in-law's appeal to stop living in the past. His reply was that his past is also his present. Brian on the other hand has no physical wounds but displays emotional and social scars. He talks about the sense of humiliation that he and his community suffered, both because of the attack and because of the lack of action by the authorities in response to the incident. Anger in both men is evident as they reflect on the injuries inflicted unjustly on them and their community. While Martin looks directly, challengingly, at the camera, his look exaggerated by the wide-angle close-up, Brian casts his eyes down, apparently trying to control his rage, the better to articulate his thoughts as clearly as possible.

Their differences also mirror social and economic differences in the wider society of the North that need to be taken into account when considering healing processes. Martin has a dependency because of his injuries. He is dependent on physical and economic support. He is unemployed and his disability makes isolation more difficult to overcome. Brian, on the other hand, has a professional job and the social mobility that comes with that. His injuries are easier to hide and less obstructive in seeking work and relationships.

In both cases their memories are vivid and powerful. But while Martin's past dominates his present and prevents him from seeing a future that offers hope, Brian can separate the past from the present and can imagine a future that is different from, and more just than, the present. Martin's future is not only physically the same as his present but he carries the guilt of knowing that neighbours died trying to save him. He carries the survivor guilt that makes closure more difficult, even if an investigation were to uncover the perpetrators and justice redeemed. But Brian can see a closure. While Martin carries a personal burden, Brian envisages a closure for the community. He believes that a public inquiry will lay the ghosts to rest for a community that has been criminalised, where the victims have been blamed. That such a narrative development will help heal Brian is probable. Whether it will be a closure for him personally, given the intensity of the experience and the lack of personal counselling that he refers to, is a more open question.

These issues of personal and public narratives recur throughout the testimonies. Although the interviews were conducted individually, they each refer to the experiences of others and this is reinforced by the editing which tells the same story from different viewpoints. The chronology is linear, but the witnesses are multiple. They display an awareness of community that needs to be addressed in any healing process. This reflects a strong sense of the collective in Belfast's working-class districts. This has been heightened during the Troubles where whole communities felt under attack either from the paramilitaries or from the state security forces. Brian states, 'It has given me an insight into how fragile we were living in this area, how expendable we were living in this area that our lives counted for very little'. From Brian's concern for the criminalisation of the community to Martin's concern for his neighbours who tried to help, they both illustrate Dipesh Chakrabarty's theory, based on testimonies from the partition of India, that trauma narrative is usually a narrative of the community and not just an individual narrative.[20] Most psychoanalytic approaches underestimate this duality and any attempts at narrative closures need to address it. One value of recording and making accessible audiovisual testimonies may be as a contribution to this process.

The documentary has been seen widely, by local community groups in Belfast, at film festivals in Britain and by survivors' groups in other countries. It has also been used as a lobbying tool in meetings with government officials to raise the issue of a public enquiry and with funders to campaign for more resources for similar work. The aims of the documentary for both the survivors and VAST have been modestly met. It is a small production which has had most effect on those who participated. VAST itself now records and edits its own video productions. Any wider impact will be judged by how many other testimonies are recorded and acknowledged by that immediate community and by the wider society, implicated by our silence. The potential of audiovisual recording of testimonies, with its unique contributions of location as character and of performance in storytelling, has yet to be fully realised in both the personal and public processes of healing.

Notes

1 A notable exception is the report 'Belfast's Bloody Sunday', in *Andersonstown News,* 3 June 2000.

2 The June 2002 Newsletter (Issue 7) of the Northern Ireland Office's Victims Liaison Unit identified thirty such groups.

3 The Victims and Survivors Trust website is http://www.vast.iol.ie

4 Broadcast documentaries include *Moving Myths* (1988), C4, and *Behind the Walls of Castereagh* (1992), BBC2. Community documentaries include *We Never Give Up* (2002), Human Rights Media Centre, Cape Town.

5 For a more detailed insight into the effects of war on a West Belfast community see Ciaran De Baroid (1989) *Ballymurphy and the Irish War*, Dublin: Aisling Publications.

6 *The Springhill Massacre: 9th July 1972.* There is no attributable author, publisher or date of publication.

7 Marie-Therese Fay and Marie Smith (2000) *Personal Accounts from Northern Ireland's Troubles: Public Conflict Private Loss.* London: Pluto Press.

8 Shoshanna Felman and Dori Laub (1992) *Testimony: Crisis of Witnessing in Literature, Psychoanalysis and History.* New York: Routledge.

9 Papadopolous, Renos (1998) 'Destructiveness, Atrocities and Healing: Eptistemological and Clinical Reflections' in *Journal of Analytical Psychology*, 43, 4, 24–5.

10 Stanley Cohen (2001) *States of Denial: Knowing About Atrocities and Suffering.* Cambridge: Polity Press.

11 See Liz Curtis (1984) *Ireland and the Propaganda War: The British Media and the Battle for Hearts and Minds*. London: Information on Ireland; and Bill Rolston and David Miller (eds.) (1996) *War and Words: The Northern Ireland Media Reader*. Belfast: Beyond the Pale.

12 In *Newsnight*, BBC2, 06.08.98, the reporter walks with an 'expert' along the streets of north Belfast providing the thread of the report, with survivors interspersed and backing up their theses.

13 Media Arts Department, Royal Holloway University of London.

14 Jean Rouch's 'participatory ethnography' or 'shared anthropology' is exemplified in *Chronique d'un Éte* (1960) and in the fictionalised *Jaguar* (1967).

15 The term protocol is also used in a discussion paper that deals with related issues such as intellectual copyright of Aboriginal stories, traditions and images: *Issues Paper: Towards a Protocol for Filmmakers Working with Indigenous Content and Indigenous Communities,* Woolloomooloo: Australian Film Commission, 2003.

16 For more information on the Workshop movement in Belfast and Derry, see *Fast Forward: Report on the Funding of Grant-Aided Film and Video in the North of Ireland*. Belfast: Independent Film and Video Association North of Ireland, 1998.

17 Stella Bruzzi (2000) *New Documentary: A Critical Introduction*. London: Routledge

18 Bill Nichols (1991) *Representing Reality: Issues and Concepts in Documentary*. Bloomington: Indiana University Press.

19 See Ardoyne Commemoration Project's (2002) *Ardoyne: the Untold Story*, Belfast: Beyond The Pale for examples of this difficulty of 'telling' at the time of trauma.

20 Chakrabarty is quoted in Gyan Pandy (1999) *Memory, History and the Question of Violence*. Calcutta: K. P. Bagchi.

Hyperlinks, Changelings and the Digital Fireside

Paul O'Brien

This chapter looks at some ways in which contemporary (and future) media are in a sense circling back to older forms (and cultural content) and the resonance for Ireland, simultaneously seen as a repository of mythic 'pre-modern' values and as the locus of cutting-edge developments in technology.

It has to be said at the beginning that there is a problem in looking for specifically 'Irish' artistic connections in the realm of digital media. This is partly because of the size of the country and partly due to slowness in getting involved in the interface between art and technology. One could speculate as to the reasons: structural conservatism regarding traditional boundaries in third-level colleges; lack of cultural awareness on the part of potential business sponsors, bureaucrats and politicians; a generational divide. But a major difference between new media and their predecessors is that the digital phenomenon transcends national borders – the Internet abolishes space to the extent that it has become truly irrelevant where the person sitting behind a computer screen happens to be at any one time. Is a Swedish graduate of an Irish art college based in Tokyo and working collaboratively over the Internet with colleagues in Ireland – and elsewhere – on an entry for a computer-art festival in Austria producing 'Irish' art? What element of 'Irishness' would have to be present to qualify it as Irish work? Merely asking the question demonstrates the near-impossibility of definitions in this regard. The internet thus challenges cultural nationalism in a radical way, a challenge with potentially liberating consequences.

A crucial element of contemporary culture is the re-marriage of art and science (divorced some centuries ago) in bio-art, interactive art, digital film, computer animation, and the developing VR/web/gaming interface (Stocker 2001; Schenck 2001; Sommerer and Mignonneau 1998). At the same time, ancient echoes are becoming heard in elements of contemporary culture. Yeats recounts an episode from a folkloric interview: '"Have you ever seen a fairy or such like?" I asked an old man in County Sligo. "Amn't I annoyed with them," was the answer' (Yeats 1986: iii). Irish folklore (Evans-Wentz 1977) has resonances with the proliferation of contemporary folklore on conspiracy sites on the web-changelings have given place to alien abduction. Paranormal paranoia has not been obliterated by new technology – it has just been given a new medium in which to proliferate.

Hypertext – the ability to jump directly into another textual dimension by clicking on a hyperlink, just as fairies (or alien invaders) are imagined to pass directly from their own domain to ours – is the basis of the Internet and the World Wide Web. Lev Manovich notes the connection between hyperlinking and the operations of the human mind: 'The very principle of hyperlinking, which forms the basis of interactive media, objectifies the process of association, often taken to be central to human thinking' (Manovich 2000: 61).

Hyperlinking privileges metonymy (Manovich 2000: 77). When elements such as sound and visuals are involved a more appropriate term is hypermedia. Reading in the context of hypertext differs from the traditional 'beginning-to-end' process: readers start at a point they pick themselves from a large array of choices, following links from document to document and leaving at any point they like (Snyder 1997: 69). Ted Nelson, the originator of the concept of hypertext, argued for the need for a system that would afford access to the complete sum of knowledge, a 'docuverse' project whereby all discourse would be available in one great matrix (Nelson 1992a: 2, 9; Snyder 1997: 24).

The consequences of the proliferation of hypertext via 'hyperlinks' on the Internet include the desire for instant gratification and impatience with the delays involved in standard linear narrative. There is also the issue of information overload and the risk of getting lost in information; further, the difficulty in judging between material of value on the one hand and rubbish on the other. Sean Cubitt adds the point that hypertext exacerbates the great Adornian bugbear, instrumental rationality, since it forces us to stay within its categories (Cubitt 1998; Marks 1999: 219).

Conspiracy sites, of which the alien/UFO sites are a (considerable) subset, range from the apparently plausible to the clearly psychotic. What is the criterion of truth or falsity given the unregulated flow of information on the Net? One consequence of this widespread cultural *anomie* is the attenuation of the concept of truth itself, already weakened by postmodern discourse from Nietzsche to Baudrillard. Hypertext might also be seen as potentially subverting the primary narrative with its beginning, middle and end, encouraging a creative, active process of involvement rather than inactive consumption. The viewer becomes in a sense a participant in the creative process itself (O'Dwyer 2001: 6–12). 'In hypertext, the common distinction between "writer" and "reader" begins to collapse in a way that has long been theorised for printed text but never before realised in such a visible form' (Snyder 1997: 79).

Hypertext, traversed by gender-shifting users in search of the multiplicity of identity, also resonates with the commonplace 'death of the subject' in postmodern theory: 'The groundless shifting subject articulated by poststructuralist theory and represented in postmodern art and literature is actualised in the virtual space of hypertext' (Gaggi 1997: 115). Hypertext constitutes an embodiment of such concepts as Derrida's notion of 'decentring' and Barthes' idea of the 'writerly' text, where the reader becomes co-creator (Landow and Delaney 1991: 6; Snyder 1997: 40). Noting that both Barthes and Derrida define the text as a network (Snyder 1997: 119), the author points out the distinction made by Barthes between traditional literary 'work' and 'text'. In distinction from the traditional notion of the literary 'work', Barthes sets up the concept of the 'text', a web linking the 'work' to other kinds of discourse: 'The Barthesian 'text' … views reading as the site of an activity, a place where the experience of reading suddenly branches out in many directions in order to establish links with an ever-expanding world of meanings' (Snyder 1997: 47).

With its possibilities of collective input and the blurring of the notion of individual originality to the point of disappearance, hypertext and the 'hypernarratives' it encourages, challenge notions of intellectual property and original authorship in a truly radical way (O'Dwyer 2001: 21). The issue of originality – already under serious threat in the era of postmodern theory – is further undermined by the collaborative, altruistic and ego-sceptical 'post-capitalist' culture of young practitioners in the realm of new media.

The literary precursors of hypertext (the basis of the World Wide Web) have been found among other sources in Joyce's *Finnegans Wake*, a work deeply rooted in Irish myth and tradition (Gibbons 1996: 6, 161). Unlike the – to us – virtually-unreadable realist novels of the Victorians, employed to keep at bay the *ennui* of long winter evenings, a work like *Finnegans Wake*, which one can dip into anywhere, is perhaps becoming increasingly appropriate and potentially accessible in the era of information-overload. This is a time, after all, when over-stimulation and a plenitude of choices – often not much different from each other – is the problem and peace, tranquillity and leisure are expensive and increasingly hard-to-find luxuries.

Michael Heim refers to hypertext as an unnoticed or added dimension – the distinctive operation of hypertext is not a step but a jump (Heim 1993: 29–30). The style of *Finnegans Wake* in his view foreshadows hypertext:

> *Finnegans Wake* spins nets of allusions touching myriad other books and often alludes to other parts of itself. Its complex self-references and allusions have daunted and frustrated many a reader: few books outside the Bible call for so much background knowledge and so much outside commentary. The secondary literature on *Finnegans Wake* is enormous, with glossaries of puns and neologisms and etymologies of the many foreign and concocted words. More important, this book embodies the structural shape of hypertext. It is the *ne plus ultra* of nonlinear and associational style, a mess of hidden links and a tangle of recurring motifs. (1993: 31)

Heim points out that Joyce laboured on the work for more than seventeen years in a non-linear way, comparable to how a contemporary writer uses word-processing. He notes that 'everything in *Finnegans Wake* dovetails like a woven pattern, turning back on itself linguistically like a wave of fractal structures … the hermeneutic structure of the novel matches hypertext' (ibid.). Soke Dinkla points out that Joyce in *Finnegans Wake* is concerned with 'generating' as distinct from 'representing' reality:

The text constantly creates new constellations, which are open to changing relations and to the tying of ever-new knots. Reading progressively turns into 'networking' … *Finnegans Wake* is characterised by a circular structure, that at least partially dissolves the principles of traditional logic. In this maelstrom of narrative the principles of cause-and-effect, causality and a progressive conception of history are simply inconceivable. (2002: 31)

Dinkla points out that the same 'circular' principles can be found in the structure of new media works by artists such as Ken Feingold, Jeffrey Shaw and Grahame Weinbren. These principles stand for a postmodern view of history wherein the concept of progress is outmoded (ibid.). It could also be pointed out that the circular structure of *Finnegans Wake* recalls the idea of the 'loop as a narrative engine' in the new media (Manovich 2000: 314–22). Dinkla cites the role played by Joyce's work in the art practice of Lynn Hershman, whose 'female protagonists … possess unstable identities – they are "shifting personalities" whose inner logic pre-supposes the non-existence of boundaries between different layers of reality' (2002: 33). Dinkla argues that Joyce had 'developed aesthetic strategies for which there was no adequate medium at that time'. But the possibilities he opened up could not achieve full development within (pre-computer) literature, which did not allow functional action on the part of the participant (2002: 32). The notion of the 'floating work of art'

makes it possible to try out a new conception of the world, where there is no longer a linear relationship between cause and effect and no distanced point of view, where one participates, at the same time, in the creation of such a new conception. In order to achieve this, however, it needs to change some of the characteristics of the traditional art work: in contrast to the latter the *floating work of art* is not an entity, but a state transformed by changing influences. The *floating work of art* is mobile and dynamic and therefore only recognises temporary hierarchies. Its uniqueness lies precisely in the fact that it is recreated with every moment of perception. (2002: 38)

Texts such as Joyce's *Ulysses* 'reveal new principles of organisation or new ways of being read to readers who have experienced hypertext' (Landow 1992: 102, cited in Snyder 1997: 83). (*Ulysses* has also inspired work in new media: artist Hirsham Bizri, based at MIT, is currently working on a digital film adaptation of the work.) Other literary 'anticipators' of hypertext include authors such as Sterne, Borges, John Fowles and Lawrence Durrell (Snyder 1997: 82–93).

Tuman, cited by Snyder (1997: 42) notes that rather than moving more and more deeply into one text, with hypertext 'one moves … playfully between texts, from side to side as it were.' Hypertext thus facilitates a wider movement from a serious, introspective, relentlessly psychological (and often Germanic) hermen-eutic tradition of interpretation – one often associated with modernism ... and toward a decidedly more ludic (and often Gaelic) postmodern concern with defining reading, and cultural criticism generally, as the play of signs. (1992: 62)

In a further Irish connection, Nora Barry (with her concept of 'Digital Shanachies') finds links between contemporary developments in web cinema and the 'archaic' medium of rural storytelling (Barry: 2001, 102–5). Barry points out that the form of Internet films is shaped by the 'digital, interactive, upstream/downstream' nature of the medium, factors which differentiate Internet films from cinematic films. (On the complicated relationship between cinema, film, video and digital media – and their associated concepts – see Spielmann 1999; Manovich 2000.) The viewing environment for Internet films is a desk and a screen rather than a traditional cinema. The size of the screen means that epics do not work, and the (current) pace rules out action-adventures (Barry 2001: 102–3). Barry notes that some of the films that have had most success on the Internet involve a static camera with the actors moving in the frame. For her, storytelling on the web recalls the traditional practice of oral storytelling, hence the term 'Digital Shanachies':

Oral storytelling was a very fluid and interactive medium, offering the teller the ability to change both the shape and direction of the story, often in real time. Oral storytellers also had complete control over the outcome of their story – there were no layers – no editors, cameramen, publicists in between them and their audience. The same is true in many ways of web cinema makers. (2001: 103)

Web filmmakers, with the aid of Digital Video and desktop editing facilities, are enabled to work individually without having to rely on crews for support, and there is consequently a 'single' voice in their creative work. They can also obtain interactive audience feedback through the web, consequently being enabled to change the story in the light of audience response (ibid.). In distinction from traditional media, storytellers on the Internet are not restricted in terms of narrative structure, since the technology allows for interactive and non-linear possibilities. Manovich coins the term *hypernarrative* to denote an interactive narrative, defining it as 'the sum of multiple trajectories through a database' (2000: 227).

Barry cites the emergence of a number of different kinds of narrative, including 'Shorts', 'Interactive' and 'Pass Along'. Short linear films on the Net are the closest to orthodox narrative, though they deliver the story in a much more restricted time. She notes that 'these web shorts tend to be moments, either dramatic or humorous, or they are silent films that rely on the moving image and a soundtrack to carry the story' (2001: 104).

Interactive narrative either (a) offers the possibility of viewer-intervention through a set number of choices within the story, or (b) presents a framing story where the viewer is free to choose where to start and end the narration. Examples from literature are Boccaccio's *Decameron* and the *1001 Nights*: within the frame story, the stories can be read in any order. As Barry points out, the Internet lends itself exceptionally well to this kind of frame structure:

> The filmmaker provides an 'About the Film' section on the home page that sets up the context, and then provides a menu of short videos. The viewer can choose what he wants to see, and when – so the viewer has total freedom as to where and how to construct the beginning, middle and end. In addition to giving greater freedom to the viewer, the frame story also offers greater freedom to the filmmaker because he or she can continue to add on to the film over an extended period of time, without having to go back in and re-cut the whole film each time (ibid.).

'Pass Along' she defines as an updated version of the juvenile game 'whisper down the lane'. One child starts a narrative, whispers it to another, who changes the story and passes it on to the next: the final story is told at the end – often much altered from the initial version. In Pass Along cinema, a filmmaker posts the first episode of a film on a site. Participants can either create their own video to add to the story, or send in suggested developments of the film (ibid.). A non-film version of this on the web is entitled 'Exquisite Corpse', an updated version of the surrealist game of the same name, which is similar to 'whisper down the lane'. Participants send in suggested additions to the story by e-mail, which consequently develops along independent lines (Denning 2000: 32–5).

Barry also cites the emergence of web genres, such as short Joke films that travel at lightning speed via e-mail around the Net (Barry 2001: 104). (Current examples that come to mind at the time of writing include the Microsoft Word paperclip that comes alive and entangles the operator, and the Smiley face that turns around revealing a bare posterior as it climbs up a ladder). Michael Punt cites formal similarities between the Internet and early cinema, 'not least in the digital film loops (animated GIFs) which appear on many web pages as lures for the *flaneur's* eye' (2000: 65). The GIFs, for example the Netscape and Internet Explorer icons, structured on the 'compelling repetition of the palindrome' are compared by him to techniques in the early Lumière films (2000: 66).

Another genre noted by Barry is that of Impressionistic films, like paintings set to music. An example that might be cited here is the haunting *L'Enfant de la Haute Mer* (Laetitia Gabrielli *et al.*, 2000) a short film about a child living in a deserted town by the sea, which was a runner-up for the computer animation section in the Prix Ars Electronica 2001. There are also Life Stories, employing person-to-camera or voice-over narrative – Barry lauds the Internet as experimental forum, a way of discovering alternatives to the tired Hollywood formulae. She notes the influence of a 'new language of film' on such theatrical films as *Time Code* (Mike Figgis, 2000), *Run Lola Run* (Tom Tykwer, 1998) and *The Pillow Book* (Peter

Greenaway, 1996) (Barry 2001: 105). (Echoing the opportunities of simultaneous narration opened up by new media, *Time Code* uses four screens simultaneously.)

Some examples of the web cinema material under discussion may be found on-line at *The Bit Screen*, *Atomfilms*, *New Venue* and *Hyperbole*. Of note in this connection also is David Blair's interactive film *WaxWeb* (1994–9), and Stephen Mamber's interface to Hitchcock's *Psycho* (1996) (see Manovich 2000: 208).

In an Irish context, the Darklight annual festival has provided a much-needed forum for the development of digital cinema, and the DATA web site provides current information on these developments. (DATA – Dublin Art and Technology Association – is an informal grouping of artists, technicians, academics and others working in or around new media.) Artists including Michael Lew and Valentina Nisi attached to MLE (Media Lab Europe) in Dublin are involved in the exploration of new media forms, including interactive film, while new media artist Neill O'Dwyer has produced a fully-fledged interactive film entitled *Diversions* (2001). New York artist Kate Sullivan has made web movies based on Irish themes, and Irish artists working in the realm of digital video include Linda Quinlan and Eamonn Crudden, who has made it a project to document the anti-globalisation demonstrations around the world in recent years. Crudden's *Berlusconi's Mousetrap* (2002), a record of the anti-globalisation demonstrations in Genoa, is not just a documentary but brings up issues of postmodernism versus realism in a theoretically sophisticated way. Operating in an informal circuit characterised by mutual aid, the digital culture is a kind of burgeoning invisible empire whose effects are nevertheless increasingly felt throughout the culture as a whole.

It has to be said, though, that in a global context much of the promise of web cinema in particular remains unrealised. Web cinema is often characterised by indifferent quality and difficulty of access. Manovich points out some of the deficiencies of interactive narrative: the author needs to control meaning and logic as well as simply forming trajectories – the user is not necessarily able to construct a unique narrative or any at all (2000: 228). Scott McQuire argues that 'The flirtation with "non-linear" and "interactive" films was a shooting star that came and went with the CD-ROM' (2000: 53). It is certainly the case, though, that ground-breaking work has been done in the realm of the CD-ROM by artists like Laurie Anderson with *Puppet Motel* (1995), and Jean-Louis Boissier with his work *Flora petrinsularis* (1995) (see Manovich 2000: 320).

It may even be the case that the real realm of contemporary media innovation is not that of film/video/cinema at all, but the (dollar-rich though theory-impoverished) sphere of computer games (see Gorman: 2001). Manovich, however, actually argues that 'the majority of the computer games of the 1990s can actually be considered interactive movies' – the distinctions between forms of new media are increasingly blurred. In an Irish context, it should be noted that while there are some extremely creative and innovative young people working in the area of computer game development in Ireland, the conservatism of

Irish venture capitalists has tended to stifle development in this area. (This was true even in the time of the dot.com boom.) Mark Tribe, founder of Rhizome.org, writes:

> At a recent coference on the theory and culture of computer games, a panellist asked this provocative question: 'If in the early years of cinema we already had seminal works that defined the language of the medium, why haven't we seen the computer-game equivalent of D. W. Griffith's *Birth of a Nation*?' The answer, of course, is that we have. The question is how to recognise it. (2001: xiii)

On the other hand, Manovich argues for the overriding cultural importance of cinema in the realm of new media. Cinema, he believes, 'has found a new life as the toolbox of the computer user':

> Element by element, cinema is being poured into a computer: first, one-point linear perspective; next, the mobile camera and rectangular window; next, cinematography and editing conventions; and, of course, digital personas based on acting conventions borrowed from cinema, to be followed by make-up, set design, and the narrative structures themselves. Rather than being merely one cultural language among others, cinema is now becoming *the* cultural interface, a toolbox for all cultural communication, overtaking the printed word. (Manovich 2000: 86)

As is often the case with new media however, web cinema suffers from a general fetishism of the technology itself at the expense of meaning and aesthetics. Furthermore, at the time of writing at least, it is not always easy to run web movies without having to make time-consuming adjustments to one's computer. In addition, the limitations of the interface – screen and keyboard – mean that there are inherent difficulties in competing with the experience of sitting in a darkened cinema. It is true that digital technology has already made its mark in a major way on the traditional cinema, in films like *Jurassic Park* (Steven Spielberg, 1993), *Titanic* (James Cameron, 1997) and *Independence Day* (Roland Emmerich, 1996). Big-screen films are already undergoing the transition from being narrative-driven to dominance by spectacle and special effects (McQuire 2000: 42). Furthermore, even 'traditional' films like *The French Lieutenant's Woman* (Karel Reisz, 1981) and *Sliding Doors* (Peter Howitt, 1998) anticipated the alternative-narrative possibilities opened up by the digital revolution. *Sliding Doors* does this in a particularly interesting way, as the plot-line (different dimensions of reality, a device recalling issues in contemporary quantum theory but reminiscent also of the folkloric elements already mentioned) neatly mirrors the diagetical possibilities offered by hyperlinks.

Some of the foregoing issues are already familiar in terms of the comparison between watching films on television and in the cinema. If the television screen replaced the fireside

– the focus of the family gathering for millennia – the computer screen might be seen as a solipsistic version of the television. (The upside of course is the extension of one's social contacts to the world as a whole, or at least that portion of it that has access to the Internet.)

To summarise the foregoing discussion, the tradition-modernity debate with which we have become familiar in Ireland may be to some extent misplaced: what is new is often a re-finding of the old. Hypertext is anticipated in Joyce, whose work in turn incorporates pre-modern ludic structural patterns characteristic of traditional Irish (Celtic or Gaelic) culture. (It is also anticipated in traditional – and contemporary – folkloric beliefs whereby denizens of a parallel domain are believed to be able to pass to and from ours.) New cinema forms on the web reinvent ancient traditions of fireside storytelling characteristic of Irish culture.

It should be remembered, though, that Joyce was an exile for most of his life, and his biography radically challenges the comfortable notion of an inherently 'Irish' culture. A consistent implication of the Internet is a challenge to the concept of a specifically national culture by digital developments where both creative input into, and experience of the work, are collective, participative and non-locally-specific. This kind of work is (like Joyce himself) consequently by no means confined – or capable of being confined – to national boundaries.

With the possibilities of interactivity through the medium of the web, the distinctions between the contributions of teacher and student, 'canonical' text and marginalised text, text and commentary are becoming increasingly blurred, as are traditional discipline-boundaries (Snyder 1997: 103, 109). One might also add the erosion the distinction between artistic creation and aesthetic experience. In the context of the blurring and broadening of creative experience in the era of new media, 'Irishness' may increasingly be defined as a non-locally-specific state of mind rather than as something confined to a narrowly geographical location. A mystical and amorphous concept, but perhaps no more than the concept of Irishness ever was.

References

Atomfilms. On-line. Available http://atomfilms.shockwave.com (28 August 2002).

Bit Screen, The. On-line. Available http://www.thebitscreen.com/af/home/ (28 August 2002)

Blair, D. *WaxWeb*. On-line. Available http://jefferson.village.virginia.edu/wax/ (28 August 2002).

Barry, N. (2001) 'Digital Shanachies', in G. Stocker and C. Schoepf (eds) *Ars Electronica 2001: Takeover – Who's Doing the Art of Tomorrow*. New York: Springer, 102–5.

Cubitt, S. (1998) *Digital Aesthetics*. London, Sage.

DATA. On-line. Available http://groups.yahoo.com/group/data (28 August 2002)

Darklight. On-line. Available http://www.darklight-filmfestival.com/ (28 August 2002)

Denning, S. (2000) 'The Exquisite Corpse', in Schrenk, C. (ed.) *Cyberarts 2000*. New York: Springer, 32–5. On-line. Available http://www.repohistory.org/circulation/exquisite (28 August 2002).

Dinkla, S. (2002) 'The Art of Narrative: Towards the Floating Work of Art', in M. Rieser and A. Zapp (eds) *New Screen Media: Cinema/Art/Narrative*. London: British Film Institute, 27–41.

Evans-Wentz, W. Y. (1977) *The Fairy Faith in Celtic Countries*. Atlantic Highlands, NJ: Humanities.

Gaggi, S. (1997) *From Text to Hypertext: Decentring the Subject in Fiction, Film, the Visual Arts and Electronic Media*. Philadelphia, PA: University of Pennsylvania Press.

Gibbons, L. (1996) *Transformations in Irish Culture*. Cork: Cork University Press/Field Day.

Gorman, I. (2001) 'Second Skins: An Analysis of the Rising Phenomenon of Multi-Player Gaming', unpublished BA thesis, National College of Art and Design, Dublin.

Heim, M. (1993) *The Metaphysics of Virtual Reality*. Oxford: Oxford University Press.

Hyperbole. On-line. Available http://www.hyperbole.com/lumiere/ (28 August 2002).

Interactive Cinema Homepage. On-line. Available http://ic.media.edu (28 August 2002).

Landow, G. P. (1992) *Hypertext: The Convergence of Contemporary Critical Theory and Technology*. Baltimore: Johns Hopkins University Press.

Landow, G. P. and P. Delaney (1991) 'Hypertext, Hypermedia and Literary Studies: The State of the Art', in P. Delaney and G. P. Landow (eds) *Hypermedia and Literary Studies*. Cambridge, MA: MIT Press, 1–50.

Manovich, L. (2000) *The Language of New Media*. Cambridge, MA: MIT Press.

Marks, L. U. (1999) Review: 'Sean Cubitt, *Digital Aesthetics*', Screen, 40, 2, 218–22.

McQuire, S. (2000) 'Impact Aesthetics: Back to the Future in Digital Cinema?', *Convergence*, 6, 2, 41–61.

MLE (Media Lab Europe). Available on-line. http://www.medailabeurope.org/index.html (28 August 2002)

Nelson, T. H. (1992a) *Literary Machines 93.1*. Sausalito, CA: Mindful Press.

_____ (1992b) 'Opening Hypertext: A Memoir', in M. C. Tuman (ed.) *Literacy Online: The Promise and Peril of Reading and Writing with Computers*. Pittsburgh: Pittsburgh University Press, 43–57.

New Venue. Available on-line. http://www.newvenue.com (28 August 2002)

O'Dwyer, N. (2001) *Digital Film*. Unpublished BA thesis, National College of Art and Design, Dublin.

Punt, M. (2000) 'Parallel Histories: Early Cinema and Digital Cinema', *Convergence*, 6, 2, 62–76.

Schrenk, C. (ed.) (2000) *Cyberarts 2000*. New York: Springer.

Snyder, I. (1997) *Hypertext: The Electronic Labyrinth*. New York: New York University Press.

Sommerer, C. and L. Mignonneau (eds) (1998) *Art@Science*. New York: Springer.

Spielmann, Y. (1999) 'Expanding Film into Digital Media,' *Screen*, 40, 2, 131–45.

Stocker, G. and C. Schoepf (eds) (2001) *Takeover – Who's Doing the Art of Tomorrow: Ars Electronica 2001*. New York: Springer.

Sullivan, K. On-line. Available http://www.nyu.edu/projects/sullivan/ap.html (28 August 2002)

Tribe, M. (2001) 'Foreword' to L. Manovich, *The Language of New Media*. Cambridge, MA: MIT Press, x–xiii.

Tuman, M. C. (1992) *Word Perfect: Literacy in the Computer Age*. London: Falmer Press.

Yeats, W. B. (ed.) (1986) *Irish Fairy and Folk Tales*. New York: Dorset.

The Boy from Mercury: Educating Emotionally through Universal Storytelling

Diog O'Connell

To ignore certain Irish films released in the 1990s because they fail to fit a paradigm defined by traditional discourses of national identity is to ignore what is at the very heart of the cinematic experience. Overlooking storytelling, as many scholars do, is merely a convenient academic confirmation of Walter Benjamin's thesis that the art of storytelling has died out. Yet throughout human history, our stories have been concerned with universal themes enacted at the level of the symbolic and the emotional rather than the literal or intellectual. Sophocles' *Oedipus Rex*, for instance, is concerned with fidelity, truth and morality; themes dramatised in a story about what makes a good king great. The tensions between free will and fate taking place on the macro level are explored on the micro level against the background of the local, namely the 'history' of the city of Thebes. Similarly in Irish mythology, the story of Deirdre of the Sorrows explores themes of love, loyalty and betrayal against the backdrop of half-remembered political events in the remote and now mythic history of Ulster and Scotland. Such stories have endured by combining the specific details of the local with the broad themes of the universal. Passed on very much in their original forms, they have withstood the test of time. Myths and fables continue to be repeated as often as they are recycled and revised. The universal desire for story is still fuelled by the child within us all.

Discourse on Irish cinema has traditionally concentrated on ideological and local readings at the expense of an engagement with 'universalism'. When a 'universal' story is addressed, it is pitted against the local, and viewed as negating the emergence of an indigenous, inward-directed voice that can give legitimate expression to aspects of Irish cultural identity. Furthermore, the concept of universality is viewed as anathema to the notion of a 'national' identity, suggesting that mere storytelling prevents the 'national' voice from asserting itself. While this analytical approach has proved illuminating with regard to the first and second waves of Irish cinema and the conflicts and tensions between the struggling indigenous cinema and the dominant international representation of Ireland on screen, it has shed little light on film since 1993.[1] Privileging the local at the expense of the global leaves several key issues regarding the development of cinema in Ireland unaddressed.

Reclaiming the art of storytelling

In 1968 Benjamin wrote that the decline of storytelling that 'gives counsel, disperses wisdom' was in direct proportion to the emergence and acceleration of a global culture of technology. Like other critics of the left including Barthes and Baudrillard, and those of the right including Steiner and Henri, he argued that storytelling was being replaced by information in what would later be known as the electronic age. In a highly pessimistic way, Benjamin saw civilisation as entering a space of 'depthless simulation inimical to the art of storytelling' (Kearney 2002:10).[2] The first step, according to Benjamin, was the rise of the novel, a medium which he said 'neither comes from oral tradition nor goes into it', and which displaced public listening with private acts of reading.

It is ironic then that classic Hollywood should take the novel as its lynchpin. Though we could argue that even Hollywood narrative has itself undergone changes throughout the twentieth century, such paradoxes constantly emerge as pronouncements of the death of storytelling go hand-in-hand with the success of the motion picture industry. In *On Stories* (2002), Richard Kearney acknowledges that old stories are giving way to new ones, 'more multi-plotted, multi-vocal and multi-media … truncated or parodied to the point of being called micro-narratives or post-narratives' (2002: 126). Yet his basic approach to story is one of defending the act of storytelling. He constantly challenges the claim that the 'postmodern cult of parody and pastiche is … fast replacing the poetic practices of narrative imagination' (2002: 10). Furthermore, he argues, the most enduring traditions of storytelling can be retrieved and re-examined by combining ancient and contemporary theories. It could be said therefore that narrative cinema, as the contemporary equivalent of the 'universal' style of storytelling, thus offers a critical site of examination for the stories we tell ourselves about our 'global' human experience.

Despite his fatalistic approach to storytelling, Benjamin's dialectical process, whereby the subject becomes one with the object, is useful as a point of demarcation for story analysis. It can be said that storytelling is an organic process whereby a story evolves as it is passed from one individual to another. The act of re-telling is therefore central to the evolution of story on the whole. Committing a story to memory ensures its re-telling, and central to this process, according to Benjamin, is a 'chaste compactness which precludes psychological analysis.' When the storyteller forgoes explanation, the story has the potential to integrate into the listeners' experience. Once lodged in memory, the chances for the story to be passed on are greatly enhanced.

The achievement of this dialectical process, or oneness between subject and object, is the primary communicative aim of storytelling in cinema, and is central to the 'word of mouth' phenomenon that helps, or conversely hinders, film from achieving wide audiences. It appears, as Benjamin suggests, that technological development and the globalisation of culture are making it more difficult to achieve. While homogeneity of culture in the global village, in theory, should render the universal more readily, it appears to have the opposite effect. What is being lost, by speaking to a homogenous group rather than one that the storyteller feels a rapport and affinity with, is this clear sense of unity between subject and object. What Benjamin's storytellers shared with their audience was 'wisdom'. Through this act something intelligent, emotional, enlightened or perceptive was passed on. In recent times characterised by advancing technologies, global cultures and the information society, such terms appear outdated. However, this chapter argues that these ideas may facilitate and re-focus an analysis of cinema by returning to what is fundamental to this art form, the act of storytelling.[3]

The Boy From Mercury

The Boy from Mercury (1996), a film notably largely absent from the most recent books on Irish cinema, tells the story of Harry, a nine-year-old boy who believes he is from the planet Mercury. The victim of bullying at school and problems of an absent (dead) father at home, Harry's frequent retreats into his imagination become the premise for the eruption of stories within the story as Harry mythologises his own 'local' experience through a 'universal' one drawn from his experiences viewing episodes of *Flash Gordon Conquers the Universe* at the cinema. As Harry sees it, he has been sent to Earth on a special mission: to live with and study an Earth family. He believes that this situation is only temporary and that one day he will be called back to where he truly belongs. The world of his 'Earth mother' and brother Paul is a familiar working-class urban environment, set in 1960s Ireland. This engagement with imagination, it can be said, is typical in childhood and psychologically normative; children often believe fanciful realities that are misunderstood or not understood at all by the adult world. Far from being dysfunctional, it is part of the living out of childhood. The film's writer and director, Martin Duffy, uses this representationally splintered world symbolically to play out the universal aspects of Harry's story.

Here I wish to present *The Boy from Mercury* as an example of the exploration of universal themes, in this case themes such as loss, grief and identity, the roots of which extend back to ancient dramatic works.[4] The film also addresses issues central to a child's life such as guilt and friendship, explored on a child's level, a level often misunderstood by adults. It is this child's-eye approach that distinguishes the film from its predecessors in Irish cinema. It works at the level of the emotional rather than the ideological while also incorporating the local and the global in terms of its visual references. As Ruth Barton notes of Duffy's work in general in *Contemporary British and Irish Film Directors*: 'A recurrent motif, the child looking through a window at the night sky in search of meaning, links all the feature films both visually and thematically' (2001: 83). In doing so the film uses a form of storytelling that unifies object and subject through the exploration of the universal.

As pointed out by Derek O'Connor in his review of the film, 'European cinema has produced many great films about childhood experience … but it's the Irishness of the film that gives it a unique quality, a feeling of seeing something never shown before on our screens, a small part of our own lives'. What Hollywood has been doing for over a hundred years, many other national cinemas have been doing also, that is, telling the universal story against a local setting. This kind of storytelling is both a process and a medium for universal themes. Even Benjamin pointed out the need for the storyteller to establish common ground between himself and the audience, often achieved by exploring a universal theme. In narrative, it is at the level of process that the writer and audience can establish a rapport or affinity. It is through the medium that the story is delivered.[5]

Educating the emotions

It is often held that the value of fiction lies largely in what it can contribute to the 'education of emotions'. In *Poetica*, Aristotle argues that the pleasure we take in mimetic works is a pleasure that comes from learning. Our pleasure in Tragedy, for example, is derived from the arousal and subsequent catharsis of pity and fear, thus linking pleasure in Tragedy to learning and to emotional response. The analytical philosophy of art is a useful starting point to tease out this idea, whose purpose is to explore the concepts that make creating and thinking about art possible. These notions can include 'the very concept of art itself as well as the concepts of representation, expression, artistic form and aesthetics' (Carroll 1999: 5). Central to this is the exploration of aesthetics: aesthetic experience and aesthetic properties or qualities. The aesthetic theorist holds that the audience uses artworks to seek out aesthetic experiences. Given that artists seek out audiences, they intend their artworks to be sources *of* aesthetic experience. This approach to art allows for the piece of art to be the focus of attention *for itself*, rather than the piece of 'art' in a wider context. It allows the discussion, in the case of film, to be concerned with that which is fundamental to film: the story.

Central to art emotions is the notion of empathy. Some theorists argue that the audience achieves new emotional states through fiction as a result of empathetic responses (Neill 1996). Susan Feagin (1988) advances this further by stating that the way we achieve these empathetic responses is by way of 'second order beliefs', that is, holding beliefs about other states (not necessarily ones we experience ourselves). Feagin's position is problematic when we consider that in some instances in fiction, a character may not hold the beliefs that prompt the audience to hold second order beliefs. In *The Boy from Mercury*, Harry clearly does not hold the beliefs that would correspond to the audience's second order beliefs, because he does not have the life-experience behind him to do so. The film explores key emotional states that children go through such as fear, guilt and abandonment, but it is only in adulthood that these emotions are understood intellectually through either familiarity or interpretation. In response to this, Feagin would argue, this is where imagination comes into play rather than belief, a position that Neill finds 'results in a distorted conception of empathy' (Neill 1996: 183).

The imaginative activity involved with the emotional state of empathy therefore must be the assimilation of the characters' situation. According to Noël Carroll (1999), this involves having a sense of the character's internal understanding of the situation; understanding how the character sees their situation or having access to what makes their assessment intelligible. For Neill this requires imagining the world or the situation that the character is in, from his or her point of view, and engaging with their emotional state either through empathy or imagination. Having imaginative and emotional responses is therefore part of appreciating an artwork, and an important part of what we appreciate about art in general is that it breaks us out of ordinary patterns of thoughts and feelings. Fiction trades on what we already know and how we can usually be expected to respond, but it should not do only that. Art can expand experience by leading us to engage in imaginings whose overall patterns are identified after the fact (Feagin 1988: 500), and thus presents the audience with meaningful emotional experiences. Furthermore, this gives fiction its value by allowing us practice 'in a mode of engagement and response that is often crucial in our attempts to engage with and understand our fellow human beings' (Neill 1996: 188–9).

Although not applied to film specifically, the concept of 'educating the emotions' is useful for cinema and story analysis. It provides a theoretical framework that is separate and distinct from the ideological readings that have been prevalent heretofore. It suggests the importance of cinema in a cultural and universal sense, by allowing us to 'see *our* world and *our* possibilities anew' (Neill 1996: 192). Part of the value of fiction is the broadening of our perspectives through empathy and imagination, thus 'educating the emotions'. *The Boy from Mercury* works on this level by exploring childhood feelings in a way that the audience can identify with. It does this by commanding the audience to use their imagination too. This is called, to borrow Robert McKee's term, 'aesthetic emotion'. It can be argued that whereas life separates meaning from emotion, art unites them. Story, therefore, is an instrument whereby this unity takes place. Story is the experience of aesthetic emotion, the simultaneous encounter of thought and feeling.

In this sense, story is non-intellectual. The idea is expressed directly from artist to audience through the senses, perception, intuition and emotion (McKee 1999: 111). Constructed in this way, it requires no interpretation or explanation. To achieve this is the mark of a great storyteller: the experience of this in Irish cinema is rare. A story must function, according to tradition, only within the dynamics of the events it portrays and not through interpretation of a mediator. To realise this is to reach a wide audience, because what is at stake is not knowledge, but human emotion. While the first 'new wave' of Irish directors (in the 1970s and 1980s) were more closely aligned to the *avant-garde* or modernist practices, contemporary scriptwriters and directors, whose experiences of Hollywood cinema are less informed by political and aesthetic engagements at this level, are less reluctant to use narrative to tell stories that engage at an emotional level. This places them more centrally within the mainstream.

Emotional storytelling

The Boy from Mercury explores what is specific to the particular situation at the centre of its story, namely fears of abandonment, and the absence of a protector. It also addresses aspects of childhood experience which are general, namely the development of a response to fear and guilt. It calls on the audience to combine their imagination and experience to empathise with the main character, as some of the emotions explored are of a universal nature and some are specific to individual experience. The film embarks on this exploration from an adult's point of view in that many of the insights into the realisation of these emotions are only achieved with the benefit of life-experience. It is a personal story, a memoir, of the writer and director. The pressure brought to bear on children by the adult world is a consistent theme in the film. This represents certain tensions in the storytelling process inevitable when telling a story from a child's point of view when the storyteller is an adult. For many children the only space to retreat from the pressure of an adult point of view is their imagination. For Duffy, creating the story of *The Boy From Mercury* is a way to explore his own experiences of an Irish childhood though a tale that is fantastic.

Harry is brought to his father's grave on a regular basis, dressed formally in a suit with his hair greased over to the side, where he is instructed to tell his dead father whether he has been a good boy or not. The first visit to the graveyard is followed by a scene in the Christian Brothers' school, which is clearly not a child-friendly place. In this typical scene from an Irish childhood, infused with religion, ritual and obedience, the only escape for Harry is his imagination and in the cinema where he makes contact with another world and feels free to be a child. As Martin McLoone notes: 'In a culture which validates the afterlife more than the material world and which spends most of the time venerating the past and the dead, it is hardly surprising that Harry should fantasise that he is really from Mercury and merely passing through Earth temporarily' (2000:188). However, paradoxically, his imagination is not always a place of refuge. In many instances it brings further burdens on him. For example, when he believes he has injured his new friend, Seán, he returns home only to see (in his imagination) two gardaí peering out from the sitting-room window.

The co-existence of an imagined 'global' world and an experienced 'local' one is at the forefront of Harry's experience. In the first visit to the graveyard, an event grounded in reality, Harry sees a black claw emerge from a partly-opened grave. His fear is signaled by an identifiable cinematic convention. The second time he visits, his mother instructs him to tell his father that he has been a good boy. This time the grave explodes, and Harry runs away. The presence and absence of his father affect Harry throughout the set up of the film, and is a site of emotional confusion. The third visit to the cemetery is with his new friend, Seán, when Harry explains: 'He couldn't really be my father, my father lives on Mercury and I'll meet him when I finish my special mission.' The child attempts to off-load the burden placed on him by the adult world, that of acknowledging the fact of death. His father and all that he symbolises is present to Harry only as a grave, an object and a place that does not relate to his childhood world. This explains the need for Harry to reconfigure his father in his imagination. His anxiety continues when he is tucked up in bed: he sees a hand at the window and shadows across the room, again a 'classic' cinematic visual reference identifiable on a universal level. What these sequences achieve in the film is the exploration of the gulf of understanding between the adult and child world and the private anxiety that many children experience. They also draw the specific experiences of the child in the real (Irish) world and the imaginary (universal) one together in a narrative that encourages an emotional response.

This manner of storytelling is continued throughout the narrative in the comic character of Uncle Tony. Harry's mother drafts him in to talk to Harry, 'man to man'. However, in keeping with the centrality of the child's world within the narrative, Uncle Tony fails miserably at trying to talk to Harry at his level, communicating instead in stock phrases, 'God bless all beer', 'the job is oxo', 'O-D-Kay'. While his function in the script is comic relief, it is poignant in suggesting the gulf that exists between Harry and the rest of his family is even encoded on a linguistic level, and the absence of anyone who empathises with him is at the centre of his sense of isolation from his 'real' environment.

The key emotion of *The Boy from Mercury* is grief, the experience of which raises a set of unfamiliar emotions in the child. As many writers on story concur (McKee 1999; Thompson 1999; Vogler 1999; Voytilla 1999), the structure of narrative is based on a journey, whereby the main character goes through change as they advance along their destined path. The *Boy from Mercury* skillfully achieves this by exploring Harry's personal journey in overcoming his fear and guilt as he deals with grief and loss. It is only when he meets Seán that this change can come about, because of the gulf between the adult and child's world. Harry's coming to terms with the death of his father starts when he meets Seán. Where Uncle Tony fails, Seán succeeds, not in an active way, but rather by living in the same childish world that Harry occupies. Confessing his guilt to Seán in a way that he could not to an adult, he puts words on his emotional state, 'I shot you!' he tells Seán, thus starting his journey to recovery. In a sense, Uncle Tony issues the 'Call to Adventure' (Vogler's term, 1999) but Harry refuses. It is only when he meets his 'Mentor' (Seán) that he 'Crosses the Threshold' (Vogler again), and then begins to face his challenge. He gives his laser gun to Seán, symbolising a moving away from his escape or fantasy world to face the challenge head on.

Seán, therefore, acts as a bridge between the adult and child's world, from a child's perspective. These two worlds meet when Harry finally trusts adults to help, by Seán telling Paul about Mucker Maguire. 'You stuck up for me', says Harry, 'of course I did. You're a Cronin aren't ya. You're me little brother.' Harry looks up at him in great admiration. Paul bends down to him and rests an arm around his neck. 'I'd always stick up for ya. Right. Always. That's what Cronins do. Now. Are ya finished with this dying malarkey?' Harry nods yes, Paul rubs the back of his neck. Paul assumes the role of 'Protector', filling the gap in Harry's life since the death of his father. By closing this void, he overcomes his grief and loss, and has someone from the adult world to look up to. One task remains for Harry, to make Paul a hero in Sarah's eyes. As he says in voice-over:

> The Mercurians had it all planned. They knew what was going to happen, and I just had to wait to find out what it was … You see they wanted Paul to be the hero so that Sarah would fall in love with him and make him not go to England like me other brothers.

This completes Harry's journey. He overcomes his grief and loss; he confronts his fear and guilt and he moves a little step forward in the direction of maturity. As he says himself:

> You see, the Mercurians want me to grow up on this planet, so they can't just keep coming down anytime something goes wrong. So now they know Paul will come to the rescue and now I can stay here and make friends, and learn loads of things about earthlings, and when the Mercurians land, I'll be able to tell them everything. (Duffy 1996a: 72, 74)

Conclusion

The Boy from Mercury captures what McKee calls aesthetic emotion and what Neill, Feagin and Carroll argue is the function of fiction: the education of the emotions through empathy and imagination. It 'authenticates its ideas solely within the dynamics of its events' (McKee 1999: 114) by adopting a narrative structured around emotional engagement. It does not require 'clever language' or intellectual explication to communicate meaning. Its story operates through a combination of form and content grounded in the norms of universal storytelling. Its 'controlling idea' is clear and consistent throughout and it clearly obeys its own internal laws of probability and internal coherence. Duffy successfully creates, in McKee's terms, a 'small, knowable world', knowable both in the sense of being an Irish story and a universal tale of childhood experience evoking identifiable emotions.

According to Feagin, 'the capacity of a work of fictional literature to elicit (some) emotional responses is part of what is valuable about it, and having (relevant) emotional responses is part of appreciating it' (1988: 485). However, this is no guarantee for the success or otherwise, in critical or commercial terms, of a film or story. As a tool of analysis, the works of Feagin, Carroll and Neill are useful in presenting a measuring device for film that can leave a more tangible impact and contribute to a debate that gets to the heart of the art of storytelling.

Benjamin pointed out that 'each sphere of life has produced its own tribe of storytellers' (1968: 85) and that the nature of every real story is to contain, openly or covertly, something useful. The usefulness may be a moral, a maxim or some practical advice. It is half the art of storytelling to keep a story free from explanation, thus allowing the audience to decide upon its nature (ibid.). As Benjamin says:

> The most extraordinary things, marvelous things, are related with the greatest accuracy, but the psychological connection of the events is not forced on the reader. It is left up to him to interpret things the way he understands them, and thus the narrative achieves an amplitude that information lacks. (1968: 89)

It can be said that *The Boy from Mercury* achieves this amplitude at a universal and local level through accomplished craft. By addressing universal aspects of the human condition and situating the exploration at a local level, the film reveals a fundamental change in the engagement of recent Irish cinema. Despite the ideological struggles of the past and the onslaught of fragmented, multi-media narratives in the 'digital age', storytelling that 'gives counsel, disperses wisdom' on a universal level has still a role to play. *The Boy from Mercury* acts as an 'educator of the emotions'; it gives insight to adults and children alike of an approach to the world embodied in the point of view of a child; and it can enlighten the unconscious. In so doing, it is part of an Irish cinema that tells stories which seek to transcend borders and cultures, connecting with a tradition of storytelling which is universal.

Notes

1   The first wave refers to the work of directors such as Pat Murphy, Joe Comerford, Cathal Black and Thaddeus O'Sullivan and spans the period 1979–88. The works produced under this wave are generally described as politically experimental at the level of form and content. The second wave (since 1993) is regarded as conservative in comparison to its predecessor (Linehan, 1999; McLoone, 2000).

2   Now that new technologies and the 'dot.com' bubble appears to have burst, it is timely to revisit the fundamentals of 'story' as being intrinsic to human nature. Only a few years ago those advocating the new technologies were claiming that the basic structure of narrative was to change beyond recognition (see Paul O'Brien in this volume). As this has not happened looking at narrative structure and classic storytelling devices seems all the more pertinent at this historical juncture.

3   In recent times, the death of storytelling has been heralded, particularly in postmodern discourse. However, in even more recent times, writers and critics, in Ireland and elsewhere, appear to be championing the story (Foster 2001; Kearney 2002). Richard Kearney states in *On Stories* that he wishes to retrieve and rethink 'those enduring functions of storytelling in the light of contemporary hermeneutic readings ... to bring the most ancient theories into critical dialogue with their most cutting-edge counterparts today' (2002: 128). Here I am arguing for the story, re-examining Irish cinema from the perspective of story, to look at Irish cinema in a new light and re-place it in the universal domain of storytelling.

4   In Greek culture, as Kearney (2002) notes, the virtue of courage was told through the story of Achilles or Iphigenia and the meaning of vice was told through the story of Circe or the Cyclops (2002: 62), thus combining the local and the universal in storytelling.

5   Audience and critic alike largely ignored *The Boy from Mercury*, arguably because it did not fit the contemporary paradigm of what makes a 'marketable' movie. In his personal diary of the making of *The Boy from Mercury*, Martin Duffy describes the experience of viewing the film to cast and crew that, naturally, gave it a resounding thumbs up. However, after the film, Brendan McCaul of Buena Vista said that while on the whole the film was a credit to Martin Duffy (writer and director), it was unmarketable because it was not aimed at a young or old audience. At the Berlin Film Festival he was told repeatedly by distributors that 'it was a lovely film but it wasn't big enough to market'. The film received a theatrical release in Dublin, Galway and Cork and received 'mixed or indifferent reviews' (Duffy 1996, unpublished). It took the paltry sum of £IR6,457 at the box office, screening to a total audience of 2,348. This compares unfavorably in market terms to a similar film, the small-budget Irish feature *The Last of the High Kings* (1996), which was screened around the same time and took £IR240,000 at the box office. However, when *The Boy from Mercury* was screened on television, 468,000 viewers or 45 per cent of the audience share saw it at the time of screening. This compares favorably with an 'economic success' of the previous year, *Circle of Friends* (1995), which received 49 per cent of the audience share (Barton 2004: 191–2).

References

Aristotle (1992) *The Poetics*. Translated by Theodore Buckley. Buffalo: Prometheus Books.

Barton, R. (2001) 'Martin Duffy', in Yoram Allon, Del Cullen and Hannah Patterson (eds) *Contemporary British and Irish Film Directors: A Wallflower Critical Guide*. London: Wallflower Press, 83.

_____ (2004) *Irish National Cinema*. London and New York: Routledge.

Benjamin, W. (1968) 'The Storyteller', in H. Arendt *Illuminations: Essays and Reflections*. New York: Schocken, 83-109.

Bordwell, D. and K. Thompson (1990) *Film Art: An Introduction*. New York: McGraw-Hill Publishing.

Branigan, E. (1998) *Narrative Comprehension & Film*. London: Routledge.

Carroll, N. (1999) *Philosophy of Art: A Contemporary Introduction*. London: Routledge.

Duffy, M. (1996a) *The Boy from Mercury – Final Script*. (Unpublished).

_____ (1996b) *The Road to Mercury: the story of a personal voyage as the maker of a first feature film*. (Unpublished).

Feagin, S. (1998) 'Imagining Emotions and Appreciating Fiction', in *Canadian Journal of Philosophy,* 18, 3, 485–500.

Foster, R. (2001) *The Irish Story: Telling tales and the making it up in Ireland*. Penguin.

Gibbons, L. J. Hill and K. Rockett (1987) *Cinema and Ireland*. London: Routledge.

Kearney, R. (2002) *On Stories*. London: Routledge.

Linehan, H. (1999) 'Myth, Mammon and Mediocrity: The Trouble with Recent Irish Cinema', *Cineaste*, 24, 2/3 (Contemporary Irish Cinema supplement), 46–9.

McKee, R. (1999) *Story: Substance, Structure, Style and the Principles of Screenwriting*. USA: Methuen.

McLoone, M. (2000) *Irish Film: The Emergence of a Contemporary Cinema*. London: British Film Institute.

Neill A. (1996) 'Empathy and (Film) Fiction', in D. Bordwell and N. Carroll (eds) *Post-Theory: Reconstructing Film Studies*. Madison: University of Wisconsin Press, 175–95.

O'Connor, D. (1996) '*The Boy from Mercury*', *Film West*, 25, 48.

Propp, V. (1968) *The Morphology of the Folktale*. University of Texas Press.

Thompson, K. (1999) *Storytelling in the New Hollywood*. Harvard University Press.

Vogler, C. (1999) *The Writer's Journey*. Pan Books.

Voytilla, S. (1999) *Myth and the Movies: Discovering the Mythic Structure of 50 Unforgettable Films*. Michael Wiese Productions.

part 4 **real places: navigating visual spaces**

Topographies of Terror and Taste:
The Re-imagining of Belfast in Recent Cinema

Martin McLoone

In a brief survey of the relationship between the cinema and the city, Geoffrey Nowell-Smith has identified a 'broad-brush distinction' between the studio-shot and the largely location-shot film. The studio-shot film, he argues, utilising sets and a certain amount of visual and special effects, 'often offers a generally dystopian vision of an undifferentiated "city" which is either unidentifiable with any actual place or only loosely so' (2001: 101). The cinematic tradition which he identifies here is a rich one indeed, encompassing, for example, Fritz Lang's *Metropolis* from 1927 and any number of other science fiction films which followed. It includes as well the American *film noir* of the 1940s and 1950s and many much more contemporary versions of this such as Ridley Scott's *Blade Runner* (1982) which mixed genres to great visual effect.

The dystopian or dysfunctional world created in this way – the expressionist city – pushes the film's meaning in a certain direction. Most commonly, this type of film creates a feeling of melancholy, weariness and deep pessimism. The prevailing mood is one of metaphysical angst and alienation, a world in which modernity itself seems to have corrupted individual human behaviour and at the same time dissipated all hope of community and home. The location-shot film, on the other hand, establishes an identifiable, often named place, an urban environment that impels a sense of realism and captures the grain and texture of the city's buildings and streets. The high-point of this location style was, according to Nowell-Smith, post-war Italian neorealism, where the actual city (or, in some cases, the countryside) became itself a protagonist in the story. There is inevitable logic, too, to the film's meaning when so much effort has gone into showing the environment unembellished with style. Here, the meanings are more social than metaphysical, the themes more political in the broad sense than they are philosophical. For Nowell-Smith, the neorealist city says more than 'this is how things are'. In post-war cinema, and especially in the cinema of Rosselini, he argues, 'the city is often a ruin, and the film's testimony is to the prior existence of an integral city, prior to war, destruction and decay which demands to be restored. Neorealism is above all a cinema of reconstruction, and its aesthetic in this respect follows its politics' (2001: 105).

Geoffrey Nowell-Smith is aware that the history of the cinema and the city is much more complex than the simple binary opposition suggested here. Indeed, most cinematic representations are a mixture of these two strategies and he draws attention to them as separate aesthetics mainly to argue that the real cinematic strengths and possibilities of location shooting are often lost in a celebration of style and visual effects. His thoughts are useful here for another reason, though. The studio/location dichotomy provides a way into a consideration of recent cinematic representations of Belfast, itself a city that has lately emerged from a period of conflict, destruction and decay. It also allows us to consider Belfast at street level, as a built environment that has rarely been allowed to signify in and of itself but which has been the subject of intense media representation down the years.

In the studio: the pariah city

It has to be said that even after nearly a decade of the peace process in Northern Ireland Belfast still suffers from a profound image problem. Its reputation as a centre of religious bigotry and inter-communal violence has made it, in William J. V. Neill, Diana S. Fitzsimons and Brendan Murtagh's (1995) graphic phrase, 'a pariah city'. In 2001, for example, as the world braced itself for the consequences of the 11 September attacks on the US, the news pictures out of the Ardoyne area of north Belfast were of militant Protestant crowds attempting to stop Catholic children from attending school in their area. Belfast's streets are of course, notoriously territorial. At the height of sectarian murder in the 1970s and 1980s, it was extremely dangerous to be caught in the wrong street at the wrong time with the wrong religious background (and this is the subject of a number of films in recent years, as we shall see). In his 1910 poem *No Second Troy*, W. B. Yeats worried that the political agitation of his beloved Maud Gonne 'hurled the little streets upon the great', a telling patrician phrase for a class conflict. In Belfast, however, it is the little streets hurled upon other little streets that continues to be the problem and the so-called peace lines zigzag around the embattled enclaves to keep in and keep out seemingly irreconcilable communities. In a range of recent films the real geography of this street-based conflict is re-imagined cinematically for symbolic or allegorical purposes. The result has been to prolong Belfast's pariah status and to obfuscate considerably the underlying politics of Northern Ireland. This is not, however, a recent phenomenon.

One of the earliest and most famous cinematic portrayals of Belfast streets was Carol Reed's *Odd Man Out* (1947). The relationship here between location shooting and the studio is extremely interesting. The opening aerial shots and some brief street scenes are the only location shots of Belfast in the film, the rest having been shot in the studio at Denham. The aerial sequence ends with the camera closing in on the Albert Clock, which, for those familiar with the city, is one of Belfast's most identifiable landmarks. Over these opening shots, however, the film's famous (or infamous titles) seemingly disavow the 'truth' of the location shooting:

This story is told against a background of political unrest in a city of Northern Ireland. It is not concerned with the struggle between the law and an illegal organisation, but only with the conflict in the hearts of the people when they become unexpectedly involved.

Despite the almost documentary realism of the aerial shots, the titles seem to insist on imprecision and disavowal. The Albert Clock itself plays a hugely important symbolic role as the narrative unfolds, appearing in shot from a variety of locations as a reminder that time is running out for the film's doomed protagonist, Johnny McQueen (James Mason). The looming presence of the clock in so many different locations and at so many key narrative moments can only be achieved through creative set design. Despite the actuality of the opening scenes, in other words, there is in the film an aesthetic shift from the concrete to the symbolic, from location shooting to the studio.

We can see this most clearly in the use made of Belfast's most famous pub, the Crown Bar, with its magnificent Victorian interior bequeathed from the city's heyday in the 1880s and 1890s. The scenes set in the pub are important for establishing the various attitudes that a range of characters strike in relation to the wounded Johnny. However, these sequences are also among the most highly stylised in the film, as Reed pushes his expressionism to the limit to capture subjectively Johnny's growing delirium. The irony is that the interior of the Crown Bar was recreated in the studio in Denham and the sequences shot there, not to establish some objective reality, a rooted and recognisable place, but to convey the increasing subjective unreality of Johnny's journey towards an inevitable demise. As John Hill argues the film's stylised and anti-naturalist aesthetic suggests the pessimistic, fatalistic world of the *film noir*, recasting the political world as a metaphysical one in which human actions are explained in terms of fate and destiny (Hill 1988: 158).

The street scenes in *Odd Man Out* are similarly stylised and abstracted, shot using the full range of cinematic stylistics that we identify with the *film noir* – low-key lighting, wide-angle lenses, disorienting high- and low-angle shots, big close-ups and claustrophobic framing. This is most obvious in the chase sequence when Johnny's friend, Dennis (Robert Beattie), plays decoy to distract the encircling police and allow the wounded Johnny to escape from the gloomy backstreet bomb shelters in which he is hiding out. As Dennis runs through the dark alleys and narrow back streets, the visual style becomes more expressionist. The shadows lengthen, angles tilt dizzyingly and in a series of oblique cut-away shots, lights are dimmed and doors and windows are closed against this netherworld. These dark, shadowy streets are the antithesis of hearth and home and Dennis resembles a fugitive being chased by something more elemental than the mere police.

Through the *noir* aesthetics and the highly stylised sets, perhaps the contemporary eye can still recognise a post-war working-class British city of bombsites and bomb shelters. Despite this, however, the politics follow the film's aesthetic and what we get is an expressionist city of darkness and fatalistic doom, a dystopian vision of decay rather than an image of reconstruction. Fifty years later, cinematic Belfast had still not been reconstructed.

In *Resurrection Man*, his novel about a Loyalist murder gang in 1970s Belfast, Eoin McNamee describes the city evocatively as 'textures of brick, rain and memory' (1994: 27). In the film adaptation of the novel, scripted by McNamee himself and directed by Marc Evans, a great deal of cinematic energy is expended in recreating visually this evocative image (*Resurrection Man*, 1997). Belfast is imagined here as a city of bleak warehouses, back alleys, deserted docks and joyless pubs and clubs where the cold garishness of the décor matches the emptiness of lives lived out at the extremes of human behaviour.

The action takes place mostly at night and is shot in a style that creates a nether world of the half-light and the half-dead. The whole film is suffused with cold blues and dark shadows, capturing a city in the depths of post-industrial decline. The film's deciding final scenes are set in the faded tiled splendour of an abandoned public bath house, the contrast between cleanliness and sordid decay matching perfectly the vampiric blood lust that is acted out there (see Steve Baker's analysis in this volume). The bath house and the warehouses are curtained off with plastic sheets, obscuring and blurring much of the action set there – a visual underpinning of the blurred moral landscape that the characters inhabit.

The protagonist is Victor Kelly (Stuart Townsend), driven to extreme sectarian violence by a need to assuage his Protestant guilt at having a Catholic father (a reference to the real 'Shankill Butcher' of 1970s Belfast, Lenny Murphy, who indulged in a murderous sectarian campaign against Catholics that involved mutilation of his victims). Victor's anti-Catholic brutality (literally up to his neck in fenian blood) is, therefore, a form of self-loathing, each killing a form of patricide that only underpins his unhealthily close relationship with his loving mother. Thus, both the original novel and the film provide an over-determined psychoanalytic frame to explain Victor's psychotic violence.

However, Victor is also just as much a product of his bleak post-industrial landscape as he is of oedipal tensions. As the novel makes clear, 'He felt the city become a diagram of violence centred around him' (McNamee 1994: 11). In the film, Victor is shown eyes-closed in the back seat of the car, framed by his two accomplices in the front. The tightly framed and claustrophobic shot contrasts with the suggested off-screen space around them – the unseen city streets that Victor knows by heart. He guides the driver unerringly without looking as if he has internalised the geography of every street corner and every turning. The city streets are mapped onto his brain – 'Joy Street, next right, Palestine Street, next right, Now! Agincourt Avenue.'

The journalist, Ryan (James Nesbitt), keeps an ordnance survey map of the city on the wall of his newsroom office and tracks the street geography of Victor's killings with pins and red string. In trying to understand what message Victor and his gang intend through the mutilation of their victims, he surmises that they are attempting 'to claim the town for themselves'. As an outsider to the city, Ryan has to plot his way before setting out on his journeys around the killing fields of Victor's streets, and especially for his murderous rendezvous with Victor at the appropriately named Tombe Street Bath House.

What is remarkable about the Belfast cityscape of *Resurrection Man* is its utter desolation. The film lacks even the melancholy, romantic fatalism of *Odd Man Out*. These are bricks and mortars without humanity, empty streets without a community. These streets are conduits of death – dumping grounds for mutilated corpses and escape routes for the killers. These streets are also markers of territory – borders and limits circumscribing movement out or in and like Ryan's red strings on a map, the bloody binds of sectarian hate and suffocating social atrophy.

The post-industrial dystopia that is conjured up is a cinematic imagining and not in anyway a portrait of a recognisable Belfast. The location shots are not even genuine. The film was shot in run-down and decaying parts of Manchester, Liverpool and Warrington, faded Victorian relics of Britain's industrial nineteenth century that are, after all, singularly appropriate to Belfast, a sister city of the same developments. Certainly, these location shots are important for establishing the dystopian cityscape, whether the hulking edifices of the past, like the public bath house with its memories of community or the abandoned bleakness of docks and warehouses with memories of commerce, trade and work. The locations are lit and dressed as a film set. There is no sense here that the real bricks and mortars of the locations, its built environment, speak in and of themselves, in the sense that neorealist locations do. The film's bleak rendering of the city is remarkably studio-bound. Its visualisation of near-death existence is the result of its claustrophobic framing, its harshly-lit interiors, its dark inner recesses.

In this way, the Belfast of *Resurrection Man* is more akin to Geoffrey Nowell-Smith's studio-shot than it is to his location-shot city. It is a cinematic construction, a nightmare city of the imagination. However, what the film does is to insist at another level on the real city that lies behind the cinematic vision. The emphasis on mapping and the naming of streets is important to the film's imaginative geography. At one point we get a series of high panoramic shots of the city at night over which the names of Belfast's republican strongholds are listed in almost reverential voice-over, presumably by Ryan as part of his street education programme. So, while the vision here is certainly an imagined, rather than an actual city, nonetheless the film insists also on the identity of the dystopia as an actual place. Here, we again see the same kind of dichotomy we located in *Odd Man Out* between a rooted location and an allegorical disavowal of the real. The aesthetic and the politics follow one another and the conflict in Northern Ireland is rendered here as a grotesque horror movie in which all passion is destructive and self-destructive and people exist on the fringes of the rational world.

Both *Odd Man Out* and *Resurrection Man* are stylised, anti-naturalist films that create a Belfast which is highly allegorical. In doing so, the films comment on the politics of Northern

Ireland in a similarly obfuscatory manner. There is, however, one important political difference between them. The paramilitaries of Carol Reed's film ('the organisation') are clearly Irish Republicans while the brutal gang of *Resurrection Man* are Loyalist. For Brian McIlroy, a critic sympathetic to the Protestant and unionist cause, the problem with *Odd Man Out* is that the nobility of suffering personified in Johnny McQueen's fate represents an acceptable and even a sympathetic portrayal of Republicanism. The politics may indeed be evacuated but all the sympathy is with 'organisation' and with James Mason's attractively romantic demise. McIlroy even reads the ending of the film as a positive endorsement of the IRA in which Kathleen (Kathleen Ryan), in love with Johnny, takes up the gun to join him in an act of martyrdom (1998: 43–53).

This does rather miss the point of the film's rich anti-naturalist style, its increasingly allegorical tone and its pervasive mood of doomed fatalism but it is testament to the film's political ambiguity that such an argument can be made at all. McIlroy's rather inventive reading is motivated by his belief that Protestant and unionist culture in Northern Ireland has been poorly represented in the media generally and in the cinema particularly. Certainly the romantic fatalism of *Odd Man Out* looks more attractive than the brutal savagery of *Resurrection Man* but in truth, neither film engages with the politics of the situation – neither is a political film. It requires a considerable political commitment on the part of the individual viewer to read these films against the grain of their style and aesthetic. Coming as they do at an interval of fifty years, whatever the aesthetic differences, there is still a remarkable consistency in the way in which the city is represented and a similar disregard for the social, historical and political contexts in which the violence happens.

The cinematic manipulation of the built environment evident here is also a characteristic of a number of other films made in the 1990s. Interestingly, Thaddeus O'Sullivan's *Nothing Personal* (1995) and Jim Sheridan's *The Boxer* (1998) were both shot on location in Dublin. (Indeed so many Belfast-set films have now been shot in Dublin that one almost imagines that the narrow streets of the city's Portobello district or the looming gasometer of Ringsend exist today solely as a permanent film set for the sectarian streets of Belfast.) *Nothing Personal* makes very good use of the streetscape offered by Dublin's Ringsend, shot mostly at night using dominant blues and misty greys to create a real feeling of inner-city claustrophobia. However, *The Boxer*, in particular, manipulates its Dublin locations and its studio sets to create an urban geography that, in relation to the real topography of Belfast, borders on the absurd. (It could be argued, though, that there is a degree of self-consciousness in the film, maybe even a sense of mischief about many of its absurdities of theme and *mise-en-scène* – see McLoone 2000: 74–9).

In one scene, local IRA leader Joe Hamill (Brian Cox) visits his daughter. To get there unseen by the security forces, he progresses down the street from the inside of the terraced row, curtains and bedroom furniture pulled aside to reveal the false walls and secret doorways in the interiors of the houses. In similar fashion, the wider city of Belfast is reconfigured as a claustrophobic, bounded area where opposing forces live cheek by jowl with one another, kept apart by barricades and walls and patrolled by constant helicopter surveillance. The parameters of the city are so constricted by the film's sets and *mise-en-scène* that across one barrier, the characters can move from one side of the city to the other. 'You are now entering East Belfast', the wall sign informs us and three square miles of urban topography are collapsed into a few yards of cinematic space.

The point here is that the vision of the city is not without political meaning. Like most recent films about the political situation in Northern Ireland, *The Boxer* approaches the situation through melodrama, in this case, the story of true love thwarted by suffocating political and sectarian tensions. The frustrated lovers try to escape the suspicious attention of their own republican community by 'crossing over' into East Belfast's loyalist territory but are recognised as 'other' the minute they leave home turf. This, then, is a film about surveillance and guilt, an exploration of internal community oppression and individual frustration as much as it is about the oppression of outside political forces. The film's ultimate endorsement of cease-fire politics and the peace process does little to alleviate the stifling effect of the *mise-en-scène* and the sense of confinement and pointlessness that it suggests – the pariah city, its warped and suffocating malevolence captured cinematically in an absurdly reconfigured topography. However, if this is ultimately a peace process film, then it is worth noting another type of Belfast film that has emerged from the general context of the peace process and which offers a different construction of the city.

On location: the reconstruction film

The two most interesting of these new films are Michael Winterbottom's 'adult comedy' *With or Without You* (1999) and Declan Lowney's amiable romantic comedy *Wild About Harry* (2000). Both of these were shot on location in Belfast and are set in a contemporary Belfast which is 'anywhere-but-Northern Ireland', at least a Northern Ireland of violence and sectarian conflict. The sectarian geography of Belfast with its dominant iconography (wall murals, slogans, orange marching bands, army and police land rovers, peace walls, barricades and checkpoints) is here replaced with images of urban renewal and brightly-lit historic buildings. The iconography of both films is that of an affluent middle-class with its culture of high-spend consumerism and metropolitan aspirations

Winterbottom's *With or Without You* sets out to rehabilitate the cinematic pariah of old. Unlike the films discussed so far this film was shot on location in Belfast (and on the north coast of Northern Ireland, the Causeway Coast, to give its tourist name). These actual locations are important and, as we shall see, the way in which the city is represented suggests the beginnings of a cinema of reconstruction. However, *With or Without You* is not neorealism – indeed it might be more useful to describe the film as both an allegory and a promotional film.

One of the film's main urban locations is the Waterfront Hall in Belfast, an ultra-modern concert, conference and exhibition centre that has come to symbolise the new, aspiring, and increasingly affluent Belfast of the late 1990s. The film's protagonist is Rosie Boyd (Dervla Kirwan) now thirty and desperately, though unsuccessfully, trying to start a family with her husband, Vincent (Christopher Eccleston). Rosie works as a receptionist in the Waterfront so that much of the film is shot inside and outside the Hall, its art galleries and chic restaurants giving an unusually modern and cosmopolitan view of contemporary Belfast. Rosie's French penpal of her adolescent years suddenly shows up, considerably adding to the strains on her marriage and the anxieties she feels because of her inability to become pregnant.

In one remarkable scene, shot in the roof-top restaurant of the Waterfront Hall, Rosie and the newly-arrived Benoit (Yvan Attal) chat about how their lives have developed since their correspondence ended ten years earlier. As the camera pans 360 degrees around the couple we see the downtown cityscape stretched out below, Rosie linking specific landmarks to key moments in her own life. As Benoit starts to fill in some details of his life, the camera seemingly loses interest in this boring couple and assumes a purpose of its own. Moving past the characters, it focuses on the downtown architecture of Belfast. Benoit's small-talk reminiscences are then juxtaposed with a montage of shots of urban Belfast that are totally unmotivated by narrative logic (civic buildings and 'classic' civic sculpture, modern commercial buildings, city streets). It is a quite incredible sequence, one that stands outside the diegesis drawing attention to itself because of its seeming disregard for the narrative.

This montage seems to emphasise the ordinariness of downtown Belfast while, perversely, also underlining just how unusual this urban banality is in terms of dominant representations, especially those images of territoriality marked out on gable walls and kerb stones. The setting, iconography and themes of the film are, therefore, located in an urban milieu that is unspecifically contemporary and far removed from the representations of Northern Ireland that have dominated film and television for many years. While the film ultimately offers a conservative message about the nature of true love and the sanctity of marriage, it is hard not to read Rosie's eventual pregnancy and reconciliation with Vincent as an upbeat metaphor for the affluent, middle-class and consumerist Northern Ireland that is itself struggling to be born in the wake of the peace process.

Vincent and Rosie are Protestant and the strongly Loyalist culture that forms part of their backgrounds – Rosie's father is still something of a bigot and Vincent used to be a policeman – adds considerably to the metaphorical meanings in the film. The film ends with a shot of the whole family celebrating the christening of the baby Vincent and Rosie finally produce. It is an image of conspicuous success and affluence, the sign of achievement and the promise of more to come. In this way the film clearly implies that unionists in general, perhaps the Protestant middle class in particular, have most to gain from the reconstruction that is implicit in the peace process. Just as the traditional images of conflict have been evacuated so too have the problematic working-class Loyalist. The unionist middle class is being offered a new dispensation that promises them an affluent future, if only they will embrace the new order. There is no going back – for Rosie to the adolescent escape that Benoit provided or for Vincent to the easy sex life that he enjoyed as an unmarried police officer. For the unionist in general, there is no going back to the era that Rosie's father laments and even he accepts that change is inevitable.

Benoit's role is ultimately to secure Vincent and Rosie's relationship, maybe representing in the process a kind of European, metropolitan influence that their community in general can benefit from. In fact, there is a strong sense throughout the film that it is a European bourgeois society that is struggling to be born out of the peace process. There is great emphasis on classical music, wine and cuisine, consumption and culture and if the feeling is that Rosie's father is maybe a bit too dyed-in-the-wool, nonetheless, the future belongs to Vincent, Rosie and their baby. This bourgeois unionism is a long way from the psychotic Loyalists of *Resurrection Man*, just as this comfortable middle-class Belfast is far removed from the carefully stylised sectarian streets of *Nothing Personal* or *The Boxer*.

As well as a metaphor, however, the film is also something of a 'promotional video' for the kind of urban renewal that the Waterfront Hall represents. The Waterfront was itself merely a stage in the massive regeneration of Belfast's decaying dockland area, now called Laganside. The model for this kind of urban renewal came from the US and the UK. Many old and decaying inner-city areas were earlier beneficiaries of this form of government-encouraged but market-led regeneration, including the docklands areas of London, Liverpool and Glasgow. Often, the development of these problem areas required a complete image-makeover. In the case of the pariah city of Belfast, as William J. V. Neill has argued, the Laganside development called for a substantial 'reimaging'. The central plank of Belfast's planning strategy, he argues, 'has been the cultivation of a neutral and normal city centre' (Neill, Fitzsimons and Murtagh 1995: 53). The main means to achieve this have been to promote urban development that has been spearheaded by flagship and prestige projects, like the Waterfront Hall. This has involved 'the toleration of a market-led postmodernist design aesthetic which for all its incongruities carries neutral symbolism intended to create images and spaces which dilute the backward looking symbolism evident in the present' (ibid.).

Discussing the Laganside Corporation's promotional briefs, Neill goes on to argue that the advertising and public-relation companies working on the project 'extended an invitation through brochures, concept plans and development briefs to leave behind sectarian space and to identify with a new neutral symbolic terrain in the "anywhere" of postmodernist space' (1995: 61). The rather extraordinary, unmotivated shots in *With* or *Without You* begin to make more sense when seen in the context of such reimaging. Indeed, what the montage seems to say is that Belfast's commercial and civic city centre is a neutral zone, now *hors de combat*, as it were, with substantial historical importance as well as contemporary commercial potential. It is a montage that could easily have come from the Laganside Corporation promotional video.

In *Wild About Harry* Belfast is re-imagined as part of an Anglo-American media universe. Certainly there are culturally specific references and asides throughout the film; but the small provincial television station which celebrity chef Harry McKee (Brendan Gleeson) works for represents media marginality in a general rather than in a nationally or regionally specific way. In the film's climax, Harry is threatened at gunpoint on live television ensuring that his local cookery programme finally gets onto the network, eventually going global as 'breaking news'.

The main premise of the film is that, after a random mugging in which he is severely beaten about the head, Harry suffers from a form of amnesia that wipes out all memory of the last twenty-five years of his life. This includes not only the memory of his local fame as a celebrity chef but also the memory of his philandering, his drunken escapades that are followed salaciously by the local tabloids and the hurt and suffering he has visited on his alienated wife and children. The amnesia is timely, in other words, giving him a second chance to repair his broken marriage before final divorce proceedings are concluded and to find again the excitement, idealism and optimism of his eighteen-year-old self. Around this contrived premise, the film plays out a variation on the currently fashionable romantic comedy genre.

The film's setting and its Belfast locations are crucial to the film's meaning. In fact the conceit of the film is that it calls for a kind of political amnesia in which twenty-five years of political strife and urban violence are excised magically. The film creates a Belfast that is, strangely, both beyond and before the Troubles. Like Harry's life, it is a Belfast of reconstruction and re-building, a second chance to re-imagine and re-image the pariah. There is, as in *With or Without You*, an emphasis on affluent, corporate professional Belfast – luxuriously appointed offices, comfortable, even wealthy homes with well-stocked drinks cabinets. Harry's amnesia provides the opportunity for some visual commentary on the Belfast of the consumer society. As he is driven home from hospital he sees contemporary Belfast through the eyes of an eighteen-year-old from a quarter of a century earlier. 'McDonald's? Is that a restaurant?' In a way, we the audience, used to cinematic images of the sombre Belfast of sectarian violence, are being shown a different city and are invited to marvel as well. The affluent, commercial downtown – even the global presence of McDonald's and other international brand names – all seems so normal, so ordinary and so uncontentious.

The crucial reconciliation scene in the film between Harry and his estranged wife Ruth (Amanda Donohoe) is shot at night on location in Royal Avenue with the illuminated dome of the City Hall framed in the background. Harry apologises to Ruth. 'I know what I was', he says, 'what I became. I hate what I did to you.' It is hard not to read this scene metaphorically, to see it being as much about the rehabilitation of Belfast as it is of Harry, as if the dome itself were speaking on behalf of the pariah city. Beautifully framed and lit in romantic light, this dome is the new civic, historical Belfast reaching out for a new beginning. Ulster has decided to say yes.

Funding, promotion and politics

One last aspect of the location shooting of *With or Without You* and *Wild About Harry* is worth commenting on. In both films, the action moves out of the city to seaside locations, in the case of the former to Portstewart Strand on the Causeway Coast and in the latter to the affluent Co. Down coast on the outskirts of Belfast. The journey allows for the inclusion of travelling shots of the city, like those described earlier, that show off the modern contemporary nature of post-conflict Belfast. The narrative shift to the coast (where Harry and Ruth maintain an ultra-modern house with a view) allows for a whole range of elegantly framed shots of sea and shoreline, showing off the beauty of Northern Ireland's scenery to great effect. Especially in the case of *With or Without You*, not only is Belfast revealed as an attractive place in its own right, it is also the gateway to some of the most spectacular scenery in the country.

After seeing these films, it is difficult not to find something strangely familiar in Diana Fitzsimons' discussion of planning, promotion and urban regeneration:

> The generic themes that can be identified in the marketing of cities are: emphasis on an upbeat future ('tomorrow', 'growing', 'new'); centrality of location ('middle of everything', 'doorway to...', 'gateway to...'); low rents and good quality space; good workforce; and quality of life ('liveable place', 'unspoilt beauty'). This similarity in the promotion of cities, despite their intrinsic character, in order to achieve an acceptable marketing image, can best be described as the commodification of place. This often results in the marketing of a kind of placelessness, to the extent that the content of the place promotion bears little relationship to the actual place being promoted. (1995: 10)

The two films discussed here could almost have been made to this promotional blueprint. We have to suppose, of course, that they were not (though the credits in *Wild About Harry* do thank the Laganside for co-operation). They were both made by television, *Wild About Harry* by the BBC and *With or Without You* by FilmFour. Both received public funding (Lottery money, Northern Ireland Film Commission support) and both were expected to work commercially with popular audiences. At best, one could argue that the films represent the optimistic, peace process climate in which they were made and that their seemingly blatant promotional dimension is merely coincidence. At worst, one can see them as examples of the shameful compromises that are now being demanded by the commercial imperatives that govern publicly-funded films. Screen Commissions are, after all, about the promotion of locations and film funding is seen first and foremost as an economic rather than a cultural activity.

There is a price to pay, however, for the kind of reconstruction that both films, wittingly or unwittingly promote. Fitzsimons notes both a political and an aesthetic criticism. In political terms, she quotes David Harvey's trenchant comments about the prestige development model of urban regeneration as an attempt to mobilise 'every aesthetic power of illusion and image … to mask the intensifying class, racial and ethnic polarisations going on underneath' (ibid.). Not everyone is a winner in the peace process (just as not everyone is a winner in Celtic Tiger Ireland). Perhaps the middle classes have most to gain, and it would be churlish to deny that things in peacetime are much better than they are in times of violent conflict. However, as the sectarian tensions in Ardoyne have shown, there are still unresolved issues, especially in the vast wastelands of working-class estates where bourgeois culture and affluent lifestyles remain foreign. If the pariah city was always only a partial image, then so too is the postmodern consumerist city of recent films.

Fitzsimons makes an interesting aesthetic point too. 'Belfast', she argues, 'in reimaging itself as if it is a normal post-industrial city and in welcoming the American styles of waterfront postmodernist development … risks losing its own identity as a remarkably complete Victorian city with overtones of Ulster-Irishness' (1995: 10). The concern, in other words, to produce a neutral space and to manufacture a recognisable 'normality' runs the risk of abandoning or downgrading that which is distinctive and which gives the city its unique cultural identity. Belfast does indeed have a major problem in this regard, as Fitzsimons acknowledges: 'Although a city culturally divided is a difficult one to reflect in logos and slogans, in open space design and in building styles, the challenge must be faced' (1995: 41). The metaphor of amnesia or the game of 'let's pretend' that is at the centre of *Wild About Harry* is not an option in the real world of the real city of Belfast. The continuing violence of working-class Belfast and the sectarian nature of this conflict cannot be ignored politically and no amount of trendy urban regeneration will disguise the fact. The people of Belfast, in other words, need to recognise the city that is being re-imagined and re-imaged and need to feel that they belong in this city. Otherwise, they will be alienated and isolated even further into their deprived ghettos.

Frank Gaffikan and Mike Morrisey make a similar point, again considering the possible shortcomings of urban regeneration in Belfast. They acknowledge that a sense of communal pride is predicated on a policy of 'parity of esteem' for both religious communities in Northern Ireland, a form of cultural recognition rather than amnesia or displacement. Cities do indeed need to sell themselves to the outside world but, they argue,

> they can be marketed in forms recognisable to their inhabitants rather than in ways which sanitise all contention and contest inherent in city life …This involves the integration of the physical with the social and economic (1999: 215).

This architectural judgement offers pointers for cinematic discourse. There is an inherent danger that in targeting films at the commercial international market – in defining cinema merely in economic terms at the expense of the cultural – a similar form of 'sanitised' cinema is the result. There remains politically an unresolved question of those left behind in the rush to development – especially the largely male working class for whom the service-led economy offers little prospects. Aesthetically, there remains a real worry that filmmaking is now so closely allied to commercial imperatives that there is little scope any longer to make the kinds of films that might probe exactly just these kinds of social tensions. In terms of the image of Belfast, between the *film noir*, pariah city and the promotional video there is now a substantial representational gap and little hope that the concerns of the little streets can ever find cinematic expression. To do so would require the integration of the aesthetic with the social and economic, not its evacuation into allegorical stylistics or its subsuming into bland commercial promotions.

References

Fitzsimons, D. S. (1995) 'Planning and promotion: city reimaging in the 1980s and 1990s', in W. J. V. Neill, D. S. Fitzsimons and B. Murtagh (eds) *Reimaging the Pariah City: Urban Development in Belfast and Detroit*. Aldershot: Avebury, 1–49.

Gaffikan, F. and M. Morrisey (eds) (1999) *City Visions: Imagining Place, Enfranchising People*. London: Pluto Press.

Hill, J. (1988) 'Images of Violence', in K. Rockett, L. Gibbons and J. Hill (eds) *Cinema and Ireland*. London: Routledge, 147–93.

McIlroy, B. (1998) *Shooting to Kill: Filmmaking and the 'Troubles' in Northern Ireland*. Trowbridge: Flicks Books.

McLoone, M. (2000) *Irish Film: The Emergence of a Contemporary Cinema*. London: British Film Institute.

Neill, W. J. V., D. S. Fitzsimons and B. Murtagh (eds) (1995) *Reimaging the Pariah City: Urban Development in Belfast and Detroit*. Aldershot: Avebury.

Nowell-Smith, G. (2001) 'Cities: Real and Imagined', in M. Shiel and T. Fitzmaurice (eds) *Cinema and the City: Film and Urban Societies in a Global Context*. Oxford: Blackwell.

Pobal Sobail: *Ros na Rún*, TG4 and Reality

Ruth Lysaght

Exploding petrol pumps, rape, skulduggery, abortion, rural renewal, cot death, drink driving, planning corruption … such are the topics recommended for the transition year curriculum in secondary schools throughout Ireland. Their source? Storylines from the Irish language soap opera, *Ros na Rún*.[1]

Ros na Rún (*Headland of the Secrets/Lovers*) is the anchor drama serial on TG4 (formerly Teilifís na Gaeilge/TnaG). Broadcast over 35 weeks a year, it depicts the intricacies of life in a small town somewhere in the west of Ireland. This chapter will argue that the existence and nature of the show, as well as deconstructing traditional representations of the west of Ireland on screen, illustrate to some extent the transformative relationship between language and reality. This relation is evident in a physical way, as the production of *Ros na Rún* has itself created an area similar to the hub of its imagined community, with An Spidéal becoming a mirror of the *Ros na Rún* set. Young go-getters hunt for media jobs, and the *seanleaids* (old timers) are acceptable in their own right, and no longer simply as icons of postmodern irony.

Since the inception of the Irish language television station TG4, there has been an exponential increase in the independent production sector, and in the numbers of people interested in Irish-language culture. For a new generation of television audiences, the Irish language has become the medium and is no longer the message. Although this is not characteristic of current linguistic practice, it is a sign of changing attitudes. I argue that this change in attitude, leading to actual change, is related to the presentation of alternative, if as yet 'unreal' situations on-screen.

In many respects, *Ros na Rún* is representative of the TG4 image. Its streamlined production (employing around 100 of the station's 350 total workforce, in a script-to-screen-facility with weekly delivery), and the relative youth of those involved in creative decision-making means that it is a rural drama which lies, if not light years, than at least several acres away from earlier RTÉ efforts such as *Glenroe* or indeed its current urban serial *Fair City*. *Ros na Rún* exists independently of other soap operas, whilst being strategically scheduled not to clash with them. Its obvious difference is the language used, of which more later – but this is by no means its only point of originality. In tandem with TG4's short-film initiatives (*Oscailt* and *Lasair*), a new vision/version of Irish is posited, escaping stereotype through fictional narrative.

The soap appeals to a younger audience, and whilst relying on all the usual storylines (family strife, public order offences, sudden illness, legal wrangles, love quadrangles…), it is not afraid to approach issues from an unusual perspective. *Ros na Rún* was the first Irish soap to show a gay kiss, in January 1997. Strong and distinctive characters clash and form alliances in this Gaeltacht town in an atmosphere refreshingly free of maudlin moaning. The following table indicates how *Ros na Rún* bypasses outsider views of the Perfect and Primitive West of Ireland:

conventional images of the West	*Ros na Rún*
pure, mountains, empty land	petrol station explosion, small town – ribbon development
wild sea	sea as afterthought, site for 'documentary'-style musings
rural	bus into Galway (10k)
animals	no farmers as characters
escape from complications of city life	intricate web of relationships and dealings
mystical elements	pragmatic characters
nostalgia, unattainability	no wish to escape
mysterious people/language	as venal as anyone, wry view of blow-ins, mix of dialects

Without wishing to insist on the realism of this portrayal, I would argue that the programme is entertaining without being patronising – always important in seeking a young audience. The universe of *Ros na Rún* is self-sufficient, and real to itself.

TG4/Teilifís na Gaeilge [2]

Teilifís na Gaeilge made its first broadcast on Hallowe'en night, 1996. The opening ceremonies, a blend of traditional and modern dance, fireworks and Afro-Celt rhythms set the tone for what was to follow: a new perspective on Irish language, culture, people and society. The origins of TG4 are a mixture of community activism and a personal commitment on the part of Minister Michael D. Higgins (the Minister for Arts, Culture and the Gaeltacht, 1993–97),[3] combining civil rights and aesthetic elements. The campaign for a specifically Irish station dates back to the late 1950s, when Gael-Linn made a bid to establish and operate Ireland's first television channel.[4] This was ultimately won by RTÉ whose remit was to include the task of 'restoring the Irish language and preserving and developing the national culture' (Barbrook 1992: 208, quoting Dáil Éireann, 1960 Broadcasting Authority Act, Section 17).

RTÉ, the first Irish television station, was charged with the task of reflecting the national condition, but in the few programmes made in Irish after the enthusiasm of the early years, it followed the line of least resistance, and did not fully represent the people of Ireland.[5] In her 1965 article, Antoinette Fortune finds the elusive Irishness present only 'in snatches, at intervals, and almost always from some unexpected source. It comes to us in programmes for minorities – differing minorities, each one of which is a reflection of a facet of the whole' (1965: 26). Niche programming, therefore, was early recognised as an effective means of catering for the interests of a non-homogenous nation. The idea that specificity might be more representative than generality is one taken up by TG4 in its commissioning, as will be discussed later.

The original aspirations behind TG4 were to cover local and regional topics of interest, with a special emphasis on Gaeltacht issues, to provide non-Dublin-based television without alienating Dubliners, to screen European films not usually found outside Ireland's four, metropolitan art-house cinemas, and to promote the Irish language, particularly among a younger audience. The motto, *Súil eile* (another perspective), is the criterion for many of TG4's projects.[6] Funded to produce two hours of Irish programming per day, by July 1998 TG4 was showing four, and by 2000, six hours per day. In October of that year, 60 per cent of its broadcasting had been through Irish, and a further 20 per cent was home-produced. The advent of TG4 ushered in a shift in topological as well as linguistic focus. Having begun as more of a distinct alternative than an opposition to the Dublocentric RTÉ, TG4 now must be careful not to fall into the trap of creating a new Pale on the other side of the country. A travelling studio (Aontel) was established in February 2000, to further extend local filming and to ensure full coverage of major events around the country (Siggins 2000).[7] Commissioning editor Proinsias Ní Ghráinne sees Irish as integral to the station's alterity: '[using a] minority language gives us a licence to be different' (2001).

The 2001 Broadcasting Act does not mention the Irish language as an integral part of the station's *raison d'être*, but in Part VI, Section 45 (4a) it is stated that programmes should be 'primarily in Irish'. The role of TG4 is to 'facilitate or assist contemporary cultural expression and encourage and promote innovation and experimentation in broadcasting' (4b), and thus to 'cater for the expectations of audiences who are not generally catered for by other broadcasting services' (5). However, as there is no definition of these expectations – or indeed of the audiences, there may be no specific obligation. Section 46b (ii) refers merely to variety: 'special regard for the elements that distinguish that culture [of the whole island of Ireland], and, in particular, the Gaeltachtaí'. The extent to which these aims are realised is difficult to measure. The term 'public service' is used, but not defined, in the Act. As is obvious from this legal instrument, language is an imprecise tool: 'Language is the mid-way between objective reality and man's conceptualisation of it' (Basilius 1968: 458).

The Irish language as a radical alternative

Confused state policies, an unimaginative education system, economic difficulty and linguistic fundamentalism have combined to produce a majority of Irish citizens who cannot speak the language, but paradoxically have a strong emotional response (whether positive or negative) to the idea of its conservation. Despite the failure of previous policies (after 3,186 hours of instruction over thirteen years, most school-leavers, according to the 1996 census, are unable to express themselves in Irish), a significant number of adults have at least a passive knowledge of Irish. The *idea* of the language nonetheless continues to appeal to the public. In the 1993 study published by Institiúid Teangeolaíochta Éireann (Linguistic Institute of Ireland), 75 per cent of people approved of the use of Irish on television, and 70 per cent saw Irish-language schools as a civil right (20–30 per cent would send their own children to one) (Ó Riagáin and Ó Gliasáin 1994: 18). That the language would die was never certain, but its prospects were not healthy. However, fatalism was challenged by a revival of awareness in cultural and community interests. As Marshal McLuhan and Quentin Fiore (1967) remind us, 'There is absolutely no inevitability as long as there is a willingness to contemplate what is happening.'

Long regarded as the 'language of a minority, of an underclass, of the threatened and impoverished', Irish is still seen by many as belonging 'to another world, that is dim and fast-fading from us now' (Mercier 2001). Until recently, characters' use of the Irish language in film and television was portrayed as a last link to ancestral ways – a talisman.[8] '*Déanann dearcadh den chineál seo imeallú ar an nGaeilge arae tugann sé le fios nach bhfuil aon tábhacht lárnach leis an nGaeilge sa saol 'réalaíoch' agus séanann sé aon domhainthuiscint ar an rud is oidhreacht bheo bhisiúil ann. i. modh machnaimh, tuisceana agus braistinte…*' (Such an outlook marginalises Irish, as it regards the language as having no central role in 'real' life, and it denies any deep understanding of the living heritage it comports: a way of thinking, of understanding and of perceiving…) (Denvir 1997: 337). Such nostalgia is similarly anathema to the characters on *Ros na Rún*. For them, the language is living, however things may be in the 'real' world. The very presence of such a town, even if imaginary, serves to strengthen the position of the language as a modern means of communication.

In relation to independent programming in general, Michael D. Higgins sets out a challenge to the status quo: 'The only way is not to moan about it, but to provide alternatives. We provide the alternatives there first, and secure audience support afterwards' (2001). This important element also features in the Breton broadcaster Mikaël Baudu's (2001) critique of French television, and its corollary explained by Ó hIfearnáin: 'if a major part of the population never hears nor sees a minority culture on their televisions it ceases to be part of their reality. The perception by non-speakers of the status of a minority language has a consequent effect on the actual status of that language' (2001: 8). It follows from this that what is portrayed on 'television … can have an effect on cultural production' (2001: 19). Thus does the virtual become the real. The dialectic of periphery and centre is obsolete. The centre is imaginary; it is the place where the subject exists, and the periphery changes depending on this perspective.[9] As Déasún Fennell said, during the civil rights era, '*Cibé áit ina bhfuil tú, is tú lár an domhain, má creidfeá é*' (Wherever you are, you are the centre of the world, as long as you believe it).[10]

The creation of TG4 and especially *Ros na Rún*, may be seen as a virtual zone, a place of the imagination, where Irish is spoken almost universally and is a normal part of daily life. What was first a vision depicted as reality is now becoming more real, as there is a resurgence of interest in the language amongst younger people.[11] For adolescent viewers in particular, whether impressed by or mocking a fictional television character, television performance may result in an alteration of real behaviour. As far as language is concerned, catch-phrases and other constructions used in the media frequently enter the vocabulary of real-life speakers, becoming assimilated into daily discourse. One example of this phenomenon is the adoption of '*fliúic*' as expletive – a euphemism introduced by the *Ros na Rún* character Síle.[12]

The Irish language as reality

Our perception of reality is, in most cases, enabled or impeded by language. This has been debated by theorists for centuries, and may equally apply to the relations between minority languages and the media. Based on the ideas of Wilhelm von Humboldt, Jost Trier argues that language makes our reality: 'Every language is a system of selection over and against objective reality … [it] creates a self-sufficient and complete image of reality. Every language structures reality in its own manner and thereby establishes the components of reality which are peculiar to this given language' (1934, quoted in Basilius 1968: 453).

The idea of a language creating its own reality is perfectly consonant with general issues of representation in television. In the era of reality-TV, we are accustomed to the notion of truth being always provisional. Ireland today no longer contends with the Joycean nets of religion and nation – but netless, flounders for some version of reality that is closer to home. Television may be used to mediate outside events to a given community, it may reflect local developments – or it may serve to isolate its viewers, who see in it nothing that relates to their lived reality. 'To make a spectator … is to maintain an alienation that is the real form of power' (Huet 1982, quoted in Sennett 1994: 312). Whether personally or politically, as an individual or as a citizen, the viewer should feel connected to the events shown on television. Bombarded with external images of the 'realities' of other places and other languages, Irish audiences seek a structure reflecting *their* realities. Through factual or fictional programming, television should reflect and challenge regional and national life.

Iarfhlaith Watson asks if the only possible model for individual relationships with mass culture is in terms of: 'a minority public sphere existing inside or alongside the dominant one?' (Green Paper on Broadcasting, 1995: 205). As Gaeltacht boundaries are challenged once more by analysts such as Donncha Ó hÉallaithe (1997, 2003), and Irish grows in trendiness in unexpected urban areas, perhaps it is time to embrace the idea of a linguistic community as fluid and non-geographic. Like national populations composed of native and diasporic elements, a linguistic community may find cohesion through mediated cultural expression – television or internet. Broadcasting valorises the language, and creates shared references for its speakers.

The presence of *Ros na Rún* is as yet more of a challenge to, than a reflection of, reality. It encourages change through its relaxed approach to serious issues and its easy relationship with the Irish language, so long the lackey of grammatical totalitarianism. This new Irish is safe in the hands of even the youngest characters, though they may use the language to express non-traditional desires. A recent exchange between little Dylan and his New Age dad Rory demonstrates an unreconstructed ambivalence to alternative cultures. Rory has brought his son on a nature walk and is urging the child to taste some organic snacks (peppers and hummus). Dylan regards them dubiously, and asks instead for '*chips agus coke*'.

Television as a 'sounding board for a community' (Doolan 2001) is replacing the idea that it might be the sounding board for an entire country. The TG4 penchant for docudrama, which has led to several highly accomplished productions (for example, *Ár Dover Féin* (2001) and *An Scealaí Deireanach?/The Last Storyteller?* (2002) (see Desmond Bell's chapter in this volume)), makes a strength of the small-screen specificity of televised versions of events. There is also a significant audience for local programming. The idea of local or community television, together with other regional initiatives (publishing, radio) is considered by Declan Kiberd to be one of the defining cultural developments over the past thirty years: in the 1960s movements, 'the Gaeltacht [was] at the cutting edge of all that was most forward in national thinking' (2001: 32).

To target a niche is not necessarily to ignore the masses. TG4 broadcasts a variety of niche programmes, so that there is something for everyone – westerns, sports (Spanish soccer), documentaries, cartoons. Since the foundation of the station, broadcasting in Irish has been directed at the entire country instead of merely at the smaller specialist group, and this is its most innovative feature.

Ros na Rún

The largest ever single commission for an independent television production in Ireland, the soap opera *Ros na Rún* was first broadcast on TG4 in the 1997–98 season, and has proved very popular, having spawned unofficial fan websites before the current official site. Antoine Ó Flatharta and Con Bushe devised the programme, and a pilot was shown in the summer of 1992 on RTÉ 1, where it attracted 400,000 viewers (Ní Chinnéide 1994). The production companies involved are Eo Teilifís, Léiriúcháin Thír Eoghain and Léiriúcháin an Spidéal Teo. *Ros na Rún* was sponsored by Telecom Éireann/Eircom for the first five years of its existence, and is now supported by Foras na Gaeilge. Advertising is carried out on radio and the in-house promos from TG4 are broadcast on the station. Features on *Ros na Rún* have been published in *The Irish Times*, *Woman's Way* magazine and *Magpie*, the cultural magazine for the west of Ireland. *Ros na Rún* also features in most 'soapwatch' columns.

There are around twelve script-writers (from America and Holland, as well as Ireland), who work on the ideas put forward by the two storyliners. The writers have three weeks to write each episode, and two drafts are usually prepared. The process (script-to-screen facility) involves three weeks of preparation, followed by two weeks of shooting (two episodes are shot per week) and a further week of AVID editing. Inspiration for the storylines derives from conversations with friends, and general interests. As the episodes are filmed in advance, there is no possibility, even if there were an inclination, to integrate contemporary 'issues' into the script. Organic storyline development is preferred to gratuitous exploitation. The strange illness of Jo (Eithne Nic Enrí) (Munchausen's syndrome) and even the somewhat unusual red-necked phalarope episode, where conservationists and building developers clashed over the preservation of a rare bird (and incidentally, the old brothers' house), were factually-based.

The action is set in a small town, and focuses on the people who live there. An occasional visitor may arrive, but usually these are related or otherwise connected to the main characters. There might appear to be a predominance of young people, but the older characters play significant parts in the action as well. Stereotype is generally avoided, although as in most soap operas, there is a degree of hyperrealism, in that certain characters possess traits which might not always be considered as normal. The old-timer, Séamus (Diarmaid Mac an Adhastair), values traditions like strong tea and *poitín*, and carves a wooden *currach* for his young grandson.

Leaving aside issues of the actual reality of the eponymous headland, let us investigate what kind of space *Ros na Rún* is. It is a thriving town, with good transport links to the city (Galway). Its inhabitants form a largely tolerant community (particularly in relation to accent!), but who are not above a 'beggar my neighbour' attitude in their respect for cunning. As in more than one soap opera, a significant amount of the action revolves around the town's pub, Tigh Thaidhg. Its proprietor Tadhg Ó Díreáin (Macdara Ó Fatharta) is the most Machiavellian character of all, and nonetheless has a large following: 'Everyone loves a rogue', as Ó Fatharta has said. He enjoys seeing various tensions of his making unfold before him at the bar. Complex relationships drive the plot forward from episode to episode, and the stories are based on characters rather than issues *per se*. Examples of dramatic situations arising from this include the return of emigrants (relations, 'friends'), tension between generations in family business (importance of inheritance and continuation), gay relationships, deception, babies born of rape and, of course, personal vendettas between grasping chancers.

Unlike other soap operas, however, *Ros na Rún*'s female characters have jobs equal to or better than those of the male characters (women: doctor, teacher, radio journalist, owner of radio station, shop owner; men: garda, vet, radio journalist, photographer, pub owner, hackney driver). Partnerships are generally depicted as between equals, with a few notable exceptions (married couple: Nancy is bullied by her new husband Daniel, who was suspected of killing his first wife; elderly brothers: Séamus is constantly dismissive of his younger brother Cóilín, with a nod to Laurel and Hardy).

In the town of *Ros na Rún*, institutional religion is sidelined, but alternative spirituality occasionally appears (even if sometimes derided). One of the earlier storylines involved Máire the shopkeeper (Máire Phíotair Uí Dhroighneáin) dialling a psychics' phone service to discover her future (advertisements for similar ventures were being broadcast on TG4 at that time). The story ended with a wiser Máire, having received an exorbitant phone bill, ringing the service one last time to berate them for their dishonesty – this was one of the rare occasions in which snatches of English were used. The type of language used, as in any situation where people are aware of linguistic difference, is important to note. For example, although religion does not feature overtly in the show, pious and impious references recur in the speech of older characters and the metaphors of younger ones. This is a function of the real language, where '*Dia linn*'/'*Dé seal*' (God be with us) is the natural response to a sneeze.

The *Ros na Rún* set is situated only metres from An Spidéal, on the Maigh Cuilinn road. Interiors range from the café to people's houses, the doctor's consulting room and the community radio. *Ros na Rún* is the only set in Europe (as far as can be ascertained) where the camera may follow the characters in or out the doors, as there is continuity between interior and exterior sets (that is, the café door is real, and opens on to the street, so that a character might be observed from the inside passing the window, and then entering the café). Other exteriors include a small house in a field, the beach, and the custom-built main street of *Ros na Rún*. The website of the original designer, Sinéad Clancy, includes a virtual tour (http://www.sineadthibault.com/website/rosnarun/splash/rosnarun.htm). (The current production designer is Sandra Turley.) Realism is salient on site. The floors of the De Burca house are all concrete, but painted to represent tiles (kitchen) and wood (hall), so that even to stand on them one would not notice the illusion. The shop and pub are fully stocked with real food and drink (best before 1997, in most cases), although the stamps in the post office are colour photocopies.

Ros na Rún has had a positive effect on the surrounding area. An Spidéal is currently experiencing a building boom (three new housing estates in the past five years), and there has been much employment created in the television and spin-off industries. The cast includes respected *de souche* Gaeltacht actors with theatre experience as well as newcomers of varying ability. Although the soap is a new venture, it retains a sense of continuity, as several of the main characters are acted by local people. For example, Peadar is played by Joe Steve Ó Neachtáin (1960s activist, playwright and author of long-running radio soap *Baile an Droichid*).

Nevertheless, the programme is not without its detractors. Purists disapprove of the dialectal mixing and *béarlachas* (anglicisms) in the series, and the unusual dialect mixtures and linguistic variety in a single location give cause for concern. Because *Ros na Rún* is set in a place that does not exist, some writers believe it is without root. In an article entitled 'An Fís a Fíorú?' ('Realising the Vision?'), Muiris Mac Conghail writes: '*Is fada ó bhaile compás Glenroe anois agus tá an éidreoir chéana ar Ros na Rún … [tá sé] dírithe ar phobail féachana chathrach*' (Glenroe has lost its sense of place, and the same lack of direction is evident in *Ros na Rún* … [it's] aimed at a city audience) (1997: 22). Whilst Mac Conghail draws attention to the risk of alienating the traditional audiences for Irish-language programmes, he does not take into account the attraction that the show has for younger viewers, and indeed for people with poorer Irish. Again, TG4 attempts to cater for the broader society, using the language casually, even to the inclusion of the occasional mistake. This realism is one of the station's greatest strengths. Unlike the antecedent lipservice which pretended that English did not exist, TG4 acknowledges the outsider view of Irish.

The comedy show '*RíRá*' uses fragments of English juxtaposed with Irish, although it is quite clear which language is there on sufferance. There is a sense of freedom when characters ask of the channel within the programme '*TnaG: an bhfuil an cac sin fós ar siúl?*' ('TnaG: is that rubbish still on?'). This self-mockery belies the success of the station among unexpected sectors of society. A show which attracts fans as diverse as the archbishop of Cashel and Emly, and the critic Liam Fay (who both chose *Ros na Rún* as their favourite serial of 2001), cannot be accused of appealing to a single audience. The series is aimed at a general audience, but as initial viewing figures showed a strong interest amongst the 14–18-year-old age group, efforts have been made to build on this. In order to strengthen the soap's appeal to this tranche, a new family was introduced in the 2000/01 series (teenage twins as pin-ups). The current viewership stands at 25–35,000 during the week, and 40–50,000 for the *ollchlár* (omnibus) on a Sunday night (Ní Ghuidhir 2002). Audience reach for the station is in the region of 700,000, with 2 million viewers per week.[13] At least one series has been sold to Tara TV, S4C and Scottish television. *Ros na Rún* travels well as it is character-driven, rather then being specifically 'Irish'; indeed, it depicts an Ireland that does not 'really' exist, but which is incrementally becoming more plausible.[14] The character Éilín on *Ros na Rún* sums up the situation: '*Seo Ros na Rún dhuit. Níl sé mar áiteacha eile!*' ('That's Ros na Rún for you. It's not like other places!').

Conclusion

The wish for a better place to exist, a Utopia, almost by definition outside reality, no matter how far away, is a human impulse long reflected in religious and secular narrative. The west of Ireland has often been regarded as the authentic heart of Gaeldom, and TG4 and the production companies involved are conscious of this cultural lode. Ironically for those in search of a rural idyll, the 'real' rural is traditionally Aristotelian in nature (Harris 2002), where there are indeed two sides to every story and twelve versions of every song. In literature such as that of Máirtín Ó Díreáin, who represents a generation of civil servant migrants to the unreal city, there is a recurrent yearning for the real life of home in the country. In this home place, messy reality is accepted in all its polyvalency, and the frantic search for one ultimate, central truth is put aside with relief.

Ros na Rún in the context of the TG4 enterprise is set to contribute to an alteration in the image of Ireland both as portrayed on screen and as experienced in actual life, and to open new possibilities for future television and film producers in depicting the space between the rural and the urban. Connected to this is the rehabilitation of the image of the Irish language, forged in the crucible of a place which, if not yet possible, is certainly potential.

Notes

1   Community service and self-access learning are integrated in this initiative, as the production companies provide weekly discussion topics and guidelines via e-mail for teachers to use in conjunction with current episodes. But, as the opening sentence suggests, the programme *Ros na Rún* is far from the traditional school-subject fare – and was not originally intended as an educational tool.

2   The station was called Teilifís na Gaeltachta (Gaeltacht TV) in the original plans, TnaG (Irish-language TV) for its launch, and finally TG4 (Teilifís na Gaeilge 4) in order to ensure a good position on the remote control.

3   Gaeltacht: Irish-speaking area, of which there are seven in Ireland.

4   Although primarily an Irish-language organisation, Gael-Linn also emphasised culture (music label, etc.), and this interconnection between the Irish language and Irish culture is still very strong.

5   In 1975, the Irish language output of RTÉ had dropped to an all-time low of 2.8 per cent, and by 1980 RTÉ was importing more foreign programmes than any other station in the EC; 1965 – 4.21 per cent; 1970 – 6.44 per cent; 1975 – 2.8 per cent as Gaeilge. See Ó Caollaí 1980: 2.

6   Pádhraic Ó Ciardha (advisor to Maire Geogheghan-Quinn (TD) and involved in setting up TnaG, current leas-cheannasaí (deputy controller/director) of TG4) invented this term.

7   The Aontel Outside Broadcast Unit was established by Telegael and Barcud-Duerwanand, and employs 38 people. The Aontel truck is parked just outside the *Ros na Rún* set.

8   Irish is associated with social shame, and treated as a mark of the past in *The Quiet Man* (1952) and *The Secret of Roan Inish* (1994). Films set in contemporary times treat the language as a throwaway gag: one line in *The Beach* (2000), and ironic subtitling in *When Brendan Met Trudy* (2000).

9   Peripherality is a learned response – every child believes the self to come first, until socialised into a broader community. The attendant loss of self-certainty and confidence characterises the teenage years, a condition which most people are glad to leave behind them. Those who persist in categorising capital cities as centres and all other places as peripheries are missing the point of a relativist reality.

10 Déasún Fennell quoted on *Splanc – Deireadh na Gaeltachta* TG4, 1 November 2001.

11 Urban-based development also deserves attention and support. Whilst the Gaeltacht areas are in a slow decline, conversely, the level of interest in the language in Gaeltacht areas is growing. Dublin now has the fastest growing proportion of Irish speakers. Of the 144 Gaelscoileanna (Irish-medium schools), 125 are outside Gaeltacht areas (Saidléar 2003).

12 In fact, the original ambit of this word's usage was limited to the actress's family!

13 *The Irish Times* 29 October 2001, 2. According to the MRBI, 85 per cent of Gaeltacht people watch TG4 regularly, and 600,000 watch every day: *'isteach is amach le 2 m duine a bhí ag féachaint ar chláracha na seirbhíse i rith sheachtain dheireadh Mhí na Samhna'* (approximately two million people watching (TG4) in the last week of November) *Saol*, Márta 2001: 18 March; source: Neilsen/Mediaworks.

14 There are plans to create a new mini-Gaeltacht community in Co. Meath, at 'Brugh na Mí'; www.gael.ie.

References

An Roinn Ealaíon, Cultúr agus Gaeltachta (Department of Arts, Culture and the Gaeltacht) (1995) *Green Paper on Broadcasting*. Dublin: Government Stationary Office.

Barbrook, R. (1992) 'Broadcasting and national identity in Ireland', in *Media, Culture and Society*, 14, 2, 203–27.

Basilius, H. (1968) 'Neo-Humboldtian ethno-linguistics', in J. A. Fishman (ed.) *Readings in the Sociology of Language*. The Hague: Mouton, 447–59.

Baudu, Mikaël (2001) personal correspondence, 20 August.

Dáil Éireann, *Achtanna an Oireachtais*, www.irlgovt.ie/oireachtas/frame.htm (1960 and 2001 Broadcasting Acts).

Dáil Éireann, 1995, *Díospóireachtaí Parlaiminte*, Iml. 450, 2–23 March.

Denvir, G. (1997) *Litríocht agus Pobal*. Conamara: Cló Iar-Chonnachta Teo.

Doolan, L. (2001) personal interview, 14 July.

Fishman, J. A. (1968) *Readings in the Sociology of Language*. The Hague: Moulton.

Fortune, A. T. (1965) 'Holding a mirror up to the Irish', *Vision*, 1, 1.

Harris, E. (2002) address to Cúrsa Ilscileanna Físeáin, 17 April.

Healy, J. (1993) *No one shouted Stop! The death of an Irish town*. Cork: Mercier Press.

Hegarty, J. (2002) 'Love rat Eddie will be the Rún of soap twins', *Evening Herald,* 26 March, 19.

Higgins, M. D. (2001) personal interview, 4 July.

Huet, M-H. (1982) *Rehearsing the Revolution: The Staging of Marat's Death, 1793–1797*. Berkeley: University of California Press.

Kiberd, D. (2001) 'Gael force', *The Sunday Tribune* (Magazine), 24 March, 32.

Mac Conghail, Muiris (1997) 'An Fís a Fíorú?', *Foinse* 2 November, 22.

McLuhan, M. and Q. Fiore (1967) *The Medium is the Message: An Inventory of Effects*. Penguin Books: Harmondsworth.

Mercier, P. (2001) personal interview, 5 July.

Ní Chinnéide, D. (1994) 'What's Goan on with TNG?', *Film West*, 19, Winter, 28–30.

Ní Ghráinne, P. (2001) speaking at the *Lasair* seminar, 19 February.

Ní Ghuidhir, S. (2002) personal interview, 29 November.

Ó Caollaí, M. (1980) *Tiarnais cultúir craolachán in Éirinn Fochoiste na Mór-mheán Cumarsáide*. Baile Átha Cliath: Conradh na Gaeilge.

Ó Direáin, M. (1949) *Rogha dánta*. Baile Átha Cliath: Sáirséal agus Dill.

Ó hÉallaithe, D. (1997) 'TnaG is great if it could be got', *Film Ireland, 27,* 30–1.

_____ (2003) 'Scéim labhairt na Gaeilge, anailís ar fhigiúirí 2001/2', *Foinse,* 5 January, 8–10.

Ó hIfearnáin, T. (2001) 'Irish Language Broadcast Media: The Interaction of State Language Policy, Broadcasters and their Audiences', in H. Kelly-Holmes (ed.) *Minority Language Broadcastin:, Breton and Irish*. Clevedon, Buffalo, Toronto, Sydney: Multilingual Matters, 6–30.

Ó Riagáin, P. and Ó Gliasáin, M. (1994) *National Survey on Languages: Preliminary Report 1993*. Tuarascáil Taighde Baile Átha Cliath: ITÉ.

Quinn, Bob (2001) personal interview, 28 June.

Saidléar, H. (2003) telephone interview, 14 April.

Sennett, R. (1994) *Flesh and Stone: The Body and the City in Western Civilization*. London: Faber.

Siggins, L. (2000) 'Travelling Studio covers the west in style', in *The Irish Times,* 21 February, 2.

Trier, J. (1934) 'Das sprachliche Feld', *Neue jahrbucherf. Wissenschaft u. bildung*, 10, 428–49.

Waters, J. (1997) *An Intelligent Person's Guide to Modern Ireland*. London: Duckworth.

Watson, I. (1997) 'Tna G as a public sphere', *Irish Communications Review*, 7, 69–80.

'A Taxi from the West': The Ireland Text in Yves Boisset's
Le Taxi mauve/The Purple Taxi

Paula Gilligan

In spite of the much vaunted reputation of Ireland as an 'island of writers', many Irish writers of the immediate post-Independence era chose exile rather than remain in a society in the process of constructing itself as a 'paradise peopled with virgins', a space where 'sterilisation of the mind and apotheosis of the litter suited well together' (Beckett 1990: 140). Many of these Irish writers went to France. The second half of the twentieth century and the early years of the twenty-first century have seen a reverse in this trend. A sizeable number of French writers have fled from France to the 'Island of Saints and Scholars'. Among those who have found themselves 'secret kings' of this 'wild country' are the writers Paul Guimard, Bernard Clavel and Michel Déon. These authors have not only made important contributions to Ireland as subject in French literature but also to notions of Ireland circulating in French cinema.[1]

Just what is it that has so inspired these French literary and cinematic visitors to Ireland? I would like to argue here that it is not just the conventional tourist attractions that have drawn them and which they have shared with their readers and viewers but a more insidious desire to rediscover in Ireland a lost reactionary paradise that is no longer available in their own country. The most popular expression of this quest is the filmic version of Michel Déon's popular novel, *Le Taxi mauve*, and its most recent proponent, controversial novelist Michel Houellebecq.[2]

Le Taxi mauve

The cinema version of Michel Déon's novel was the last full-length French fiction film to be set wholly in the Irish Republic and the first French film financed with a cash investment from Irish sources.[3] Directed by Yves Boisset, *Le Taxi mauve* (1977) was a box-office hit in France, figuring among the top three highest-grossing French films for the year. It attracted audiences of more than 350,000 in Paris and the eleven principal towns alone.[4] *Le Taxi mauve*'s construction of Ireland has influenced its French audience to the point where French visitors to Connemara still base their itinerary entirely on the film (Farren 1996: 11). The women's magazine *Prima* cites French authors such as Déon as essential reading for the French traveller about to embark on a voyage to Ireland (Le Brun 1994: 45). The *Prima* list omits any books from the Irish literary canon although many of these have been translated into French and are widely available.

Le Taxi mauve opens with the arrival of French journalist Phillippe Marchal (Philippe Noiret), in Connemara, Ireland, following the death of his son. He falls ill and is treated by Doctor Skully (Fred Astaire) who drives the purple taxi of the title. While there he makes the acquaintance of a young American, Jerry Keane (Edward Albert), who, having disgraced his wealthy family in the US, has been sent to Ireland to reform himself. They also meet Taubleman (Peter Ustinov), a Russian exile of somewhat dubious character, and an apparently-mute young girl named Anne (Agostini Bella). Taubleman presents Anne as his daughter although there is some mystery about that and more than a hint of a sexual relationship exists between these two. Later Marchal strikes up a relationship with Jerry's sister, the titled wife of an extremely wealthy European who has arrived with her Asian servant. In spite of the sexual tension between brother and sister, Jerry falls in love with Anne. She runs away one night on her horse and is found lying on Caimín Ól strand. In hospital it is revealed that she can talk. Taubleman, distraught at losing Anne to Jerry, sets fire to the stables attached to his house. His 'idiot' alcoholic Irish ostler runs into the flames to save the horses and dies. Anne turns up and comforts Taubleman. Jerry elects to stay in Ireland, Sharon goes back to her life in Europe, and Phillippe decides to return to France. Stylistically the film is shot in realist mode although the extensive use of voice-over continuously recalls the film's literary origins.

Ireland, France and the cinema

Ireland as subject in French cinema has been marked by its close connection with themes linked with the Right in France (Gilligan 2002). In *Le Taxi mauve* this is expressed as an Ireland of primitive landscape, natural unchanging structures, feudal glories, pure of capital and immunity to history. The passage to this mythic Ireland is the purple taxi of the title.

Anticipating the car in *Diva* (Jean-Jacques Beneix, 1982), this taxi is not the index of modernity it might seem at first glance. The use of the Citroen in *Diva*, Fredric Jameson argues, shows a curious postmodern mixture of old and new. The image of the 'powerful elegant white Citroen', its 'extraordinary luminosity', emits messages of the primacy of the image and of the world's transformation into visual commodities, a celebration of the scoptic libido (Jameson 1990: 60). In *Le Taxi mauve*, the horse-less carriage, the purple dream machine, belongs in the same mythic landscape as the horse and the heather. The taxi connotes nostalgia generated by the reassuring presence of Fred Astaire. The image of the Citroen in *Diva* leads ultimately, in Jameson's view, to the disappearance of 'affect' and the sudden unexpected absence of anxiety and the effacement of negative impulses (ibid.). This is also the miraculous effect of Skully and his car which takes us on a trip to a country inoculated against the 'degeneracy' of modern French society. Marchal says of Skully that 'he knew nothing, but he divined everything – he showed us the direction we must take'. The cover of the video version *of Le Taxi mauve* also takes up this theme: 'Skully will play for each of these characters, the role of destiny'. This comment suggests that the trajectory of the narrative has nothing to do with history but is simply a manifestation of pre-ordained fate. Criticisms of the film *Le Taxi mauve*, directed at Boisset and not at Déon, reveal just how crucial these notions are to the message of the film.

Into the West: the search for melancholy

Le Taxi mauve was an unexpected departure for Yves Boisset who had made his name as a director of thrillers, particularly with *Cran-d'arret* (1970), ranked by critics as among the best of the period, and of action films on contemporary political subjects.[5] Critics were surprised when he suddenly 'lurched', to borrow a phrase from French critic Jean Tulard (1982: 92), into big-budget film making with *Le Taxi mauve*. For most French reviewers of the film it was a mistake for Boisset to direct Déon's book. Marie Steinberg complained that Boisset, by presenting Noiret's character as a man grieving for the death of his son, had offered an explanation for Marchal's flight to Ireland. In Steinberg's view melancholy and the search for solitude are sufficient reasons to come to Ireland (1977: 13).

In spite of its funding *Le Taxi mauve* has no major Irish characters, no Irish actors in key roles and relies on an international cast. The biggest stars are English and American: Charlotte Rampling as Sharon, Fred Astaire as Doctor Skully and Peter Ustinov as Taubleman. The brother and sister are American millionaires, returning to the site of their great-grandfather's house; the Taublemans are Russian exiles; Phillip is a French travel writer; the Irishness of Fred Astaire's character is over-ridden by Astaire as Hollywood icon. Only one French actor, Phillipe Noiret who was the star of Louis Malle's *Zazie dans le Métro* (1960), has a part of any note in the film.

With Déon's novel and Boisset's film we are back in the Ireland of Pierre Bourget, author of *La Chaussée des Géants* (1922), who wrote:

> Erin, sacred land of saints and giants. Erin, island of the golden harp, of grey rocks on pale sand, of blue skies and green meadows, brown streams and black bogs. To understand you, Erin and to love, one must have contemplated the purple Loire or the green Rhine and not the abject waters of the Thames (in Rafroidi 1973: 37).

Bourget suggests that it takes a certain kind of person, a member of the intellectual elite, to embrace this landscape.

Ireland: 'L'Ile refuge' for the happy few

Certain French writers are repeatedly selected in French media as commentators on aspects of the Irish scene. Bernard Clavel has been called upon as to represent his views of Ireland in travel magazines such as *Geo* (Clavel 1993: 88–90). Houellebecq is also an important source of commentary on Ireland. Michel Déon connotes Irishness in French culture to the extent that he is seen as *'un irlandais de choeur'*.[6] Clavel, Déon and Houellebecq represent Ireland not only as a cultural oasis but also as a refuge from modernity. For Clavel, Ireland is reducible to a lump of turf brought in from the outdoors: 'I look at it, breathe it, and it seems the whole of Ireland is on my desk' (1993: 89). While Clavel's construction of Ireland is located firmly within the romanticist tradition, something different is at stake with the work of a writer like Déon.

Déon is quoted on the cover of Hervé Jaouen's 1990 book on his travels in Ireland, *Journal d'Irlande, 1977–1983/1984–1989*. In this quotation, Déon's construction of 'les happy few' who truly understand Ireland recalls Pierre Benoit. Déon writes: 'Your book is reserved for the happy few, those who really understand – not the tourists.'[7] The quote is signed – Michel Déon 'de l'Academie française', a qualification which lends authority and the weight of tradition to the text.

The notion of Ireland as being a proper destination for an intellectual elite was reinforced by the popular imagery of De Gaulle on the beach at Sneem. Following the upheavals of May 1968, the general quit the political stage and travelled in the 'old countries', Ireland in 1969 and Spain in 1970, where 'his presence bore scant risk of giving rise to wrong interpretations or political movements' (Alguhon 1995: 431). De Gaulle and De Valera are strongly associated in the narrative of De Gaulle in Ireland (De Faragoce 1983: 257–61). Pierre Joannon comments that both shared:

> the visionary temperament restrained by an acute sense of reality which is the hallmark of great statesmen, a haughty sense of the destiny of their nations, a devotion to public liberties which are best guaranteed by the sovereign state and the charismatic authority of those providential men who sometimes spring from people confronted with great historical tragedies. (1991: 11)

Maurice Alguhon's description of De Gaulle's flight implies that De Gaulle found in De Valera's Ireland the kind of Republic he had hoped for: a country where authoritarian Catholicism reigned, a de-politicised rural idyll where industrial unrest and gender-driven clamours for equality were unknown. These are undoubtedly potent attractions for Houellebecq whose ideas on women and reproduction reflect the sort of thinking enshrined in De Valera's constitution (Van Eersel 2003: 1).[8] The Irish constitution's legislation on gender found favour with Vichy apologists in the war years (Pollard 1985: 46) and would appear to have struck a chord with 'les nouveaux réacs' (the New Reactionaries) in France.[9]

Déon is seen as part of another group of intellectuals who are identified with the Far Right in France. He is most often associated with the writers Roger Nimier (1925–62),

Jacques Laurent (b. 1919) and Antoine Blondin (1922–91). This group were collectively labelled 'les hussards' by critic Bernard Frank in *Les Temps Modernes*.[10] Déon at first resisted the term but he soon adopted it. Déon described himself and his fellow hussards as 'like predecessors of the Fraigneau' and 'like the Musketeers of Dumas' perpetrating 'a thousand blows' against the 'dictatorship' of the existentialists (1988: 140–41). Key features of the 'Hussards', according to French criticism, include: empathy with fascist intellectuals who were prominent in the 1920s and 1930s such as Maurras and Barrés (Deon was a journalist for the Action Française and wrote in praise of Maurras in his book *Mes arches de Noé*); a 'Stendhalian' line; anti-Sartrism: a preoccupation with generations and youth; a notion of a new aristocracy based on a classic aesthetic 'sensibility': an idealism about the literary figure which constructs the figure of the male poet/writer as 'ideal and total' man: a spiritualising mission against the corruption and disorder of history.[11] All of these elements can be seen in *Le Taxi mauve*. Déon chose to retire to Galway and in a recent documentary on his life, part of the *Siècle d'écrivains* series screened by F3 in 1995, it was in Ireland, not France, that the cameras filmed 'le dernier des hussards/the last of the hussards'. Déon's attitude to history is extreme. His experience of the Second World War inspired in him more than ever 'a repulsion for those forms of government that are the Republic and Democracy'.[12] An earlier work by Déon, *Les Poneys Sauvages* (1970), winner of the Interallié prize, is one long lament for the irreversible decadence of the West. Houellebecq is also concerned with 'the suicide of the West' (Wardle 2002: 2), yet this West does not appear to include the West of Ireland.

The landscape represented in *Le Taxi mauve* and its scenes of brawling peasants have led many commentators to compare the film with Ford's *The Quiet Man*. French critic Claude Benoit compares the two, commenting that 'Boisset films the Irish landscape as well as John Ford' (1977: 22). Although both are constructed as traumatic narratives in which Ireland functions as a healing space, there are, however, important differences between the two films and these differences are reflected in the French response to Ford's film (Tulard 1991: 293). *The Quiet Man* constructs Ireland as a pastoral idyll very different from the purifying space of the west in *Le Taxi mauve*. Further, it seeks integration for its outsider hero, Sean Thornton (John Wayne) into the community and into peasant life. Jean Tulard says that *The Quiet Man*, although not his masterpiece, is 'the most representative of the Fordian universe'. Jean Mitry describes *The Quiet Man* as 'romance as happy as it is likeable' (1954: 101). Ford said of his own point of view: 'I am often reproached for my idealism. I don't deny it. It is true that I believe in many things that it has become a habit to mock: love, friendship and even in justice, when it is fitting. I love people and I have confidence in them' (Ford in Haudiguet 1974: 20). This attitude is reflected in *The Quiet Man* where communal violence becomes a celebration and a mechanism for renewal and change.

The brawl in *Le Taxi mauve*, a homophobic attack on two Dublin potters on holidays in the area, has a different tone: it is provoked by Taubleman to break the monotony of the village pub scene and provides one more opportunity for Marchal and his cohorts to share sophisticated amusement at the savagery of the locals. Indeed this is just one aspect of a film that reflects little of the humanism and desire to level difference that characterises Ford's cinematic career. This in turn leads us to an important theme in *Le taxi mauve*: the presence of the 'flaneur', the dandyism mediated by the interaction between the members of the core group and notably by the two young Americans (Coblence 1998). These two characters, brother and sister, exhibit the key features of 'dandyism': elitism and freedom from material worries (Sharon holds the title of 'La Princesse de Honovre' and Jerry the title of heir to a massive American fortune); youth and exoticism mediated by Jerry's flirtation with opium, eastern women (he has a disastrous affair with an Iranian girl – a tale conjuring images of the poets Rimbaud and Baudelaire) and suicide; sensibility, good taste and knowledge of the world (they chill their vodka, they admire the 'simplicity and rusticity' of the ancestor's cottage); rejection of bourgeois morality (Sharon shows her breasts to Marchal, talks of masturbation and flirts with lesbianism with Anne whom she describes as an 'Orchid in an old chimney'). Sharon's relationship with her brother could be mistaken for a play on the theme of incest but it is not about that – indeed the film, in keeping with other texts in this tradition, condemns incest in its negative portrayal of the relationship between Taubleman and his 'daughter'. Sharon plays the role as 'initiatrice' to Jerry, introducing him, according to her own account, to 'flaneurism': shoplifting (not of necessity of course!), masturbation and the mystique connoted by the feminine sexual organs.

The 'community' established by the central characters is based on an aesthetic response to the landscape. It is this response that allows them entry into the realm of 'les happy few' who truly understand this space. The Irish of the film do not apparently appertain to this select company. They live in the landscape but they do not understand it. In one significant scene Marchal rises, opens his bedroom window on an idyllic pastoral vista, selects and places Chopin on his record player, and then goes and turns his landlady's kitschy landscape print to the wall. The Irish, their 'natural' peasant simplicity contaminated by contact with petit bourgeois pretension and with corrupt characters like Taubleman, not only have no role in interpreting this landscape but they are largely irrelevant to it. The island of the writers, a mythological construct, unfettered by the actual words of Irish writers, feeds into an ideology of culture which privileges 'souls and landscapes' over people and society (Vandromme 1997: 235).

This point of view is not shared by novelists like Bernard Clavel and Paul Guimard, who, in spite of their romantic views of the Irish landscape, demonstrate a desire to fraternise with the local people they encounter. Clavel defers to the oral culture of Ireland as a repository of knowledge to which he has no access (1993: 88–90). He does not present himself among Déon's 'happy few'. Guimard's novel also strikes a different chord. Although it makes references to the asceticism of the monastic tradition in Ireland, the book is dominated by talk, the voices of Irish characters whose commentary opens and closes the book. These characters are stereotyped but maintain a degree of complexity not paralleled in *Le Taxi mauve*.

Ireland in *Le Taxi mauve* summons up images of feudalism, of castles and little stone cottages, quaint peasants and the sea against the sky. It offers a background in which the middle-class play out their anguished and complex lives against a chorus of local simpletons and atavistically Catholic matrons. The presence of the castle introduces a new theme into *Le Taxi mauve*, namely a desire to return to the old order, to blood-lines, ancestry and nobility. The castles in the Irish landscape signify 'Normanism', to coin a phrase. Their inclusion has the double effect of inserting nostalgia for feudalism into the space of Connemara and of fusing Ireland and France together in a relationship which 'supersedes' the problematic history of Ireland as English colony. The theme of '*l'amour courtois*' ('courtly love') is mediated through the 'refinement' of the relationship between Marchal and Sharon.

In the framework of '*l'amour courtois*', Sharon represents not, as we first imagine the '*femme fatale*', but '*la Dame*', the married Lady who engages in an elaborate discourse of love with her 'soul' mate, the troubadour/writer Marchal, but who finally returns to her courtly destiny – her husband, the Prince of Hanovre. This narrative is to be found also in the canonical courtly novel, *La Princesse de Clèves* by Mme Layfayette (1678). Déon wrote the introduction for the most recent edition of this book (1990). Many of the conversations between Marchal and Sharon take on the tone of the elaborate and '*précieuse*' intensity of the *amour courtois* form. Sharon says that Marchal does not talk of himself. He replies that it is too early. She answers that, for her, 'it is never too early, but often too late'. This theme of the ideal impossible love based on communication of souls surfaces in earlier work by Déon: 'a mute complicity attached us to one another, and we apprehended without anguish and with, in the bottom of our hearts, a little piece of joy – a very little piece of joy, it's true, the feeling of belonging to a pure race' (1960: 213).

In Boisset's version of Déon's *Le Taxi mauve*, Sharon takes rooms at a castle-hotel, where, although it is obvious she is wealthy, no mention of money is made. The fact of the Asian maidservant connotes past colonial relationships but is never challenged. The mistress/servant relationship is enhanced by the identification of the servant with the mistress. When Sharon arrives at the hotel she asserts the authority of her title to reclaim the best rooms in the house which she then gives, in keeping with her power to be-queath, to her servant, commenting that the rooms are for the maid 'because she adores that sort of thing'. The 'big house' also figures in this space but, because of its association with the Anglo-Irish, the over-riding impression is one of decay and ruin. Marchal recounts the tale of the family, the Templars (the name is significant), whose ancestry consists of three hundred years of deer hunting. The family's over-indulgence in the sport manifests itself in a creeping palsy of the face, a genetic inheritance which destroys the family in the end. Their hope for the future, the male line, comes to an abrupt end at Ypres in World War One when the son is killed by shrapnel, a nostalgic conclusion that completely elides the economic basis for the disintegration of the feudal, Anglo-Irish system.

The fatalism of the theme of 'doomed youth' is fused with images of hunting. These two themes are also present in the opening scene when Jerry, whose prowess at fire-arms is established very early in the film, adopts a trench pose when fired on by Taubleman who instead shoots the young American's dog. Marchal, the veteran 'hussard', saves the young man and disarms the enemy in one quick manoeuvre. His action here reinforces the paternalistic relationship between master and apprentice implicit in the narrative. Unlike Marchal's Irish landlady, these young people make mistakes of taste – Anne's penchant for primitive painting is an example – because they are not fully formed and have not yet developed a disgust for society. They are 'naïve but refined' and 'full of mystery'. The connection between Marchal and Anne is based on literary sensibility: they share the same taste in books, Jack London and T. S. Eliot. Marchal literally cures Anne by poetry. There is, however, a pervasive pessimism about the film. *Le Taxi mauve* questions the value of all human relationships. Marchal advises Jerry at the end of the film that, having found his roots, he should stick with breeding horses and forget about Anne.

In *Le Taxi mauve* the Irish peasantry are ultimately a source of reassurance– the threat to the moral order comes from the remnants of a decaying, 'impure' aristocracy. The fire that ultimately destroys Taubleman's home is thus an act of purification. In its wake the old corrupt order can be replaced by the new intellectual aristocracy, represented by Jerry, whose right to the landscape is established through the sophistication of their background: moneyed, trans-national and educated but with 'simplicity of spirit'.

The anguish of the French bourgeois in *Le Taxi mauve* is 'healed' in Ireland by the return to the values of a mythic past. We can hear this notion in the narration accompanying the famous hunting sequence in the film. In this scene Marchal reflects that,

> in Jerry's company I forgot, I forgot everything, or at least the essential. We walked for hours: the fatigue erased my memories. I was searching for refuge in this country where so often the beauty makes the heart contract. My heart was so fragile then. No doubt because of this fragility, it felt to the point of anguish the beauty of this landscape of which Jerry and I allowed ourselves to believe, we were the secret kings.

The French fascist intellectual Charles Péguy, in 1898, outlined his dream of utopian society: the 'beautiful community in which 'each soul realises to the fullest degree its degree of beauty ... each soul becomes to the fullest what it *is*' (cited in Caroll 1995: 49). The opening scene of *Le Taxi mauve* constructs a landscape in which this 'beautiful community', personified by Marchal and Jerry, can exist. This dream is interrupted by the women characters and the incursions of the modern world in the form of the petit bourgeois, the 'homosexual' tourists and the kind of decaying Europe represented by Taubleman and the absent Prince. The disharmony generated by these figures prevents the 'souls' realisation of their own personal beauty (ibid.).

In the battle to prevent the ravages of history disrupting the communion of landscapes and souls, the Irish tourist industry has not being found wanting. Bord Fáilte's campaigns to attract 'the Simple in Spirit' met with considerable success in the late 1990s. Not to be outdone, the Irish literary organisations celebrated Déon as an 'Etonnant Voyager' in Dublin Castle in 2001 and awarded the IMPAC Dublin Literary award to Houllebecq in 2002. In the twenty-first century, Ireland has thus become the 'new reactionary' paradise and a space in which 'minds' like Houellebecq's, sterilised or otherwise, can flourish.

Notes

1   There are of course other writers who were interested in the subject of Ireland and the work of Irish writers. Their work reflects a dialogue with writers from Ireland and, if anything, offers a counter-discourse to the image of Ireland constructed by writers such as Déon. One such writer is Raymond Queneau (1903–76) avant-garde novelist, mathematician, philosopher, poet and editor of the *Pléaide encyclopedia*. Queneau wrote the French translation of Muiris Ó Suilleabháin's classic tale of growing up on the Blasket Islands off the south coast of Ireland, *Fiche Blian ag Fás* (reprinted, Rennes: Terre de Brume, 1997; first published, 1937) and two 'detective' novels set in Ireland under the penname of 'Sally Mara'. Another author in the 'counter' category is the writer Joseph Kessel who reported on the Irish Civil War and wrote a story based on his experiences, 'Mary de Cork' (*Les Coeurs purs*, (Paris: Folio/Gallimard, 1987; first published, 1921). The work of these two writers impacts on the Ireland text in France to a considerable degree. See Gilligan 2003.

2   Following remarks he made on Islam, Hoeullebecq was put on trial for, but later acquitted of, incitement to racial hatred in September 2002. He said at his trial that the Koran was inferior to the Bible as a literary work.

3   They were granted monies by the National Film Studios of Ireland who then received a seven per cent stake in the profits of the film from anglophone countries. See J. Hill, K. Rockett and L. Gibbons (eds) *Cinema and Ireland*, London: Routledge, 1988, 183.

4   It was also in the top 23 of the total film releases that year, competing with blockbusters such as Kubrick's *Barry Lyndon* (also filmed in Ireland), *Marathon Man* and *King Kong*

5   He made *L'Attentat* in 1972, based on a controversial Ben Barka scandal in 1965; *R.A.S.* in 1973; and *Dupont-lajoie* in 1974, a critique of the racism of middle-France. In 1976 he directed the film considered his greatest critical success in this genre, *Juge Fayard dit le shérif*, concerning the assassination of a judge in Lyons.

6   Pascale Frey, 'Michel Déon', *Lire*, June 1995, http://www.lire.fr/portrait.as, accessed 3 June 2004.

7   My translation.

8   'The question of the liberation of women in relation to their bodies is interesting. There the body of the

woman is nothing but a tool which permits a being to appear' (my translation). Michel Houellebecq in interview with Patrice Van Eersel (2003: 1).

9   For accounts on Houellebecq and 'les nouvelles réacs', a group of intellectuals labelled the 'new reactionaries', see Nicolas Weill, 'Intellectuals francais et 'coup de barre a droit' *Le Monde*, 15 November 2002. News headlines on Houellebecq and this group included 'Un puritain contre la gauche morale', *Liberation*, 28 January 2003, and 'les nouveaux réacs', *Le Point*, 8 November 2002.

10 For a detailed account of the affiliations of this group of writers see N. Hewitt and J. E. Flowers (eds) *Literature and the Right in Post-war France: The Story of the 'Hussards'*. London: Berg, 1996.

11 See for example, R–M. Albérès, *Histoire du roman moderne* (Paris: Albin Michel, 1962); P. de Boisdeffre, *Une histoire vivante de la littérature d'aujourd'hui* (Paris: Librairie académique Perrin, 1965); J–M. Maulpoix, *Itinéraires littéraires du XX e siècle*, volume II (Paris: Hatier, 1991); Gaëtan Picon, *Panorama de la nouvelle littérature française* (Paris: Gallimard, 1976); Robert Poulet, *Le Caléidoscope: trente-neuf portraits d'écrivains* (Lausanne: L'Âge d'Homme, 1982).

12 'Une répulsion pour ces formes de gouvernement que sont la République et la démocratie'. Déon, quoted in *Télérama*, 2390, 1 November 1995.

References

Alguhon, M. (1995) *The French Republic 1879–1992*, trans. Antonia Nevin. Oxford: Blackwell.

Beckett, S. (1990) 'Censorship in the Saorstat', in Julia Carlson (ed.) *Banned in Ireland*. London: Routledge, 145.

Benoit, C. (1977) '*Le Taxi mauve*', in J. Delmas (ed.) *Jeune Cinéma*, 104, 22.

De Faragoce, B. (1983) 'Charles de Gaulle et Eamon de Valera', in *Etudes irlandaises*, 7, 257–61.

Déon, M. (1960) *Tout l'Amour du Monde*. Paris: La Table ronde.

____ (1988) *Bagages pour Vancouver*. Paris: La Table ronde.

Clavel, B. (1993) 'Une ile bousculée par le vent de l'océan', *Géo*, June, 88–90.

Coblence, F. (1988) *Le Dandyisme, obligation d'incertitutde*. Paris: Presses Universitaires de France.

Farren, J. (1996) 'L'homme tranquille dans un taxi mauve', *Le Monde/Terres d'Irlande*, 16 March, 11.

Gilligan, P. (2002) *Dream Country: The Ireland Text in French Cinema 1937–77*, unpublished PhD thesis, Trinity College Dublin.

Haudiguet, P. (1974) *John Ford; cinéma d' aujourd'hui*. France: Editions Seghers.

Jameson, F. (1990) *Signatures of the Visible*. London: Routledge.

Jaouen, H. (1990) *Journal d'Irlande, 1977–83/1984–89*. Brest: Éditions Ouest-France.

Joannon, P. (1991) 'Charles De Gaulle and Ireland: a Return to Sources', in P. Joannon (ed.) *De Gaulle and Ireland*. Dublin: Institute of Public Administration, 11?

Le Brun, D. (1994) 'Balade irlandaise au coeur du Connemara', *Prima*, 143, 128.

MacKenzie, S. (2002) 'Michel Houellebecq', *The Guardian*, http://books.guardian.co.uk/departments/generalfiction/story/0,6000,783583,00.html

Mitry, J. (1954) *John Ford, Tome II*. Paris: Éditions Univeritaires.

Mitterand, F. (1986) 'Ireland and Europe', in James Dooge (ed.) *Ireland in the Contemporary World*. Dublin: Gill & Macmillan, 5.

Pollard, M. (1985) 'Women and the National Revolution' in R. Kedward and R. Austin (eds.) *Vichy France and The Resistance: Culture and Ideology*. London: Croom Helm, 45–63.

Rafroidi, P., G. Mac Conamara and M. Mac Conamara (eds) (1973) *France-Ireland*. Lilles: Université De Lilles.

Steinberg, M. (1977) '*Le Taxi mauve*', *Lumière du çinéma*, 6, 12–13.

Tulard, J. (1982) *Dictionnaire du çinema, les acteurs*. Paris: Laffont.

_____ (1991) *Dictionnaire du çinéma, les réalisateurs*. Paris: Laffont.

Vandromme, P. (1997) *Michel Déon. Le nomade sédentaire*. Paris: La Table ronde.

Van Eersel, P. (2003) 'Ou est le vrai visage de Michel Houellebecq', in *Nouvelles Clés*, 28 March, 12–15

Wardle, L. (2002) 'An interview with Michel Houellebecq', *The Guardian*, 5 April, 4–5.

part 5 **real paradigms: conceptualising the national**

Preparing to Fail: Gender, Consumption, Play and National Identity in Irish Broadcast Media Coverage of the 'Roy Keane Affair' and the 2002 World Cup
Marcus Free

> It's cost a lot of money to come out here and look ... it's preparation. Fail to prepare, prepare to fail.
>
> – Roy Keane, *Irish Times* interview, 23 May 2002

In May and June 2002, national football captain Roy Keane's expulsion from the team prior to the World Cup Finals in Korea and Japan dominated Irish broadcast media. On arrival in the pre-tournament Saipan training base, Keane complained that the training pitch had injury-threatening holes and that the training kit had not yet arrived. At a squad meeting (23 May), manager Mick McCarthy challenged Keane to reiterate his *Irish Times* interview account of the problems, published that day, whereupon Keane attacked McCarthy's management ability and McCarthy dismissed him from the squad, subsequently refusing to accept his return without apology.

Developing the arguments that sport is a key focal point for the construction of nations as 'imagined communities' (Anderson 1991), and that broadcast media narrativise and discursively construct the meanings of sporting events (Whannel 1992; Blain *et al.* 1993), this chapter examines how, in ensuing radio and television broadcasts, including phone-ins, interviews and round-table discussions, fantasies of 'hegemonic masculinity' (Connell 1995) were generated and projected onto Keane as a corporeal embodiment of Ireland's economic regeneration in the 1990s. The managerial incompetence of his dismissal, by contrast, was rhetorically cast as emblematic of an enduring and embarrassingly pre-modern 'old Ireland'.[1]

Using psychoanalytic perspectives on sport and media consumption (Richards 1994; Silverstone 1994), I argue that these constructions and projections were forms of play homologous with the oscillation between anxiety and security in on-field ball play itself: Keane became a symbolic object, through dialectical play with which a fantasy of collective identity was continually constructed and reconstructed. A key feature here was how Keane's objectification became a vehicle for the participants' – commentators and callers alike – performance of gender identity and difference (Butler 1990). Keane was an unstable signifier of 'native' Irish success. His apparent exemplification of 'hegemonic masculinity' through separation and individuation, his pragmatic attitude to representational commitment, and his professional development *abroad*, problematised his fantasised embodiment of and reproduction of collective identity and economic achievement. Nonetheless, the exhaustive debate, which far exceeded the typical constituency of football supporters, shifted the tournament focus from actual competitive outcomes to collective consumption – discussion, argument, speculation – as the focal point for imagined national community. Ironically it realised Keane's warning that 'fail[ure] to prepare' adequately for the tournament (through poor training and preparation) was 'prepar[ation] to fail' in the tournament itself. As expectations lowered, failure was 'prepared for': celebrations of participation by supporters eclipsed the significance of actual competitive outcomes, and the modest achievement of reaching the second round was considered a success.

'Old' and 'New' Ireland: the mythology of the 'Celtic Tiger'

Keane's behaviour and McCarthy's response to this ensured that the footballer became an ambivalent national representative. Blanket media coverage focused firstly on the possibility of apology, then on Ireland's diminished tournament hopes following confirmation that he would neither apologise nor return. Hard facts from Saipan, and then Japan, were lacking, time zone differences meaning that key events occurred in early or mid-morning, Irish time. In their absence, numerous presenter-led morning and afternoon radio programmes, fuelled by listener phone-ins and e-mails, presented themselves as gauges of the national mood.

The key figure, both as presenter on 'The Last Word' (Today FM), and as guest on other programmes, was Eamon Dunphy, ghostwriter of Keane's subsequent autobiography. Famous as a former Ireland player and for his scathing attacks on Jack Charlton's management of Ireland in the early 1990s, Dunphy was himself an object of ambivalence among Irish soccer supporters (Rowan 1995). A well-known populist proponent of the Fianna Fáil-Progressive Democrat coalition government's corporate sector-friendly, neo-liberal economic policies, Dunphy conjoined his football and political interests to set an agenda for other radio and television programmes. He speedily elaborated a rhetorical polarity between an idealised 'new' Irish professionalism embodied by Keane, deemed both source and symptom of the government-enabled 1990s economic boom, and an 'old Ireland' of incompetent bureaucracy and anti-individualism associated with a lazy, bogus cultural nationalism. Thus he equated Keane with 'the financial services area ... where excellence is achieved and required', echoing Irish economists' congratulations for Irish business culture's 'new self-confidence' and entrepreneurial productivity (Fitzgerald 2000: 55). At the same time he was dismissive of the Football Association of Ireland (FAI) and the 'Irish media mob' as consumers of an excellence that the FAI's managerial structures could not emulate (interview, 'Gerry Ryan Show', 2FM, 24 May 2002). This polarity entailed projecting onto Keane the characteristics of 'hegemonic masculinity', that is, those characteristics requisite for the successful performance of masculinity as a culturally and socially constructed gender identity. The projection in turn enabled Dunphy and his interlocutors to themselves perform overlapping and mutually reinforcing masculinities. Dunphy moved between three spheres: 'business world' guests from the new Ireland; 'laddish' masculinity as a guest with fellow radio presenter Gerry Ryan; and the 'intellectual' sphere of cultural commentators who were guests on his programme.

The business world guests were mobilised to pass judgment on McCarthy's (mis)management of Keane. Two aspects dominated: commentaries on the FAI and McCarthy's competence and their public relations management. The first equated sporting performance's supposedly pure measurability with business performance, so elevating and idealising business culture, although superior management knowledge was often established through the unscientific rhetoric of personalised anecdote and relativity. Hence, '[in] management and organisations, the ones most closely aligned with football teams would be professional firms ... where people are highly paid and high performers ... big merchant banks, consultants, law firms', and 'I've heard more serious language [than Keane's reported outburst] ... that would peel paint off doors at under-14 matches' (Chief Executive, Irish Management Institute, 'The Last Word', 28 May). Indicting McCarthy's childish sensitivity here simultaneously elevates the interlocutor and by implication the business community. (He's also the 'good', tolerant father – who attends kids' games!) On an imaginary scale of masculine resistance to injury it exemplifies management culture's routine deployment of sporting and militaristic metaphors to distinguish managers from non-managers (Collinson and Hearn 1994).

In another variation, the dispute's translation into a quasi-sporting game turned sporting into business management, legitimating the latter with a masculine corporeal form. Thus, a PR consultant's enthusiastic 'scoring' of the participants' public relations 'game' adopted a mock football commentary: 'McCarthy hesitating on the ball, he leaves the door open, gets caught in possession ... is wounded, perhaps fatally', etc. ('Last Word', 28 May – note the slippage into military metaphor here). The effect is two-way legitimation: football is important because it is like business, and vice versa.

McCarthy and Keane thus became objectified imaginary figures in a dialectic by which speakers performed their own hard-nosed masculinity. Projecting characteristics onto sport and business, they positioned themselves in a hierarchy of masculine toughness. Banter was a significant feature, a typically masculine form of mock mutual deprecation in which disavowed fondness is ironically articulated through reciprocation and/or mockery of a third party (Easthope 1992). The PR scoring, for example, describes Dunphy's attack on 'a national icon in John Giles' [former Ireland player and football pundit who supported McCarthy] as 'almost another own-goal', *equating* Dunphy-versus-Giles with Keane-versus-McCarthy. Dunphy's reply, 'he's gonna get another one in a minute!' ironically separates him from the old Ireland represented by Giles, forging an alliance with his interlocutor, since such a PR 'own goal' is a goal for the honesty and truth of new Ireland.

This dialectical process additionally entailed the projection of hegemonically masculine characteristics onto Keane. Dunphy moved between the above and a more deliberately vulgar laddish masculinity in such exchanges as the following with Gerry Ryan ('Gerry Ryan Show', 2FM, 24 May):

Dunphy: This great man, not just a footballer, he's a *man*, Keane, he's a lovely family, lovely wife, looks after his parents ... perfect human being ... but he's living in a world full of spivs, PR merchants, chancers...

Ryan: I don't think it's manly, the kind of things I hear coming from these players [who sided with McCarthy]...

Dunphy: McCarthy was one of the boss' men, he was close to Jack [Charlton] ... so was Packie Bonner, Gerry Peyton, they were the sort of ... establishment men.

Ryan: [overlaps] The 'Top Dogs'.

Dunphy: Well, the wagons, you know. And Keane is one of the lads, at the back of the bus.

This exchange shows several significant rhetorical shifts. Firstly, Keane becomes 'a man', implicitly suggesting a hegemonic masculinity, indirectly defined by what follows as independence, self-reliance, self-making and reproduction, power, as opposed to the legitimate dependence of family, including parents, and illegitimate dependence of consumers ('spivs') who contaminate football's pure world. Secondly, spatial metaphors ('back of the bus') indirectly differentiate Keane's manliness from non-manly Charlton associates – in turn feminised as 'wagons', Dublin masculine slang for difficult, conceited, untrustworthy women.

The indirect reliance on metaphor and negative distancing from a feminised 'other' is striking. Ryan began the exchange with 'do you know what I smell, Eamon? I smell amateur riflemen lining up to shoot the finest buck male in the herd.' This metaphor was typical of his show's adolescent sexualising, 'smell' suggesting the nervous sweat of (sexually) insecure males seeking compensation by destroying the epitome of sexual prowess. Sexual metaphors continued in Ryan's phone-in discussions. Given Keane's non-apology and final statement that he would not return, Ryan asked, 'would Mick McCarthy have apologised for behaving like a debutante spurned by her date for the night?', later remarking that 'the whole thing looks like a ballet-dancing weekend' ('Gerry Ryan Show', 29 May 2002). McCarthy is progressively feminised by association with ballet's 'effeminacy', but the recourse to mixed metaphor signifies the relativity and instability of the gender game at play.

Such exchanges exemplify Deborah Cameron's argument that in performative gendered speech, stereotypically 'cooperative ... talk among female friends ... building on one another's contributions so that ideas are felt to be group property' (1997: 55) may equally characterise men's talk. Hence a combination here of cooperation through reinforcement ('man'/'manly') and stereotypically masculine competition in the search to outdo each other's metaphors!

Dunphy shifted register yet again as his regular guest Fintan O'Toole intellectualised the narrativisation of uneasy transformation from a culture of low expectation and bogus national collectivism to professionalism in search of excellence. O'Toole added another 'Celtic Tiger' myth to Dunphy's, that the state equals the nation, the nation equals culture, and national subjects are symptomatic, in their actions, of national culture. Peader Kirby has argued that O'Toole's 'Manichean polarities' of 'old' and 'new' are 'derived from crude forms of modernisation theory and entirely dismissive of any historical complexities that may cloud [his] clarity of judgment' (2002: 23). In this instance, culture is reduced to an abstractly symbolic and innocuous plane.

Thus, in Levi-Straussian vein, O'Toole's mythologising resolves a cultural binary opposition:

> [the team] learned from Keane … that even the greatest individuals can function within a collective enterprise … something we needed to hear in Irish society at the moment where we have … individualism placed against collective institutions … because the institutions are crap. ('The Last Word', 17 June 2002)

O'Toole makes a three-way mutual reinforcement and conflation of distinct social and cultural spheres. Football becomes high culture, (in an *Irish Times* article, he compares Keane to Sophocles' Philoctetes! (27 May 2002)), high becomes popular culture and the social an idealised cultural, symbolic sphere where action takes place on a level playing field with an outstanding individual as ultimate team player, a hall of mirrors in which O'Toole symbolically resolves a mythical opposition he has helped construct.

Keane variously becomes material, human embodiment of an 'economic boom' of 'contested pedigree' (Kirby 2002). Claiming professionalism developed abroad as symptomatic of a supposedly like-minded domestic generation mystifies Keane's professionalism, the source of national wealth and the nature of the labour which produces it. Keane's success might as easily be read as working-class pragmatism motivated by desire for optimal achievement. At the same time, his bodily labour power reflects and vindicates generations of working-class Irish migrants who defined themselves by their capacity to sell and reproduce their labour (Greenslade 1997).

As for the boom, while proclamations of success routinely cite radical reduction in unemployment, growing GDP and consumerism as indicators, as Denis O'Hearn (2000: 74) argues, Ireland has 'bought economic tigerhood' by importing foreign capital, a proportion of which is effectively fictitious due to low taxation and foreign multinationals' capital 'repatriation' (Fitzgerald 2000: 54), so that GNP lags well behind GDP. The bulk of new jobs are in poorly-paid service sectors (O'Hearn 1998) and wages constitute a shrinking proportion of GDP (O'Connell 2000: 84). Consumerism has been fuelled by low EU-set interest rates and income tax reductions despite persistently poor transport, health and social services infrastructural investment and development (O'Connell 2001), while relative poverty has increased despite the boom (Cullen 2002). It is no coincidence that, given Irish economists' narrow definition of cultural change in Ireland as 'a successful business culture only' (Kirby *et al.* 2002: 13), the search for a broader cultural manifestation of the 'new self-confidence' should focus on sport.

The fantasised Keane legitimates free market and imagined Ireland alike by willing Ireland to win. But there was an inevitable contradiction, that the quintessentially self-made man should be appropriated by nationalism, however new. His own initial withdrawal indicated a tension between his status as Manchester United employee and national subject. Proclaimed as an emblem of native productivity, he was objectified by various consumption fantasies in which native productivity was ironically paramount, fantasies which emblematised Ireland's arrival as a consumer society.

Such conflation and confusion, through variously gendered play, contributed to the 'Celtic Tiger' myth of shared national economic success and ownership, rising consumption as a symptom of modernity, and the appropriation of foreign-based professionals as native successes, thus legitimating a history of economic migration which footballers like Keane, albeit contradictorily, represent.

Public service broadcasting and the 'national family'

In object relations psychoanalytic writing on childhood play, the infant's cathexis of an object (personal toy, blanket etc.) with magical significance through play is a means of negotiating the boundary between 'me' and 'not-me'. It is a first 'transitional object' (Winnicott 1971) in the path to individuation. This concept has been applied both to play in sport and media consumption. Barry Richards (1994: 27–50) sees oscillation between possession and dispossession in sport as a symbolic re-enactment of residual anxieties in individuation: the ball as 'transitional object' mediates anxiety and security. Roger Silverstone sees the play of childhood and adult media interpretation as a 'dialectical articulation of anxiety and security ... shifting between illusion and disillusion' in the search for 'ontological security' (1994: 16–17). If nations are 'imagined communities', arguably broadcast international sporting contests 'corpo-realise' the community, but in a rather unstable way. Loss is a serious risk, and collective anxiety concerning Keane's withdrawal here highlighted the community's contingency: just whom exactly did Keane represent?

A structural homology developed in Irish media between the possession/dispossession dialectic of on-field play, and Keane's objectification as an unstable symbol of national identity. There was an extraordinary interplay between radio phone-ins and television broadcasts, particularly following Keane's RTÉ television interview with Tommie Gorman (27 May 2002), in which he failed to 'apologise'. This dialectic shifted focus from football to the play of consumption. A different problematic replaced the 'new'/'old' Ireland polarity, though exhibiting a similar level of anxiety over Keane's representative status. In ensuing radio discussions focusing on Keane's emotional state in the interview, a metaphorical frame of national family emerged, though given the move from strictly sporting terms of reference, this frame developed with some ambivalence from the various interlocutors.

The interview itself was a discursive agonistic play between Keane's rhetorical device of a hypothetical alter ego questioning his motives before confirmation – an imaginary, self-justificatory dyad in a classically masculine, individualised corporeal economy – and Gorman's multiply claused, repetitive, invitational questions, re-framing the dispute in terms of the 'national' audience:

Keane: if there was any doubt in my mind that 'Roy, you were a little bit out of order' ...

Gorman: *aren't* wrongs all relative things, and *what about* the sense of wrong to those poor people *who* saved their money, *who* follow Ireland, *who* love you, *who* want to teach their kids, *'yes, you're right, he is a hero, he's a fantastic fellow', what about* the sense of confusion they feel, that ye guys can't sort this out as adults? (my emphasis)

RTÉ's television news bulletin prior to the interview led with Keane's declaration that 'I want to play for Ireland', yet this was actually the final outcome of verbal sparring and an indirect response to Gorman's hypothetical scenario: [McCarthy and the FAI] 'come to you and say 'for the good of the country ... we'd like you to be playing for Ireland'.

The constructive nature of this discursive exchange, unacknowledged in preceding and succeeding news bulletins, was complemented by the camera's remaining in mid-close-up or close-up on Keane through the lengthy questions, as though seeking out a non-verbal, emotional flicker of response. The quintessential 'action' man (famously, in the press photograph in which, bare chested, he shakes hands with McCarthy while turning away) was reduced to head and shoulders, fixed as silent, still, attentive – singularly untypical of televised football. Indeed it is the classic 'reaction' shot of the 'woman's genre' of melodrama (Modleski 1984). Television's typical 'look', the 'glance', temporarily becomes the 'cinematic' look, the 'gaze' (Ellis 1992), an image that newspapers the next day photographically reproduced as single, or multiple television screens in actual viewing locations.

This visual excess – hallmark of feminine suffering in melodrama, the image temporarily rupturing the filmic narrative – underpinned a different commentary from Gorman on the

9pm news, as he interrupted interview segments with explicit interpretations stressing Keane's shift from expressing 'pain, his hurt and his blind anger' to his wish to 'play for Ireland'. The report concluded with Keane walking alone to his car, implicitly establishing a contrast with his strident but reporter-plagued dog-walking when he returned from Saipan. The shift in focus from narrowly-defined sporting issues (training facilities, playing ability, fitness, match outcomes, and so on) to his emotional state and the possibility of a change of heart (if not mind) enabled a stereotypically feminine melodramatic narrative form to develop with a possibly negotiated, even partial pragmatic solution (Nochimson 1992) in prospect.

On the following day, RTÉ radio was dominated by discussion of Keane's, McCarthy's and other players' emotional states and the possibility that the 'hurt' might be repaired, even if ego-damaging apologies were not forthcoming. However, these discussions exhibited a tension between indulgence in, and ambivalent distancing from this feminised narrativisation. As a story of clashing masculine egos, it was elevated to the public sphere, but as a narrative with an emotional focus, it was simultaneously devalued as soap opera. So, when current affairs presenter Cathal MacCoille suggested (on RTÉ radio's *Morning Ireland*, 28 May) that, given a threatened India-Pakistan nuclear war and new revelations of child abuse in Ireland, 'Princess Diana'-scale mass hysteria had gripped the country, co-presenter Aine Lawlor, who had introduced the discussion with 'this is a soap opera', shrieked with laughter before guest psychologist Maureen Gaffney restored the emerging orthodoxy, that 'we're ... primarily emotional beings', seeing the row as a 'rift in the [national] family' and expanding Gorman's interpretation that Keane 'was actually expressing great vulnerability'. Ambivalence was contained by the privileged position of television sport (Rose and Friedman 1997: 4) as a 'mas(s)culine cult of distraction', legitimating male (and female, as evident here) viewers' absorption by multiple identifications with, in hard news terms, comparatively trivial matters.

Interestingly, transgressing the implicit code of hegemonic masculinity drew complaint from many recorded female calls through the day – 'if this was a bunch of women, they'd all be talking about hormones or PMT by now. They're a disgrace', etc. ('Today with Pat Kenny', RTÉ Radio One). Such comments both varied performance of gender difference and signalled another emerging theme in the live radio flow, the repeatedly expressed possibility that media encouragement of prurient fascination had rendered a mutual face-saving apology impossible, while inducing guilt about voyeurism and eavesdropping.

A variant mode of consumption began to emerge, then, an ambivalent humorous oscillation between indulgence in and self-distancing from this feminised consumption of masculine competition. This was encapsulated, on the eve of Ireland's opening match (May 31), in well-known feminist and 'Late Late Show' (RTÉ Television) guest Nell McCafferty's ironically expressed wish to *be* in Japan, free of 'the spectacle ... of players being brought out to be executed and then weeping and pleading exhaustion and crying for their mammies'; in other words, to avoid the mediated reconstitution of men as relationally connected (Chodorow 1978), 'human, passionate, volatile, vulnerable'.

The motor behind this ambivalence was, once again, Keane's ambiguity as a model of individuated masculinity: if he 'want[s] to play', why not apologise? To extend the 'Diana' analogy, if as Richard Johnson argues, Princess Diana became a vehicle for 'transferred feelings', a vicarious working through of hitherto 'unmourned' losses (1999: 31), transference was enabled by her media construction as a quintessentially connective figure. Roy Keane, however, was the quintessential hard man with an already established reputation for on- and off-field displays of temper and violence no more readily co-opted to a national broadcaster's construction of national family than an imaginary embodiment of Ireland's new professionalism. The play of ambivalence towards him progressively shifted the focus from a narrative of national becoming through competitive play to national being through collective speculation, argumentation and consumption.

A 'moral victory' by any other name...

From the tournament's commencement, Dunphy himself ironically contributed, with this resignation and ambivalence, to 'preparation to fail', in that acceptance of competitive failure was prepared *for*. As a 'panel of experts' member, Dunphy attacked RTÉ's upbeat build-up as 'happy-clappy public relations guff' (*Network 2* – 'World Cup Preview', May 30), so establishing an agonistic tension between the new Ireland allegorical narrative of national becoming and old Ireland celebration of national being. This tension endured in the broadcast of Ireland's opening match against Cameroon (1 June), with three notable textual features.

The broadcast effectively prepared for failure in two ways, the first a continued strain of ambivalent humour, the subtext a self-reflexive celebration of being Irish as playful acceptance, a knowing wink at the em*bodied* stereotypes: presenter Bill O'Herlihy joked, at the 7am outset, that it was 'an ungodly hour to put your reputation on the line' with a breakfast of 'bacon and pints'. As such, this was an ambivalent indulgence, shifting the textual emphasis from the play of production to consumption. The second re-framed the opening 'hermeneutic enigma' ('will Ireland win?') in terms of McCarthy's survival – O'Herlihy again: 'can McCarthy silence his critics today?' Failure, if it happens, is McCarthy's, rather than ours.

The third feature was Dunphy's continued attack on RTÉ and his fellow panellists, particularly their reading a 1-1 draw as a quasi-victory, despite a remark (John Giles) that 'the days of "moral victories" are over' – Dunphy: 'The players ... carry[ing] this monkey on our back' were 'set to be "betrayed" by 'flag-waving leprechaun[s]' (the carnivalesque supporters). The 'our' extended a fascinating slippage: 'if we ... go through to the second phase and come home feeling that this has been successful, then we will be betraying [players] like Damien Duff...' Players who achieve despite managerial incompetence represent new Ireland. Because they are already cast as old Ireland, however, (by remaining with McCarthy), they had to fail for old Ireland (colonially stereotypical 'leprechaun' supporters and 'monkey') to be exposed! Dunphy's convoluted logic was confronted with record complaints from viewers. Ironically, and inadvertently, he became 'bad cop' in a 'bad cop'/'good cop' dialectic that progressively validated moderate success in reaching the second round, precisely the 'it will do' old Ireland reading he decried.

By the second-round match against Spain (16 June), the result (defeat on penalties after extra time) was effectively rendered inconsequential through a pre-match build-up culminating in a musical sequence stitching together several 'World Cup' scenes. An *Embrace* song, the lyrics 'I've been lucky, I was lost, now I'm found', over images of individual players, led to the title refrain, 'My weakness is none of your business' as a shot of the panel celebrating Ireland's goal against Germany in the studio included Dunphy in the middle, visibly punching the air – symbolically if mutely reclaiming him. Concluding with a montage of celebrating, waving supporters in stadiums, pubs and streets, in the final shot, two young women shrugged, laughed, cried and embraced. The sequence signified a moral victory, in the agonistic on-screen battle of ambivalent modes of consumption, community progressively imagined as imagery. Loosely extending a Lacanian psychoanalytic perspective (Lacan 1977), narcissistic self-identification with a collectivity through imaginary recognition of wholeness in the waving 'other' as mirror combined with indirect construction of collective identity through voyeurism. Claiming a moral victory despite actual defeat has historically been an Irish sporting analogue of heroic failure in Irish history and culture. Despite contrary protestations, RTÉ's broadcast, including its panel of experts, contributed to its reproduction.

Conclusions

Ultimately, these modes of consumption were not dissimilar in constituting complementary searches for metaphorical embodiments of late twentieth-century Ireland. Each fed off the other in a dialectical play, the ultimate outcome the reaffirmation of collective national identity at a historical moment when the supposed economic boom was coming to an end and was increasingly exposed as an unstable function of Ireland's dependence on mobile international capital. Ambivalence, the play of indulgence and distance, is fuelled by and helps negotiate anxiety. Few national icons could be more ambiguous and anxiety-inducing than Roy Keane, whose autobiography revealed an extraordinary capacity for ambiguity and ambivalence with respect to football itself. At one point he asks, 'are footballers sometimes childish? Of course ... otherwise they'd just start believing they were only playing a game!' (2002: 184), in which case professionalism would slip. Players have to be childish to be serious. 'Play', paradoxically 'unreal' and 'real', entails, as

Bateson argues (1972: 153), an implicit 'metacommunicative' rule that 'these actions in which we now engage do not denote what would be denoted by those actions which these actions denote': the animal's 'playful nip denotes the bite … not what would be denoted by the bite'. If Keane's play is ambiguous and attitude ambivalent, so are the forms of playful consumption discussed here. They are variously gendered, nuanced, mutually extensive performances of national identity both real and unreal in articulating anxieties concerning the imagined community.

There are two final points in this regard. Firstly, the World Cup itself carries ambiguous status in football. National teams are only indirectly related to the 'serious' business of regional teams in national leagues and, of growing significance, European club competitions. The heightened contingency of outcome in contests between concocted teams of mutually unfamiliar players means that success can prove imagined national identity 'real' and that failure is bearable, both to regular football supporters and the more casual fans who appear every four years. The second point is unfashionably basic, in the context of contemporary cultural studies: the fervour surrounding the national football team may be a symbolic compensation for the redundancy of cultural nationalist rhetoric in post-'peace process' 26-county Ireland. Further it may substitute for the historically inclusive social vision of cultural nationalism, however flawed, that the intellectually impoverished and socially divisive adoption of neo-liberal economics has replaced.

Note

1   While this chapter focuses on the World Cup campaign only, the 'Keane story' endured into 2003. Keane's autobiography, published in August 2002, and serialised in *The Times* and *News of the World* newspapers, re-ignited the feud with his account of an enmity dating from their overlapping careers as Ireland players in the early 1990s. McCarthy entered the 2004 European Championship 'qualifiers' in September 2002 adamant that Keane would never play for him again. Having lost the opening two matches, he resigned as media pressure and negative criticism mounted. Supporters unprecedentedly booed him and chanted 'Keano' following the second defeat, at home to Switzerland. In November 2002, an Football Association of Ireland-commissioned report on World Cup preparations, by Genesis, a UK business consultancy, confirmed and supported Keane's original criticisms. Widely expected to return to the fold following appointment of McCarthy's successor, Brian Kerr, Keane reiterated his retirement from international football in February 2003 on medical grounds. However, he reversed this decision, returning for the friendly match against Romania in May 2004.

References

Anderson, B. (1991) *Imagined Communities: Reflections on the Origin and Spread of Nationalism*. London: Verso.

Bateson, G. (1972) *Steps to an Ecology of Mind*. New York: Ballantine Books.

Blain, N., R. Boyle and H. O' Donnell (1993) *Sport and National Identity in the European Media*. Leicester:

Leicester University Press.

Butler, J. (1990) *Gender Trouble, Feminism and the Subversion of Identity*. London: Routledge.

Cameron, D. (1997) 'Performing Gender Identity: Young Men's Talk and the Construction of Heterosexual Masculinity', in S. Johnson and U. H. Meinhof (eds) *Language and Masculinity*. Oxford: Blackwell.

Chodorow, N. (1978) *The Reproduction of Mothering*. Berkeley: University of California Press.

Collinson, D. L. and Hearn, J. (1994) 'Naming Men as Men: Implications for Work, Organisation and Management', *Gender, Work and Organisation*, 1, 1, 2–22.

Connell, R. W. (1995) *Masculinities*. Cambridge: Polity Press.

Cullen, P. (2002) 'Ireland a society of poverty, inequality, UN study finds', *Irish Times*, 24 July.

Easthope, A. (1992) *What a Man's Gotta Do?: The Masculine Myth in Popular Culture*. Boston: Unwin Hyman.

Ellis, J. (1992) *Visible Fictions*. London: Routledge.

Fitzgerald, J. (2000) 'The Story of Ireland's Failure – and Belated Success', in B. Nolan, P. J. O' Connell and C. T. Whelan (eds.) *Bust to Boom: The Irish Experience of Growth and Inequality*. Dublin: Institute of Public Administration, 27–57.

Greenslade, L. (1997) 'The Blackbird Calls in Grief: Colonialism, Health and Identity Among Irish Immigrants in Britain', in J. MacLaughlin (ed.) *Location and Dislocation in Contemporary Irish Society: Emigration and Irish Identities*. Cork: Cork University Pres, 36–60.

Johnson, R. (1999) 'Exemplary Differences: Mourning (and Not Mourning) a Princess', in A. Kerr and D. L. Steinberg (eds) *Mourning Diana: Nation, Culture and the Performance of Grief*. London: Routledge, 15–39.

Keane, R. and E. Dunphy (2002) *Keane: The Autobiography*. London: Michael Joseph.

Kirby, P. (2002) 'Contested Pedigrees of the Celtic Tiger', in P. Kirby, L. Gibbons and M. Cronin (eds), *Reinventing Ireland: Culture, Society and the Global Economy*. London: Pluto Press, 21–37.

Kirby, P., L. Gibbons and M. Cronin (2002) 'Introduction: The Reinvention of Ireland: A Critical Perspective', in P. Kirby, L. Gibbons and M. Cronin (eds) *Reinventing Ireland: Culture, Society and the Global Economy*. London: Pluto Press, 1–18.

Lacan, J. (1977) *Ecrits: A Selection*. London: Tavistock.

Modleski, T. (1984) *Loving with a Vengeance: Mass Produced Fantasies for Women*. London: Methuen.

Nochimson, M. (1992) *No End to Her: Soap Opera and the Female Subject*. Berkeley: University of California Press.

O'Connell, M. (2001) *Changed Utterly: Ireland and the New Irish Psyche*. Dublin: Liffey Press.

O'Connell, P. J. (2000) 'The Dynamics of the Irish Labour Market in Comparative Perspective', in B. Nolan, P. J. O' Connell and C. T. Whelan (eds) *Bust to Boom: The Irish Experience of Growth and Inequality*. Dublin: Institute of Public Administration, 58–89.

O'Hearn, D. (1998) *Inside the Celtic Tiger: The Irish Economy and the Asian Model*. London: Pluto Press.

_____ (2000) 'Globalisation, "New Tigers", and the end of the Developmental State? The Case of the Celtic Tiger', *Politics & Society*, 28, 1, 67–92.

Richards, B. (1994) *Disciplines of Delight: The Psychoanalysis of Popular Culture*. London: Free Association Books.

Rose, A. and J. Friedman (1997) 'Television Sports as Mas(s)culine Cult of Distraction', in A. Baker and T. Boyd (eds) *Out of Bounds: Sports, Media and the Politics of Identity*. Bloomington: Indiana University Press.

Rowan, P. (1994) *The Team that Jack Built*. Edinburgh: Mainstream Publishing.

Silverstone, R. (1994) *Television and Everyday Life*. London: Routledge.

Whannel, G. (1992) *Fields in Vision: Television Sport and Cultural Transformation*. London: Routledge.

Winnicott, D. W. (1971) *Playing and Reality*. London: Tavistock.

Keeping it Imaginary, Cultivating the Symbolic

Barry Monahan

I'll square myself with Lazarre, if you don't mind. That's why God invented cards.
  – Tom Reagan (*Miller's Crossing*, Joel Coen, 1990)

There is no Keyser Soze!
  – Dean Keaton (*The Usual Suspects*, Brian Singer, 1995)

Although these quotations have no ostensible thematic relationship, the films from which they have been taken foreground and stylise certain generic conventions of the gangster film in specific ways. *Miller's Crossing* reviews the genre nostalgically, paying homage with a slight exaggeration of performance, narrative action and production design; *Usual Suspects* is more cynical in its formal exposure of the kind of narrative construction that resulted in the plot complexity of *films noirs* such as *The Maltese Falcon* (John Huston, 1941) and *The Big Sleep* (Howard Hawks, 1946). As they self-consciously perform the cinematic styles and conventions of the gangster film, each may be considered postmodern in its approach to the genre. There is, however, another noteworthy connection between the lines of dialogue quoted above. They are spoken by the Irish-born actor Gabriel Byrne and delivered in a Dublin accent that has been influenced by a slight American inflection. Though far from his beginnings in the Irish rural soap operas *The Riordans* and *Bracken*, Byrne's position within the mainstream is by no means incongruous. There may even be something appropriate about the centrality of the actor with the perceptibly Irish accent within a patently American format at the same time the elements and structure of the genre are being renegotiated. Perhaps his parody cameo appearance as 'movie gangster' at the end of *When Brendan Met Trudy* (Kieron Walsh, 2000) – a film that satirises the visualisation and representation of 'Irishness' at home and abroad – also questions the position of the actor within certain mainstream genres.

Not long before being cast as Tom Reagan by the Coen brothers, Gabriel Byrne had played the role of a drug baron in *The Courier* (1987), a low-budget Dublin-set gangster film by Frank Deasy and Joe Lee. In noting what was perceived as its generic failure, a number of commentators pointed to the unsuitability of the landscape of the Irish capital to contain certain conventions of the thriller and gangster genres. Lance Pettitt claimed that the film was unsuccessful in its attempt 'to fuse contemporary Irish social concerns with a mainstream TV crime genre film'[1] and Martin McLoone concluded: 'What the film seems to prove is that Dublin is not amenable to the convention of the urban thriller.'[2] Shortly before *The Courier* was released, Mark Kilroy was interviewed by *Film Base News* for an article in which he stressed the importance of indigenous film for a healthy culture by stating: 'Irish people really need images of themselves made by themselves'.[3] This point has been echoed by Kevin Rockett who has suggested that despite successive waves of attempts at developing an indigenous film industry, even as late as 1999 there has been a persistent lack of 'tangible imagery' of contemporary Dublin.[4]

In different ways each of these writers is highlighting the problem inherent in producing images of the self that might not – because of their infrequency or novelty – seem to 'fit' the patterns of already existing modes of representation. The difficulty lies more in the failure to develop a sense of cinematic self and watch oneself on screen, than in the appropriateness or otherwise of the landscape to narrative. Although it might be suggested that the integration of cinematic character and landscape with generic conventions has been better effected in Hollywood films than in the Dublin-based crime thriller, or that certain settings and individuals are better suited to the cinematic image and imagination than others, perhaps it may be suggested that it is the film spectator who must be 'normalised' in the process of cinematic expectation.

Many Irish films frequently overcome the problem and relieve the spectator's position as viewer of his or her 'own' landscape by enframing voyeuristically a diegetic onlooker. A significant early example of this tendency is Bob Quinn's *Budawanny* (1987), which provides the eavesdropping islander who suspects the priest of his affair. The convention persists in 1990s cinema. The young boy in Gerry Stembridge's *Guiltrip* (1995) facilitates narrative continuity across the formally complex temporal arrangements of the film; Alan Parker and Stephen Frears' screen adaptations of Roddy Doyle's Barrytown trilogy are punctuated constantly by reaction shots of incredulous onlookers; and the children in *I Went Down* (Paddy Breathnach, 1997) looking over the wall interrupting Bunny's marital dealings calling 'Hello, Mr. Kelly!'

Over the following pages I will propose that a necessarily significant element in the development of any cinematic canon that purports implicitly or explicitly to represent a collective identity – social, cultural, national, regional, political, religious – is the continuing invention, negotiation, recognition and approval of a sense of 'cinematic self'. Without restricting my readings to Jacques Lacan's psychoanalytical models of subject development, I will make use of Lacanian terminology in order to examine notions of the represented self, and argue that despite different stylistic and thematic approaches a number of films recently produced by young Irish directors, writers and crews have formally addressed or problematised the insertion of the subject into the cinematic space. I will pay particular attention to two of Paddy Breathnach's earlier features *Ailsa* (1994) and *I Went Down* (1997), and to Kirsten Sheridan's debut feature *Disco Pigs* (2001). As these films narrate the stories of individuals who are socially alienated in different ways, and consider thematically the extent and effect of possible reintegration, they formally reproduce the positions of their protagonists cinematically, attempting to consolidate a position within filmic fields; narrative *syuzhet*, auditory and visual diegetic (*Ailsa* and *Disco Pigs*), or generic (*I Went Down*).

Contexts for the realisation of a cinematic identity

Because from its earliest examples animated photographs of Ireland and its people have been predominantly controlled by overseas production companies, the importance of reclaiming management of representation as the basis of a healthy indigenous film industry is undeniable. Ian Jarvie has written of film as the ultimate modern aesthetic apparatus for reflecting the nation, by referring to the moment at which its operations have been understood and mobilised: 'Modernity empowers partly by mastering a technology: that is, acquiring it, training the necessary support personnel, but also creating an interface so that its mastery can be widely diffused.' [5] Proponents for and cultural defenders of the necessity for sustained governmental support of an Irish film industry have frequently reiterated the disadvantages of being caught within the representation of the 'outsider'. As a particularly vociferous advocate of national film, Bob Quinn has persistently criticised the cultural colonialism of mainstream Hollywood and has lamented the fact that 'Ireland has long been a figment of the American imagination'.[6] This statement strongly suggests the need to recapture the control of representations of Ireland by the indigenous filmmaking community. But while the point has been raised elsewhere in relation to the development of European cinemas, 'film both reflects and refracts; it both mirrors and interprets the society which we inhabit, and our responses to it',[7] I wish to focus on the line separating the representation and the represented, the identified and the identity, by calling upon the metaphor of Lacan's mirror.

The relevance of psychoanalytic theory in the field of film studies has been somewhat undermined since its steady rise in application in the mid-1970s. Two of the strongest counter-arguments against its possible elucidation of the workings of the cinematic apparatus or the cognitive response of the spectator have been often cited. Firstly, there is the claim that what might be theorised as constituent of the individual subject ego cannot be generalised *ipso facto* to explain the workings of a 'collective unconscious'. Secondly, it has been suggested that psychoanalytical theory lacks a strong enough empirical foundation for transferral to other theoretical fields. Jacques Lacan's writing on the mirror stage and his use of the terms Real, Imaginary and Symbolic in the constitution of the subject have been particularly attractive to film theorists reading film as ideologically positioning the viewer with respect to (predominantly) *his* own gaze, desires and identifications. But the film screen, at which the spectator looks to see himself represented, can no longer be unproblematically compared to the primordial mirror quite simply because, as Christian Metz has said: 'The film is like the mirror [but] there is one thing that is never reflected in it: the spectator's body.'[8]

I want to recall Lacan's terminology in order to suggest that what is possible within the filmic Symbolic – the semiotic network of paradigmatic and syntagmatic cinematic operations – is not the formation of an image of the individual subject, but the establishment of a collective identity with which individuals may identify. The importance of a visualisation of identity (individual or collective) is as relevant for counter-hegemonic representations of group identities and identifications, as has been Lacan's theoretical anamorphosis for the individual who recognises himself as seeing and being seen; positioning himself and being positioned within a semiotic system. I am not using Lacan's mirror metaphor to suggest that the cinematic apparatus interpolates and dupes the spectator with an identitarian logic that establishes a transcendental subject. Rather, I want to translate the metaphor and its psychic realms of the Imaginary and the Symbolic for broader application.

To use Lacan's metaphor in the context of the formation, projection, recognition and endorsement (or rejection) of the cinematic identity is not to suggest that the notion is ideologically innocent, but it does propose that the process of identity formation through the positioning of the subject is not necessarily totally invisible in the cinema. Susan Hayward has referred to 'visibilisation' as the empowerment and enfranchisement of the previously excluded elements of society, as they emerge through the popular media, including cinema.[9] The use of Lacan's writing does not limit the sense of 'national' by establishing binaries of inclusion and exclusion, and founding essentialist or essentialising discourses through which the nation is ideologically narrativised: instead it allows for an opening to diversification at the same time as the possibility for group identification. Hayward states: 'What we can make of this enfranchisement and visibilisation is that, within a limited sphere of cultural expression at least, identity co-existing with difference(s) has become a reality – the very thing that nationalisms seek to deny.'[10]

In the sections that follow, I want to analyse how an individual or landscape is inserted into a filmic field in order to generate a sense of (cinematic) identity; in each of the examples given, acknowledgement is made of the thematic repositioning by virtue of precise formal and aesthetic compositions within the films. *Ailsa*, *I Went Down* and *Disco Pigs* not only narrate the reframing of person within landscape (society) through character within *mise-en-scène*, but in different ways they address the formation of cinematic character (*Ailsa*), genre (*I Went Down*) and identity (*Disco Pigs*).

A Symbolic space for the cinematic identity

Paddy Breathnach's first feature production is an adaptation by Joseph O'Connor of his own short story. It narrates the growing obsession of a young man with an American woman who moves into a downstairs room in the suburban house where he has been living with his wife. Over a period of time – long before he has even met the girl, whose name he hears is Campbell – Miles fantasises about her. When he finally meets her with his wife, Sara, Campbell tells them that she is pregnant. The emotional shock upsets Miles to such an extent that he has a nervous breakdown. Campbell returns to America to meet her husband, and when she sends Sara a letter to announce her imminent return with husband and child, Miles shoots himself. If Martin McLoone has been justified in drawing attention to the position of Breathnach's films within an emerging film culture 'which is attempting to find its own cinematic identity',[11] then none of them comes closer to reproducing this endeavour than *Ailsa*. The protagonist of the film undergoes a double *spaltung*: a division and separation from the *syuzhet* that he simultaneously inhabits and constructs, and a split between the coherent extra-diegetic narrative voice-over and his screen presence that is gradually fragmented and undermined as the film unfolds.

Miles occupies an imaginary cinematic space, but his visual representation is undermined by the impossibility of his narration. One evening as he lies in bed beside Sara, the room lit by the cool blue that haunts much of Cian de Buitléar's cinematography and connotes the death and absence that permeate the film, the camera begins to pan from her side of the bed to his. The shot continues across a line of ornaments and pictures on the shelf above the bed, before it returns 'full circle' to her. In an ironic inversion of his position of omniscient narrator (later to be problematised by the revelation of his death) just as he is taken out of frame, his wife begins speaking. Although the monologue is simple diegetic sound, it is detached from the picture, in an insinuation of another narrative voice-over. Only when she comes into shot, do we see her lips moving and have confirmation of the diegetic source of the sound. Miles' response to her, as she describes her imagining his character into existence, is doubly ironic:

Sara: You know, Miles, sometimes I think of you during the day. I wonder where you are and during the afternoon I wonder what you're doing, or what you're saying. I close my eyes and try to see you. Your hands, your face, the sound of your voice. [*The camera brings her slowly into the shot.*] Sometimes I can see you, but other times I can't. Makes me think that I've made you up somehow, and that you're not all real, and when I come home you won't be here at all.

Miles: I am here, I'll always be.

The synchronisation of sound with image in the case in which a dead character, in a flashback sequence which he narrates, tells another character who has just questioned his existence that 'I am always here', provides one level of dramatic irony within the story world, but resonates with another that problematises the very notion of characterisation in film.

There is evidence of the same filmic splitting in Kirsten Sheridan's *Disco Pigs*, adapted from Enda Walsh's play by the playwright himself. It tells the story of two teenagers – Darren and Sinéad – who have, from birth, come to focus uniquely on each other's world by closing themselves off from society, and communicating in a language only they understand. Marking their exclusion by calling themselves 'Pig' and 'Runt', their anti-social behaviour comes increasingly to show Sinéad's (Runt) romantic commitment to Darren (Pig), and the emergence of his more serious pathology, fuelled by a growing obsession to consummate his feelings for Sinéad. When Runt is taken to an institution in Donegal, Pig suffers a breakdown and sets off to find her. Reunited, Pig becomes increasingly paranoid that he has, over the period of her absence, lost some of Runt's affections to a school friend and, during another psychotic episode, he kills him in a nightclub. Shortly after the murder, they make love on the beach and, when they realise that there is no other option, Pig indicates to Runt that he wants her to end his life, and she does.

The diegetically divided protagonist of *Ailsa* is represented literally by two characters in *Disco Pigs* and what is established at the beginning as a harmonious synchronisation of sound and image, is gradually undone as the narrative progresses, in order to mark the tragic separation of the characters, and Pig's eventual detachment from the diegesis. The unfeasible *post mortem* voice-over narration of *Ailsa*, has become a prenatal one in Sheridan's film. The implication of impending disruption of the aural (linguistic, Symbolic) and the visual (Imaginary) is played out in the opening sequences showing Runt in her

Figure 13: **Darren (Cillian Murphy) and Sinéad (Elaine Cassidy) unsutured in *Disco Pigs* (permission – Element Films; photographer – Pat Redmond).**

mother's womb: 'That was the time when silence was some sort of friend.' Sinéad's birth does not establish the beginning of her entry into the linguistic realm of the Symbolic and society through the first of Jacques Lacan's three phases of separation from her mother,[12] because within moments of her birth a bond forms with the newly born Pig, who will prevent the process of that evolution. Having established Sinéad's position as narrator, Sheridan creates an uncomfortable tension by alignment with Pig's point-of-view (usually focusing on Runt, but also through dream and flashback sequences, and his video camera lens). As the film moves towards its climax, the aural is increasingly associated with Sinéad, while the visual is connected to Darren. The abnormal internal diegetic images align the spectator with Pig's psychosis, while Runt's narration marks their separation from the normal diegetic world presented: 'So no word we speak as the world around jabbers out stuff that goes nowheres to no-one.'

A crucial aspect of the conceptualisation of the cinematic self – the establishment of an Imaginary identity within a Symbolic representational field – is the comprehension of the relationship between subject and space. This self-consciousness is related to a double perception that has been central to Lacan's evocation of the mirror stage and that he has described as 'something that is one of the essential correlates of consciousness in its relation to representation, and which is designated as *I see myself seeing myself*.'[13] Most significantly for the present discussion is the notion of possession of the representation that emerges for the subject in this position: Lacan continues, 'The privilege of the subject seems to be established here from that bipolar reflexive relation by which, as soon as I perceive, my representations belong to me.'[14] A notable moment in Danny Boyle's *Trainspotting* (1996) occurs when the drug addicts leave the city on a trip into the rugged highland landscape. In a moment of enlightenment – and against the otherwise easily romanticised mountainous backdrop – one of the group declares:

It's shite being Scottish. We're the lowest of the low, the scum of the fucking earth, the most wretched, miserable, servile, pathetic trash that was ever shagged into civilisation.

The following year Kevin Allen's Welsh protagonists in *Twin Town* (1997) reflected upon their urban setting with reference to Dylan Thomas. Quoting the poet, one character states:

Swansea is the graveyard of ambition ... an ugly lovely town ... I'd call it a pretty shitty city.

Although these films openly acknowledge a certain critical self-reflection, I am suggesting that a similar expression emerges by implication through certain formal qualities of the films under discussion here. While the results of character development within cinematic space result in tragic consequences in *Ailsa* and *Disco Pigs*, in *I Went Down* the difficulty emerging from this insertion is framed for comic effect. If there has been a perceived incongruity between the images of Dublin (the city's '*imago*') and the cinematic generic structure (symbolic system) in the 1987 film *The Courier*, then Paddy Breathnach's third feature film plays with that perception by challenging expectations. *I Went Down* comically exposes the discrepancy between the recognised generic conventions and coding of mainstream cinema, and the seemingly ill-fitting iconography of the Irish 'local and provincial' that are being applied to them. For its primary comic effect, the film blatantly marks its own failure at 'becoming' a genre film, in a playfully absurd juxtaposition of the visual semantics of the local with the syntax of Hollywood mainstream.

Three possible generic frameworks are established within the opening sequences, and each is undermined in turn by a dramatic or comic alteration. At first it appears the film will be a serious romance focusing on the love-triangle between Git, his ex-girlfriend, and her new lover – Git's best friend – Anto. Git's release from prison and subsequent saving Anto from being beaten up for failing to pay a debt simultaneously obliterates the romantic plot, and introduces the underworld criminal scene. But this is quickly injected with a comic tone when Git injures two men working for local crime lord, Tom French. For compensation French orders him to go on a road trip with Bunny Kelly, the would-be gangster, to find Frank Grogan and deliver him to a *rendezvous* with 'the friendly face'.

Bunny aspires innocently to the status of cinematic hero, but the generic circumstances in which he finds himself constantly militate against the realisation of a role that is rooted in images of the United States. Subverting Bob Quinn's fears that cinematic Ireland remains trapped within an imagined construct of American film, Bunny's desire is to incarnate the Irishman's image of the American gangster although he confesses that all he knows about America is what he has seen on television. Bunny performs a number of 'types' usually associated with decisive masculinity. Associating himself with the western hero, Bunny buys himself a pair of cowboy boots, and reads a western novel, and when the meeting occurs with 'the friendly face' the sequence is reminiscent of the beginning of *Once Upon a Time in the West* (Sergio Leone, 1969). Irish bogs are shot like open frontier plains, and underscored by harmonica music. The ochre wash of the lighting design, the train tracks running through the wooden enclosure, and the background harmonica serve to exaggerate the absurdity of the ineffective Dublin gangsters within the generic coding of the *mise-en-scène*. Deciding to leave their charge, Frank Grogan, in the hands of the atypically named 'friendly face', Bunny answers Frank's protestations by saying 'We're not letting you go. Charles Bronson is.'

The status of gangster hero provides more room for generic parody. The credit sequence and music connote the slick performances of a Tarantino movie, and there are a number of intertextual references throughout the film to maintain this, but these are constantly displaced by inappropriate intrusions. Getaway cars break down, as an 'independent operator' the novice gangster, Git, is obliged to pay each time he fires his gun, and Bunny – whose name would sound more in place in a children's book – must eat chocolate regularly because, he announces embarrassedly, 'I have a little condition'. When Bunny and Git prepare to raid a house to capture Frank Grogan, Bunny gives the apprentice a lesson in handling the gun. Not only does this serve further to ridicule the protagonists working within the context of the cinematic 'gangster raid', but the scene also ends with Bunny giving Git a children's coloured woollen hat announcing, as he puts on his own balaclava, 'I could only get one cool one'. The child's bonnet adds a comic touch to the raid scene, but by his apology for the fact that it was not a 'cool one' Bunny's playing at being a gangster is brought to the fore once again, and signifies the film's performing through recognisable Hollywood cinematic conventions. Bunny's comic failure as character entering the established generic landscapes of mainstream cinema is the ultimate verification of his inability to 'see himself seeing himself'.

In *Ailsa* Miles – who significantly works as a genealogist – obsessively reconstructs images of Campbell's private life, trying to find out about her past and her character by stealing letters sent by her mother. Before he has any contact with her, a folder in which he accumulates her stolen post comes to symbolise how he has configured her as a character in his 'story'. Breathnach underscores this when, in a sequence after Campbell has left to go to America, Miles speaks about the extent to which he misses her, and the scene in which she is seen leaving on the train is replayed with his voice-over:

All I thought about was the last time I'd seen you: that last day when you went away. I can't tell you how many times I thought about that day. I ran it back over and over in my head. The day I tried to say 'Goodbye' to you. I ran it over and over like a film till I thought I couldn't bear it.

In *Disco Pigs* Darren, as an aspiring filmmaker, also tries to create and manipulate his own cinematic environment. Like Campbell's position with respect to Miles, he remains caught within the visual side of Runt's attempts to re-enter society (the Symbolic). The beginning of his spilt from her – representative of the *spaltung* of a single protagonist – occurs after his coming-of-age monologue, which is shot in a single take with simple framing and sound. The psychotic breakdown that Darren suffers when he discovers Sinéad's departure is echoed in the fragmentation of the cinematic coherence that had accompanied his monologue. The shots as he leaves the house the following morning are cross-cut with shots of her earlier going away, but when he reaches his front door and finds she is not beside him, a jarring music accompanies the frantic scene shot with hand-held camera as he jumps over the dividing garden fence, breaks into her house and runs upstairs to her room. The symmetry that earlier marked the imposed stability of their relationship has been shattered. What follows is a scene in which shots of Darren – seen from opposite sides in a deliberate violation of the 180-degree rule – are rapidly intercut to connote the mental collapse of the character appearing to be in dialogue with himself. Sound becomes a-synchronous, and the harmony between image and voice, and composite diegetic levels disintegrate utterly in illogical ellipsis.

Formalising degrees of realisation of the cinematic identity

The last fixed shot of Miles' personal narration in *Ailsa* is a further representation: the photograph of Campbell, her husband and their baby, which she has sent to Sara. After this, there occurs a montage of shots of Miles in his bathroom, a gun, dripping taps, and a bath half-full of water. With the first gunshot, we see Miles burning a letter he had written earlier to his wife, and (again an impossibility of the *fabula*) removing the tape from Campbell's answering machine. By the end of the film, Miles' character has been removed from the *syuzhet*. The logic established by the *post mortem* narrative voice-over undermines the possibility of maintaining his position, and his own efforts to transfer Campbell from his Imaginary into the film's symbolic fails in an equivalent way. This is formally emphasised by the ultimate displacement of synchronisation that occurs when we hear the second gun shot which is dubbed over a drop of water falling from one of the taps shown earlier: the dissolution of the filmic protagonist is complete and the end is marked by the dissociation of image and sound. The primary tension created throughout the film is between the protagonist's construction of character, and Breathnach's continuous displacement of character from the narrative core.

Pig's instability within the realm of the image in *Disco Pigs* is underscored by the irregular use of mirrors in the closing sequences of the film before he kills Markie in 'The Palace' nightclub. Shots of his final conversation with Runt are intercut with their reflection in a large mirror on an opposite wall. In successive takes, the two characters change position at the table in a shifting that once again problematises normal suturing. The ultimate breakdown occurs when Darren suffers a psychotic episode in the toilet: the soundtrack is muted, detaching his image from his voice and the background noises, until he smashes the mirror in which his shattered reflection is held briefly afterwards. The connotation is clear: Pig no longer remains in the realm of coherent cinematic representation. The fragmented image in the mirror marks Pig's failure to undergo anamorphosis through what Lacan has identified as 'the transformation that takes place in the subject when he assumes an image'.[15]

Runt's ending is not as pessimistic, and there is the suggestion of her possible social reintegration through a harmonious realignment of the film's synchronisation. Having been freed from the restriction of her relationship with Darren, unlike the protagonists from the other films analysed here, she reaches a point of cinematic coherence, successfully entering a symbolic realm. Four closing shots of Runt are played twice in succession: the first time with her a-synchronous voice-over, and the second time, as her voice-over continues, with the image and picture moving into synchronisation. The sequence begins with a frontal shot of Runt alone, facing out to sea and towards the camera. This is followed by a shot of the sun reflected in the shallow waves; a shot of Runt turning to look up towards the sun; a shot of the sun; and a shot of her again. In the final shot Runt's lips move, but her monologue does not match the image:

> And so it's all over then. Pig and Runt they leave and went all alone, it seems. It's like I really do want for something else, it seems. Yeah. That silence again. And so I know that he too is silent and safe.

At this moment, and half way through her voice-over, the set of four shots begins again, in the same order. The second time, however, her voice corresponds exactly with the movement of her lips in the final shot:

> And once alone, she calms. And do you know? The sun, it really is a big beautiful, shining thing. Oh where to, eh pal? Where to?

By the end of the film, the protagonist's struggle is resolved with the establishment of a more self-assured position in the diegesis, and a corresponding re-integration into the cinematic discourse.

Conclusion

Each of the films above deals thematically with the problematic position of individuals on the peripheries of society, but echoes formally the insertion, invention or establishment of an identity or identified landscape within a cinematic space, as character and *mise-en-scène*. I have outlined the advantage for collective identification of any social group of 'seeing myself seeing myself' in Lacanian psychoanalytical terms, and have related these to the structural and thematic operations of the films. In other disciplines, the advantage for society of developing, recognising and identifying with a visual sense of self has been reiterated frequently. Christopher Murray has written of the advantage of the theatre when it holds a 'mirror up to a nation',[16] and Declan Kiberd has also drawn attention to J. M. Synge's time on the Aran Islands with his camera that created 'a new narcissism among the islanders [because] seeing his photographs of them, the islanders tell Synge that they are seeing themselves for the first time'.[17] In conclusion it might be interesting to compare the studio audiences of *The Late Late Show* in the 1960s waving and nervously nudging the people on either side when they appeared on the studio monitors, or singing their requests for relatives and friends 'at home', with the relaxed sophistication of their present-day counterparts on *Kenny Live*, who barely acknowledge the presence of the cameras. A part of the coming-to-terms with the self as image (mirrored, photographed, televised or filmed) is the ability to relate to the imaged self as it is inserted into symbolic networks of different media: the international cinematic system is one of the most contested spaces for the foundation of a contemporary sense of visualised self, and we may have quite a distance to go before our cognitive mapping of that symbolic terrain is complete. It is a long way from the Riordan's fields in Dunboyne, Co. Meath to the burnt-out drugs vessel of Keyser Soze in San Pedro, but by no means an impossible leap of the imaginary.

Notes

1   Lance Pettitt, *Screening Ireland: Film and Television Representation* (Manchester: Manchester University Press, 2000), 108.

2   Martin McLoone, *Irish Film: The Emergence of a Contemporary Cinema* (London: British Film Institute, 2000), 204.

3   Mark Kilroy, 'The Arts Council and Film', in *Film Base News*, 5, Jan/Feb 1988, 6.

4   Kevin Rockett, '(Mis-)Representing the Irish Urban Landscape', in *Cinema and the City: Film and Urban Societies in a Global Context*, M. Shiel and T. Fitzmaurice (eds) (Oxford: Blackwell, 2001), 223.

5   Ian Jarvie, 'National Cinema: A Theoretical Assessment', in M. Hjort and S. MacKenzie (eds) *Cinema and Nation* (London, New York: Routledge, 2000), 81.

6   Bob Quinn, quoted in *Cineaste*, 24, 'Contemporary Irish Cinema Supplement', 73.

7   Wendy Everett, quoting Vigdís Finnbogadóttir in 'Framing the Fingerprints: A Brief Survey of European Film', in W. Everett (ed.) *European Identity in Cinema* (Exeter: Intellect Books, 1996), 15.

8   Christian Metz, from 'The Imaginary Signifier', quoted in *Film Theory and Criticism,* L. Braudy and M. Cohen (eds) (New York, Oxford: Oxford University Press, 1999), 802.

9   Susan Hayward, 'Framing National Cinemas' in M. Hjort and S. MacKenzie (eds) *Cinema and Nation* (London, New York: Routledge, 2000), 88–102.

10   Ibid., 95.

11   McLoone, *Irish Film*, 2000, 199.

12   Jacques Lacan, 'The Mirror Stage as Informative of the Function of the I as Revealed in Psychoanalytic Experience', from *Écrits: A Selection* (London: Tavistock, 1977).

13   Jacques Lacan, *The Four Fundamental Concepts of Psycho-analysis,* Jacques-Alain Miller (ed.) (Middlesex: Penguin, 1986). 80.

14   Ibid., 81.

15   Jacques Lacan, 'The Mirror Stage', 1977, 2.

16   This is the subtitle of Murray's book *Twentieth-Century Irish Drama* (Manchester, New York: Manchester University Press, 1997).

17   Declan Kiberd, *Inventing Ireland: The Literature of a Modern Nation* (London: Vintage Press, 1996), 173.

appendix **interview with stephen rea**

Interview with Stephen Rea

Conducted by Ted Sheehy at the Irish Film Centre, 21 April 2002, part of the 'Keeping it Real: The Fictions and Non-Fictions of Film and Television in Modern Ireland' conference

Ted Sheehy: One of the first things people would like to hear about is your working relationship with Neil Jordan. I was interested in what it is like when Neil is making a film and you are not working on it. Do you feel somehow that you are absent?

Stephen Rea: No. I don't have to be in all his movies. Someone once said to him, 'What's Stephen going to do in your next movie?' and he said, 'Stephen isn't in all my movies.' Then he paused and said, 'He's in all my good movies.' *Angel* [1982] was my first film, it was his first film and to do that together marks you. My attitude to film is defined to some extent by having done that with him. He is remarkable in a sense that he doesn't want to make a film about anything except what is in his own head; at least when he makes a good film. When he gets subverted slightly is when he gets drawn into making films to someone else's agenda. Earlier we were talking about *The Butcher Boy*, which we all agreed was Neil's best film. Of course the people who gave him the money to do that hadn't the slightest idea what he was on about and that marked the gulf between what people in Los Angeles understand cinema to be and what people here would like it to be.

TS: *Is it difficult to work with other people when you work so regularly with someone like that?*

SR: Every film is an act of trust. You read the script and think, 'this could be really something'. Then you quickly realise that maybe the director didn't see those things in it at all. So with Neil, because often he just tells what the film is going to be about, you know that it is going to work out. I worked with a woman director before and she also wrote the script. Because she was a very good writer, everything had the possibility of many meanings. She had the capacity to be ambiguous. However, when she came to direct, she lost that ambiguity. She was frightened if she couldn't pin it down to one meaning. So she was constantly asking you to do very specific acting – the worst kind of acting. The great thing about Neil is he does understand the whole broader ambiguous thing. He is a very sophisticated writer.

TS: *And there is that ambiguity in what he writes.*

SR: And he comes out of a tradition of very strong, ambiguous writing, to name Joyce but one. So that is exciting, particularly to work with someone who is attached to the same culture as yourself. In a way, we are talking about something that is ideal. Maybe it was like that in the French cinema of the fifties and sixties, maybe there were dozens of people who felt connected intellectually and culturally and of course we don't have that kind of structure here and we are relying on individuals the whole time.

TS: *You have made a number of Irish films over the years, appearing in some of them in cameo roles. For instance, there was The Last of the High Kings where you played a taxi driver, a very funny taxi driver. But others like A Further Gesture, you had more input into from an early production stage.*

SR: I wrote the treatment for that film when *The Crying Game* was supposed to be happening and then they lost the money for the film. Sadly for me, the structure of *A Further Gesture* was somewhat similar to the structure of *The Crying Game*. And it was a direct steal from a film of Jean-Pierre Melville's called *Le Deuxieme Souffle* [*Second Breath*, 1966]. So I was very connected to that but I also very quickly lost control over it. We acquired a producer who wanted to control it. Channel 4, who were putting up the money, started to dictate what the ending should be. Their preferred ending was not the ending that Ronan Bennett, who wrote it, and I wanted. I ended up being shot and I thought that the modern hell would be for everything to go wrong and still to be alive. They wanted something dramatic and I don't think they understood what we were talking about. It's very easy to lose control over a movie. I suppose Neil's trick is that he has managed to keep that control.

TS: *Among the other Irish films is one that is not perhaps as widely seen as it should be and that is Trojan Eddie [1995] by Gillies MacKinnon.*

SR: I love that movie.

TS: I like it too and I remember seeing it first in Cork [Film Festival] and there were people coming out who just didn't stay with it from an early stage and wanted something to happen sooner.

SR: I spoke only the other day to Billy Roche who wrote it and I said, 'I am really sorry that it didn't have a bigger impact at the time.' Billy said, 'We were carved up, boy!' Billy's intention, and he said that to Gillies who is Scottish, was to make an Irish movie that was Irish in a way that a French movie is French and an Italian movie is Italian. Gillies was utterly faithful to that. Oddly, the one thing that I had a big influence over was the casting of John Power – whom Richard Harris eventually played. I asked who was going to play that and they said, 'We are thinking of Paul Newman or Dennis Hopper.' I said it wasn't going to be an Irish movie any more and that the only guy who could play this was Harris. They said he was trouble and all that but I found working with him absolutely fantastic.

TS: *And he was terrific.*

SR: He was terrifying. There was one scene we were doing and he didn't know the lines. It was a difficult shot, there were mirrors in the bar, and we had to do it in one take. He stumbled through a couple of rehearsals and Gillies said, 'Let's go for it.' Richard started to do it and it suddenly became clear that he was going to kill me and it was inspired and totally terrifying! If you see the film, you can see I am scared, absolutely terrified. And he went through the thing word perfect and foot perfect. If Harris hadn't been in that, it wouldn't have been the same.

TS: *Prior to The Butcher Boy, it had probably the best ensemble of Irish actors.*

SR: And Gillies facilitated that.

TS: *When it happens just in the moment, as it did with Richard Harris, is that how it is for you as an actor when it works?*

SR: When it's at its best, it reveals itself to you when the camera is turning.

TS: *How do you prepare yourself to best allow that happen?*

SR: You have to allow the camera to watch you. You have to not predetermine what you have to offer. You have to go in with as much information as you can but if anything is going to be any good it can't be planned.

TS: *Another Irish film that you worked a day on was I Could Read the Sky. I think it is a very interesting film – can you talk a little about that and Irish cinema in general.*

SR: *I Could Read the Sky* is utterly itself and that is why it works. It doesn't seem to be diverted towards some hope for a commercial success that it can't possibly have.

TS: *I think you have said in interview before that there is an absence of political engagement in Irish cinema?*

SR: I can quite understand why people don't want to engage with the Troubles any more even in a historical way. There is something else going on which I think Des (Bell) addresses in this film [*The Last Storyteller?*]. He transposes those old stories that Seán Ó hEochaidh collected and invites us to make them relevant to things that are occurring in our society today. Of course, I think cinema should be entertaining and all that. I just don't think we should go from a narrow canvas of West Belfast to a narrow canvas of Temple Bar.

TS: *In the Field Day project, did you consider cinema?*

SR: Yes…

TS: *And did it ever…?*

SR: No!

TS: *In Irish filmmaking, there isn't anything like the Field Project in terms of trying to do something.*

SR: There was a potential for a misunderstanding of the Field Day project which grew – that we were just Northern nationalists who had tunnel vision about a thing. In fact, there were as many views around the table as there were members of our Board. We had very different opinions and what was actually paramount was developing ideas and our theatre really became a theatre of ideas. We don't have a cinema of ideas and if we completely latch ourselves onto the American cinema, we won't have one. They have a cinema of plots and effects. There are people like Altman, maybe the Coen Brothers, who have ideas but it's not how it is run.

TS: *We were talking about the casting of Richard Harris in Trojan Eddie. Do you think that in*

Irish cinema some people stick out like a sore thumb?

SR: Yes, they don't maybe to everybody but they do to us. I guess it mattered to people that Julia Roberts was playing that character in *Michael Collins*. Though in the end of the day, it didn't sell that picture.

TS: *Thank you very much.*

filmography

fiction

2by4 (Jimmy Smallhorne, 1997, US)

25th Hour (Spike Lee, 2002, US)

Ailsa (Paddy Breathnach, 1994, Irl./Ger./Fr.)

Angel (Neil Jordan, 1982, UK)

Barry Lyndon (Stanley Kubrick, 1975, UK)

The Battle of Algiers (Gillo Pontecorvo, 1965, It./Alg.)

The Beach (Danny Boyle, 2000, US)

The Big Sleep (Howard Hawks, 1946, US)

The Birth of a Nation (D. W. Griffith, 1915, US)

Blade Runner (Ridley Scott, 1982, US)

Les Blanchisseueses des Magdalenes (Christophe Weber, 1998, Can.)

Blondie Johnson (Ray Enright, Lucien Hubbard, 1933, US)

Bloom (Seán Walsh, 2003, Irl.)

The Boxer (Jim Sheridan, 1997, Irl./US)

The Boy From Mercury (Martin Duffy, 1996, Irl./UK/Fr.)

Bracken (1878–82, TV, Irl.)

Budawanny (Bob Quinn, 1987, Irl.)

The Butcher Boy (Neil Jordan, 1997, Irl./US)

Charlie's Angels: Full Throttle (McG, 2003, US)

The Cotton Club (Francis Ford Coppola, 1984, US)

The Courier (Joe Lee, Frank Deasy, 1987, Irl.)

Cracker (1993–95, TV, UK)

Cran-d'arret (Yves Boisset, 1970, Fr.)

The Crying Game (Neil Jordan, 1992, UK/Jap.)

Le Deuxieme Souffle (Jean-Pierre Melville, 1966, Fr.)

Disco Pigs (Kirsten Sheridan, 2000, Irl.)

Diva (Jean-Jacques Beineix, 1982, Fr.)

Donnie Brasco (Mike Newell, 1997, US)

L'Enfant de la Haute Mer (Laetitia Gabrielli, Pierre Marteel, Mathieu Renoux and Max Touret, 2000, Fr.)

Exiled (Bill Muir, 1999, US)

Exotica (Atom Egoyan, 1994, Can.)

Fair City (1988–, TV, Irl.)

Felicia's Journey (Atom Egoyan, 1999, UK)

Flash Gordon Conquers the Universe (Universal, 1940, US)

Flick (Fintan Connolly, 1999, Irl.)

The French Lieutenant's Woman (Karel Reisz, 1981, UK)

A Further Gesture aka *The Break* (Robert Dornhelm, 1998, UK/Irl./Ger./Jap.)

Gangs of New York (Martin Scorsese, 2002, US/Ger./It./UK/Neth.)

The General (John Boorman, 1998, Irl./UK)

Glenroe (1983–2001, TV, Irl.)

The Godfather (Francis Ford Coppola, 1972, US)

Guiltrip (Gerry Stembridge, 1995, Irl./Fr./It.)

High Boot Benny (Joe Comerford, 1994, Irl.)

Hush-a-bye-Baby (Margo Harkin, 1989, UK)

I Could Read the Sky (Nichola Bruce, 1999, Irl./UK)

Independence Day (Roland Emmerich, 1996, US)

In America (Jim Sheridan, 2003, Irl./UK)

In the Name of the Father (Jim Sheridan, 1993, Irl./UK)

Inspector Morse (1987–2000, TV, UK)

I Went Down (Paddy Breathnach, 1997, Irl./UK)

The Job (2001–02, TV, US)

Jurassic Park (Steven Spielberg, 1993, US)

Killer Instinct aka *Mad Dog Coll* (Greydon Clark, Ken Stein, 1992, US)

King Kong (John Guillermin, 1976, US)

The Krays (Peter Medak, 1990, UK)

The Lad From Old Ireland (Sidney Olcott, 1910, Irl./US)

The Last of the High Kings (David Keating, 1996, Irl./Den.)

The Lawless Years (1959–61, TV, US)

Little Caesar (Mervyn LeRoy, 1930, US)

The Long Good Friday (John MacKenzie, 1980, UK)

The Luck of Ginger Coffey (Irvin Kershner, 1964, Can./US)

Mad Dog Coll (Burt Balaban, 1961, US)

The Magdalene Sisters (Peter Mullan, 2002, Irl./UK)

Making the Cut (Martyn Friend, 1997, Irl.)

The Maltese Falcon (John Huston, 1941, US)

Marathon Man (John Schlesinger, 1976, US)

Metropolis (Fritz Lang, 1927, Ger.)

Michael Collins (Neil Jordan, 1996, Irl./US/UK)

Miller's Crossing (Joel Coen, 1990, US)

Mobsters (Michael Karbelnikoff, 1991, US)

Nothing Personal (Thaddeus O'Sullivan, 1995, Irl./UK)

Odd Man Out (Carol Reed, 1947, UK)

Once Upon a Time in the West (Sergio Leone, 1969, It./US)

Ordinary Decent Criminal (Thaddeus O'Sullivan, 2000, Irl./Ger./US/UK)

Pigs (Cahal Black, 1984, Irl.)

The Pillow Book (Peter Greenaway, 1996, Fr./UK/Neth.)

Prime Suspect (1991–, TV, UK)

The Public Enemy (William Wellman, 1931, US)

Pulp Fiction (Quentin Tarantino, 1994, US)

Psycho (Alfred Hitchcock, 1960, US)

A Quiet Day in Belfast (Milad Bessada, 1974, Can.)

The Quiet Man (John Ford, 1952, US)

Reservoir Dogs (Quentin Tarantino, 1992, US)

Resurrection Man (Marc Evans, 1997, UK)

The Riordans (1965–79, TV, Irl.)

Road to Perdition (Sam Mendes, 2002, US)

Ros na Rún (1996–, TV, Irl.)

Run Lola Run (Tom Tykwer, 1998, Ger.)

Ryan's Daughter (David Lean, 1970, US)

Scarface (Howard Hawks, 1932, US)

Scarface (Brian De Plama, 1983, US)

The Secret of Roan Inis (John Sayles, 1994, US)

Sleepers (Barry Levinson, 1996, US)

Sliding Doors (Peter Howitt, 1998, US/UK)

Some Mother's Son (Terry George, 1995, Irl./US)

Speaking Parts (Atom Egoyan, 1989, Can.)

State of Grace (Phil Joanou, 1990, US)

Le Taxi mauve aka *The Purple Taxi* (Yves Boisset, 1977, Fr./Irl.)

The Ten Commandments (Cecil B. DeMille, 1923, US)

Terminator 3: Rise of the Machines (Jonathan Mostow, 2003, US)

Titanic (James Cameron, 1997, US)

Time Code (Mike Figgis, 2000, US)

Trainspotting (Danny Boyle, 1996, UK)

Trojan Eddie (Gillies MacKinnon, 1995, Irl./UK)

Twin Town (Kevin Allen Welsh, 1997, UK)

The Untouchables (Brian De Palma, 1987, US)

The Usual Suspects (Bryan Singer, 1995, US)

Veronica Guerin (Joel Schumacher, 2003, Irl./US/UK)

Vicious Circle (David Blair, 1999, Irl.)

The Visit (Orla Walsh, 1992, Irl./UK)

A War of Children (TV, George Schaefer, 1972, UK)

The Wayfarer (Fr. Jackie Moran, 1965, Irl.)

What Happened on 14th Street (Edison Co., 1896, US)

When Brendan Met Trudy (Kieron J. Walsh, 2000, Irl./UK)

When the Sky Falls (John MacKenzie, 2000, Irl./US)

Wild About Harry (Declan Lowney, 2000, Irl./Ger./UK)

With Or Without You (Michael Winterbottom, 1999, UK)

Yesterday's Children (Marcus Cole, 2000, US)

Zazie dans le Metro (Louis Malle, 1960, Fr.)

non-fiction

Activities of a Country Town (Fr. Jackie Moran, 1951, Irl.)

Adveniat Regnum Tuum /Thy Kingdom Come (Fr. Jackie Moran, 1962, Irl.)

…and then there was silence (Simon Wood, 2000, UK)

Aran of the Saints (Catholic Film Society of London, 1932, Irl.)

Behind the Walls of Castlereagh (1992, UK)

Clubs are Trumps (Stuart Hetherington, Brendan Redmond, 1959, Irl.)

Chronique d'un Éte (Jean Rouch, Edgar Morin, 1961, Fr.)

Dear Daughter (Louis Lentin, 1996, Irl.)

Decasia (Bill Morrison, 2002, US)

Eucharistic Congress 1932 (Fr. Fr.nk Browne, 1932, Irl.)

Film of Her (Bill Morrison, 1996, US)

Handsworth Songs (John Akomfrah, 1986, UK)

The Hard Road to Klondike (Desmond Bell, 1999, Irl.)

The Irishmen: An Impression of Exile (Philip Donnellan, 1965, UK)

An Irish Village (James Clark, 1959, Irl.)

Jaguar (Jean Rouch, 1967, Fr.)

The Last Storyteller? (Desmond Bell, 2002, Irl.)

Mad Dog Coll (Pat Comer, 2000, Irl.)

Man of Aran (Robert Flaherty, 1935, UK)

Moving Myths (1988, UK)

Night Rider (Harmen Elisa Brandsma, 1999, UK)

One Man's War (Edgardo Cozarinsky, 1982, Fr.)

Sans Soleil (Chris Marker, 1983, Fr.)

Sex in a Cold Climate (Steve Humphries, 1997, UK)

Shoah (Claude Lanzmann, 1985, Fr.)

Sixty Minutes: The Magdalen Laundries (CBS News, 1999, US)

Snapshots from Church Road (Fr. Courtney, 1939-40, Irl.)

States of Fear (Mary Raferty, 1999, Irl.)

Stolen Lives (Louis Lentin, 1999, Irl.)

Telling Our Story (Cahal McLaughlin, 2001, UK)

Territories (Issac Julien 1985, UK)

We Never Give Up (Human Rights Media Centre, 2002, SA)

Wittgenstein (Peter Forgacs, 1994, Hun.)

Index

Contemporary British and Irish Film Directors

A Wallflower Critical Guide

Edited by Yoram Allon, Del Cullen and
Hannah Patterson
Introduction by Mike Hodges

Encompassing the careers of over 300 directors that have
worked in Britain and Ireland in the last twenty years, this
unique guide is an invaluable reference for students,
researchers and enthusiasts of film. Every entry provides
concise biographical information as well as insightful textual
and thematic analysis of each director's work. In compre-
hensively covering a wide range of filmmakers – from British
social realists such as Tony Richardson, Karel Reisz and Ken
Loach, through major figures including David Lean, Neil Jordan
and Richard Attenborough, visionaries Terence Davies, Derek
Jarman and Mike Figgis, to emerging talent such as Lynne
Ramsay and Peter Mullan – the evolving landscape of contemporary filmmaking is brought into sharp focus.

2001
£17.99 PBK   1-903364-21-3
£50.00 HBK   1-903364-22-1
416 PAGES

'Brilliantly and incisively documents the new British and Irish
cinema. The entries are authoratitive, persuasive and compul-
sivly readable. An utterly indispensable reference volume for
serious scholars and film enthusiasts alike.'

– Wheeler Winston Dixon, University of Nebraska

'A thoroughly well-researched and very comprehensive work
that will be a useful resource for the film industry professional,
academic and anyone who is interested in the contemporary
history of British and Irish filmmaking.'

– Adrian Wootton, Director, Regus London Film Festival

ALSO AVAILABLE
Contemporary North American
Film Directors (second edition, 2002)

'Must buy ... threatens to become indispensable.' *Empire*

'Offers an extremely useful, incisive and lucid account of an
extraordinary range of modern America filmmkaers,' – Geoff
Andrew, *Time Out*

'Excellent ... a real bargain. Highly recommended for all film
studies collections.' *Library Journal*